CW01239217

'There's a real sense of peace and magic in this beautiful book – it's filled with stories and ideas about loss and reconnection through our ancient landscapes that will help us all to heal.'

Daisy Buchanan, broadcaster, columnist and author of *Insatiable*

'An extremely relatable memoir, densely packed with the author's first-hand experiences as a committed "stone hunter". As well as an inspiring tour of the megalithic landscapes of these isles, *Stone Lands* is a human journey into grief, hope and love. It's a fantastic book for weird walkers and megalith obsessives alike.'

Weird Walk

'A wonderful story of grief, self-discovery, hope and reconnection to our ancient past and landscapes, in which Fiona Robertson takes us on her own deeply personal journey and, by doing so, shows us the power of looking back in order to move forward.'

Ben Edge, artist and author of *Folklore Rising*

'Written with great craft, sensitivity and authority, Fiona Robertson offers a wonderfully evocative and poignant account of the ancient sites and landscapes of Britain. There is a resonance here to artists and writers such as Nash, Ravilious and Blake, and that tradition of deeply embedded landscape romanticism and sense of place that runs through our engagement with traces of a prehistoric past.'

Josh Pollard, Professor of Archaeology, University of Southampton

'An utterly endearing account of seeking the ancient wonders of the prehistoric stone sites of Britain, told against the backdrop of such poignant personal heartache. *Stone Lands* brims with the intrigue and delight of the modern antiquarian who journeys to the sacred spaces of these isles to connect with the ways of our ancestors.'
Dr James Canton, Director of Wild Writing at the University of Essex, and author of *Grounded* and *Renaturing*

'A wonderful and moving book: part personal memoir and part tribute to the megaliths in our midst which – in strange and subtle ways – still have so much wisdom to impart.'
Oliver Smith, columnist and author of *On This Holy Island*

'Reading *Stone Lands* feels like coming home after a hard day's toil. This strangely comforting book is a reminder that the ancient stones can be sources of reassurance and solidity, even in our times of greatest upheaval and loss.'
Angeline Morrison, folk singer

STONE LANDS

A Journey of Darkness and Light Through Britain's Ancient Places

Fiona Robertson

ROBINSON

ROBINSON

First published in Great Britain in 2025 by Robinson

Copyright © Fiona Robertson, 2025

1 3 5 7 9 10 8 6 4 2

The moral right of the author has been asserted.

Some names have been changed.

All rights reserved.
No part of this publication may be reproduced, stored in a retrieval system, or transmitted, in any form, or by any means, without the prior permission in writing of the publisher, nor be otherwise circulated in any form of binding or cover other than that in which it is published and without a similar condition including this condition being imposed on the subsequent purchaser.

A CIP catalogue record for this book
is available from the British Library.

ISBN: 978-1-47214-918-3

Chapter opener illustrations by Philip Harris
Site plans and maps by Ben Prior
Design by Clare Sivell
Typeset in Minion Pro by Clare Sivell
Printed and bound in Great Britain by Clays Ltd, Elcograf S.p.A.

Papers used by Robinson are from well-managed forests and other responsible sources.

MIX
Paper | Supporting responsible forestry
FSC® C104740

Robinson	The authorised representative
An imprint of	in the EEA is
Little, Brown Book Group	Hachette Ireland
Carmelite House	8 Castlecourt Centre
50 Victoria Embankment	Dublin 15, D15 XTP3, Ireland
London EC4Y 0DZ	(email: info@hbgi.ie)

An Hachette UK Company
www.hachette.co.uk

www.littlebrown.co.uk

**For Stephen,
and E. and E.**

Note on dating

CE: *Common Era (the equivalent of AD)*
BCE: *Before the Common Era (the equivalent of BC)*

Most BCE dates quoted in this book should be read as cal BCE, the 'cal' referring to calibration done by archaeologists on raw radiocarbon dates, which can be out by several centuries. Calibration involves comparison with tree-ring growth in very ancient timber (among other methods) to make the radiocarbon dating more accurate, sometimes pinpointing a date to a single generation (a span of 25 years).

It is hard to date stone circles and rows. Stone itself can't be radiocarbon dated and most stone circles have not been scientifically excavated. Finds that would assist with dating are rare. Hazel charcoal unearthed in a stone-hole at Long Meg and Her Daughters in Cumbria has given an Early Neolithic date of 3340–3100 BCE, implying that this is one of the earliest stone circles in Britain. Other stone circles have been dated to the Middle Bronze Age, around 2000 BCE or later, so there's a very wide range of dating possibilities.

Chambered tombs, on the other hand, often contain burials that can be dated, and these dates tend to be earlier than those associated with stone circles, typically 3700–3000 BCE. However, it's important to remember that these burials could have been inserted in the stone monuments centuries after they were built.

Radiocarbon dating is now being combined with ancient DNA analysis to infer ever more accurate dates based on knowledge of family relationships between burials – this is very complex and pretty mindblowing modern archaeological magic!

Contents

Chapter 1	**EVERYTHING CHANGES** Avebury, WILTSHIRE	1
Chapter 2	**THE STORIES WE TELL SHAPE OUR WORLD** The Rollright Stones, OXFORDSHIRE	35
Chapter 3	**THE THING IS TO KEEP GOING** Stones of the Isle of Mull	57
Chapter 4	**HOPE IS THE MOST HUMAN QUALITY** Stones of Dartmoor, DEVON	85
Chapter 5	**ANYTHING IS POSSIBLE** Stones of Preseli, PEMBROKESHIRE Stonehenge, WILTSHIRE	115
Chapter 6	**WE CANNOT HOLD BACK THE TURNING WHEEL** Stones of the Isles of Scilly	145

Chapter 7	**THE STONES ENDURE AND SO CAN WE**	
	Calanais, ISLE OF LEWIS	173
Chapter 8	**THE LAND IS STILL ENCHANTED**	
	Stones of the Lake District, CUMBRIA	201
Chapter 9	**THE STONES BRING US TOGETHER**	
	Stones of the Medway, KENT	
	Stones of the Peak District, DERBYSHIRE	227
Chapter 10	**THE LIGHT WILL COME BACK**	
	Stones of Orkney	257
Chapter 11	**THIS IS A WORLD OF WONDER**	
	Stones of West Penwith, CORNWALL	291
Chapter 12	**THE PAST IS ALWAYS WITH US**	
	The White Horse and Wayland's Smithy, OXFORDSHIRE	323

Acknowledgements 351
Endnotes 355
Bibliography 367
Index 377

STONE
LANDS

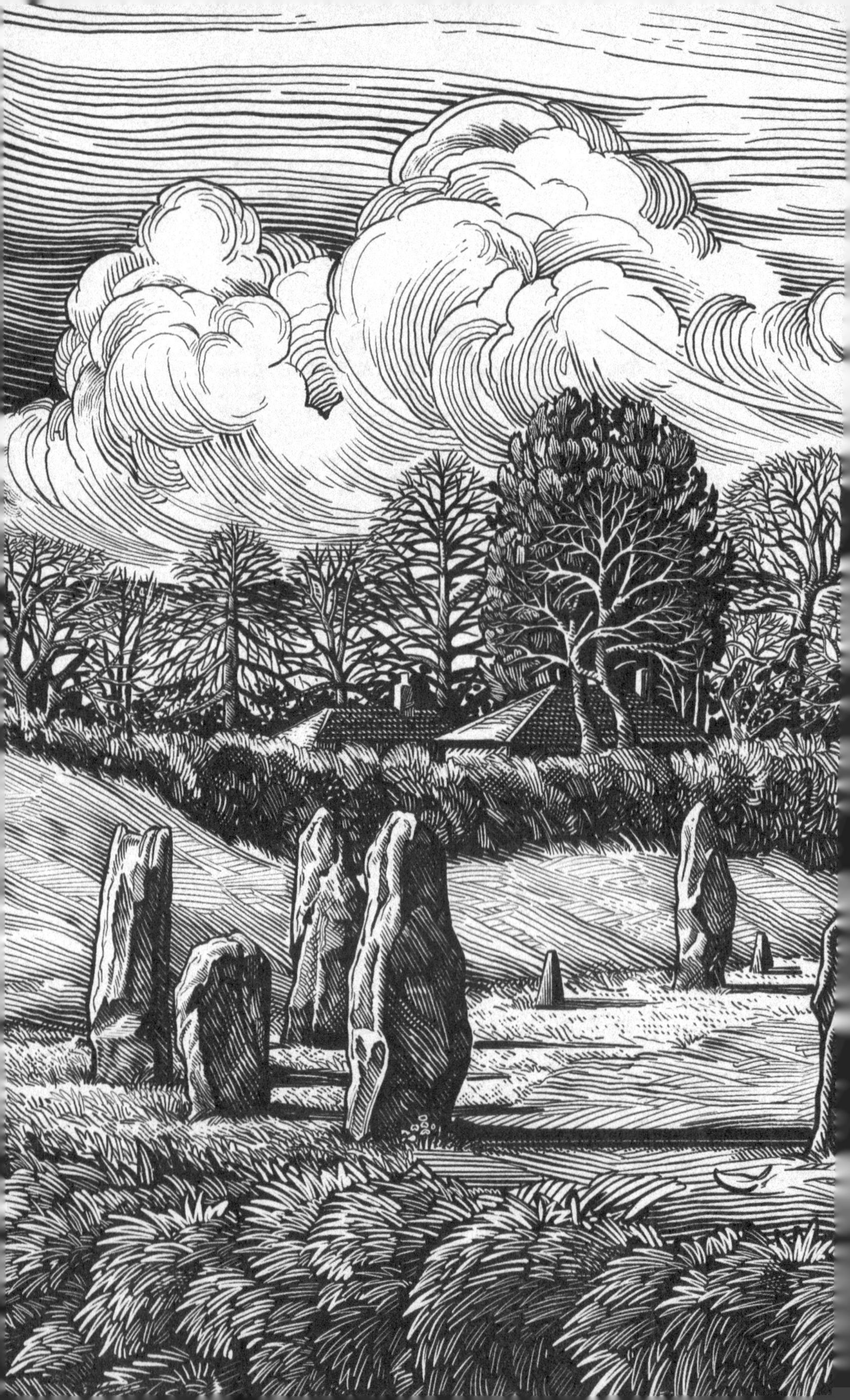

Chapter 1
EVERYTHING CHANGES

- c.3700 BCE: Work starts on Windmill Hill causewayed enclosure and West Kennet long barrow

- c.3000–2200 BCE: Avebury henge and stone circles/avenues built in phases, with activity intensifying c.2500 BCE

- c.2400 BCE: Work starts on Silbury Hill

- LATE THIRD MILLENNIUM BCE: West Kennet long barrow closed

Avebury, WILTSHIRE

WE TAKE OUR PINTS and wander into the field of the standing stones. Through the open windows of the Red Lion come the sound of a fiddle and the cheery singing of the Morris dancers, who are done with the dancing and are now embarking with equal enthusiasm on the drinking. I can barely walk, my feet blistered after two days of Ridgeway hiking in ill-fitting sandals, so I take them off and go barefoot, the grass warm and dusty against my soles, nudging me gently with every step as if the earth itself is welcoming me back to this place. The sun is lower now but the heat has not yet gone out of the day, and golden light falls like an enchantment on the whitewashed walls and lazily drooping thatch of the pub, on the drinkers at the picnic benches and on the sarsen stones that stand in an arc in the field awaiting our arrival. We choose our stone, a giant sharp-angled lozenge honeyed by the sun, and rest our heads against rough sandstone that is warm to the touch, as if the stone is a living, breathing creature.

For a moment the music and the voices all fall silent; the people are spellbound while the stones are more intensely alive than ever, trembling on the verge of movement. There are faces hidden in the rock, we decide: a clenched jaw and furrowed brow here, a turned-up nose and disdainful grimace there. The more we look, the more we see: human emotions weathered into stone that seem to speak of Avebury's 5,000 years of history.

As we sip our pints, we read the guidebook and try to work out if the stone we are leaning against is the very one that crushed an itinerant barber-surgeon*[1] in the early 14th century, trapping him there until 1938 when his skeleton, along with the tools of his trade, were liberated during Alexander Keiller's excavations. We wonder how the barber-surgeon ended up under the stone and whether there is any danger of us suffering the same fate.

On the front of my backpack, its long stem threaded through the straps, is the flower that Stephen gave me two days earlier when we met at Paddington station: a gerbera daisy, its petals fiery orange as the sun and defiantly unwilted despite being carried along the Ridgeway through an August heatwave. It's only a few weeks since we met for the first time and we are very happy.

Fast forward through 18 years and more: Stephen, his face more lined, a little gaunt, but still looking younger than his

---

* It's now thought he might have been a tailor and already dead when he was placed into a convenient stone-hole, but the crushed barber-surgeon remains ingrained in Avebury folklore.

Everything Changes

not-yet-50 years, stands within a grove of beeches that grip with their snakelike roots the earthen bank of the Avebury henge, a girl and a boy on either side of him. Our children, Alex and Ava. The boy is 12 years old, on the cusp of adolescence, his expression preoccupied, his fists clenched; he has something on his mind but that might just be the indignity of being made to pose for a photo or (very likely) the prospect of 30 sorry gaming-less hours. The girl is nine, brimming with not always helpful questions ('Can we play hide-and-seek?' 'How long will this walk last?' 'What's for lunch?'), fighting with the wind for control of her long hair. You would not tell from Stephen's smiling face that anything is wrong, except that his skin, in the pale February sunlight, has a yellowish tinge that should not be there.

The beech roots writhe across the bank and dig down deep into the earth, holding the trees fast; and though the wind grabs the beeches and shakes them violently, making the wishing ribbons flap wildly and a shower of twigs rain down, its best efforts are no match for these roots that have been gripping on to the ground for a hundred years or more. There is a numinous quality to the space where Stephen and our children stand; it is a natural chapel with a pillar of living wood at each corner, roofed by twisting branches that throw a black web across the wind-scoured sky. As I join them within the beeches, I offer up a silent pleading prayer to whatever spirit may reside there.

From the henge, the Avenue stretches south-east, a double row of stones that today seem to be leaning in like sails to catch the wind. The violent gusts are the aftershocks of a great storm that has rampaged across the country, scattering trees across roads, felling fences, blowing off roofs and prompting an

STONE LANDS

'essential travel only' announcement from the government, but what is a bit of atmospheric disturbance to these millennia-old stone sentinels? They've seen it all before.

I am keeping a discreet watchful eye on Stephen and he seems OK, but I know he will make a heroic effort to keep up with us and in doing so might push himself too far. At the end of the surviving section of the Avenue we turn west up Waden Hill and now Stephen slows, his breathing laboured, wincing at each step. My heart sinks and the nauseous sense of dread that is never entirely absent these days surges through me. This is the man who three months ago was merrily scaling rock faces in Snowdonia. He is determined not to be defeated by a bit of hill, however, and puts one foot in front of the other, making it up before the children, who have gone into a paroxysm of moaning that slows them down considerably. 'Come on, you lot, what's the hold-up?' he calls down, when he's got his breath back. 'This should be easy for you seasoned climbers!' The mix of encouragement and exasperation, and the promise of chocolate, finally gets them to the top.

And it's epic up here, on Waden Hill. In the valley below is Silbury Hill, Avebury's weirdest monument, a 4,400-year-old artificial mound that resembles a giant green blancmange, or perhaps an alien spaceship that has slipped down to earth through a golden slit in the clouds. The wind grabs our hair and tugs at our clothes, pummels our faces, snatches our words away.

There is nothing for it but to open our arms wide and fly.

It All Starts with Avebury

I was 18 years old when I first came to Avebury, long before I met Stephen; school was behind me, the start of university a comfortable number of weeks away, and in that long, hot, psychedelic-patterned summer it felt like anything might be possible. The spirit of the late '60s was abroad once more, smiley faces were everywhere and English fields were alive with the sound of techno. I read E. M. Forster and Arthur Machen, and waited for Pan in the woods. I tried acid for the first time and watched the paving stones of my then-boyfriend's parents' patio dissolve into whirling vortexes of energy. Reality was warping and it seemed like magic might, after all, turn out to be real.

And then the boyfriend and I made it to Avebury and it was like, wow, how can this place even *exist*?! Avebury was by far the most mind-blowing thing I'd ever encountered. A village inside a circle of huge standing stones. A processional avenue of paired stones that marched outwards from the stone circle into the countryside. A prehistoric artificial hill as old as, and as big as, the Egyptian pyramids but set in English farmland. An ancient ridgetop road edged with tree-spiked burial mounds that stood out on the skyline like beacons broadcasting a message encoded several thousand years ago. How could this all *be*? The landscape felt potent with spiritual meaning, the whole sweeping chalk downland imbued with a significance that I could feel if not articulate. And the people who crowded the lanes of the village in their tie-dye and army surplus, who lay on the grass soaking up the energy of the stones, who smoked weed, played guitar and danced in the circle, who slept overnight in the chambers of the long barrow – the crusties, hippies, ravers, dowsers, stone huggers, crystal enthusiasts, witches, Druids – these were my people, I felt instinctively, or at least (I was not a confident teen) I wanted them to be. I was enchanted. My love affair with standing stones had begun.

And it all started with Avebury for John Aubrey, too, the 17th-century antiquarian who fathered the modern practice of megalith hunting – stone seeking, stone bothering, megalith enthusiasm, whatever you want to call it – that thing of eagerly (sometimes obsessively) getting out there to look for prehistoric standing stones. Aubrey's *Monumenta Britannica* opens with an account of coming across Avebury while out hunting with some of his fellow country gentry soon after New Year in 1649: 'I was wonderfully surprised at the sight of those vast stones: of which I had never heard before: as also at the mighty bank and graff [ditch] about it.' Whereupon, in the manner of many megalithophiles to come, he abandoned his companions and the hunt to entertain himself 'with a more delightful' exploration of the site.[2]

Aubrey was 22 when he first encountered Avebury and it had a profound effect on him. He became the first true stones obsessive, gathering information about ancient sites all over Britain for his *Monumenta Britannica*. In 1717 or 1718 a transcript of this unpublished manuscript came into the hands of the man who would become Britain's other father of megalith hunting – William Stukeley – who just a year or so later was in Avebury himself, obviously inspired by his predecessor's enthusiastic description of the site.[3] It was to be the first of many visits during which Stukeley meticulously recorded the stones

Everything Changes

there even as great swathes of them were being toppled and destroyed.

Until Aubrey and Stukeley, no one seems to have paid much attention to the Avebury stones. Stukeley comments that 'It is strange that two parallel lines of great stones, set at equal distance and intervals, for a mile together, should be taken for rocks in their natural state' – but apparently they were, even though Aubrey had identified the Avenue as a prehistoric monument decades before.[4] But after Stukeley, megalithomania took root and from then on stones enthusiasts of all sorts began making their way into the fields and moorlands of Britain: Druid theorists, Romantic poets, antiquarians, ley line hunters, earth mystery investigators, New Agers, modern Pagans, committed megalith-community members, casual prehistory buffs, photographers, walkers, picnickers and more. And of course the professionals: hordes of archaeologists of all kinds, assisted by further hordes of volunteers.

So what is it about standing stones? This book is, in part, an attempt to answer that question. Prehistoric people took hundreds, thousands, even millions of labour hours away from the practical business of staying alive to raise massive stones and build huge earthworks, and though we can speculate endlessly about why they were moved to do so, we can never know for sure. What we *can* say is what the stones mean to us today.

I am profoundly intrigued and impressed by standing stones. Placed upright thousands of years ago, somehow (amazingly) here they still are, standing in fields and gardens, on moors and roadsides, waiting for us to go out and find them. For me, they are above all symbols of survival, set in contrast to our ephemeral human lives. The Medway megaliths, which are to be found in a motorway-encircled zone of Kent less than an hour's drive from London, are among the oldest stone monuments in Britain, still standing after 6,000 years – that's an inconceivable length of time. Maybe some of these megalithic survivors will still be upright when all we humans are gone.

There is something about the extreme longevity of standing stones that I find very comforting. Whatever people get up to, the stones have seen it all before. However long our personal span on this planet – 80 years, or 50, or eight – they will outlast us. These millennia-old witnesses to the sound and the fury of human existence put it all into perspective. Touching an ancient, weather-scored pillar of granite, sandstone or quartz can make the drama of life seem, if only for a moment, small and far away.

Standing stones are totems of mystery, a multitude of theories projected onto them and yet we have no way of knowing if any of them are true. For some people, such as the Druids, Wiccans and other neo-Pagans who gather at standing stones to celebrate the eight festivals of the Wheel of the Year, a stone circle is more than mysterious; it is sacred space. I am not a practising Pagan but like many others today I am drawn to mark the turning of the seasons at key solar moments such as midwinter and midsummer, and a stone circle, which like the year itself leads from every ending to a new beginning, seems a potent place to do that. I find it possible to believe that standing stones mark sacred ground and that divinity is present in very ancient places. Standing stones are much more than lumps of rock set on end a long time ago. Infused with wonder and mystery, they enchant the landscape.

Everything Changes

Sometimes, when my brain is whirring and I can't get to sleep, I imagine I'm a standing stone. I close my eyes and I'm up on the moor, rooted deep in the earth and resting on springy turf. All around me, stretching to the far-distant hills, is a dark expanse of bracken and gorse, speckled with pools that reflect the stars. I'm furred with lichen, crusted with quartz and scored with rain runnels, and I've been standing in that spot, battered by the storms and warmed by the sun, for a very, very long time. From time to time a crow will land on me or a colony of snails will creep up over me, and occasionally a human or two will build a fire and camp near by. All stone-me needs to do is just be. (Honestly, it is very relaxing.)

A Kind of Awakening

I had been thinking for a while, without doing much about it, of the idea of writing a book about standing stones and the meaning we might make of them today. And then something happened to focus my mind.

My most frequent companion in my standing stone adventures has always been Stephen, my partner, then husband, and fellow (albeit more sceptical, though cheerfully tolerant of my 'woo' tendencies) megalith enthusiast. In the January of the year in which we were both to turn 50, the story of our lives took an unexpected dark turn. It started, for me, with a feeling of dread, waking up before dawn with the sense that something was not right. Since New Year, Stephen had been feeling exhausted and unwell. The nausea was growing and his abdomen became swollen and painful. His pee suddenly turned amber coloured. The doctor sent him for a blood test and we expected the results to come through in a week or so, but the very next morning he received a call: the test showed he was severely jaundiced, he should go to A&E immediately. We were sure the cause would be gallstones (a friend had recently been sent to hospital for that very issue, and all had been well). It did cross my mind that it was strange the doctor had said 'they will diagnose the problem and it *may* be possible to cure it', but I assumed he was just a bit lacking in bedside manner. Of course it would be possible to cure it.

A phone call came through from Stephen in hospital. 'Where are you? Can the children hear?' he asked, his voice shaky, tears not far away. I ran upstairs to our bedroom, the phone clamped to my ear, unable to breathe as I waited for the blow to fall. It wasn't gallstones. The ultrasound had revealed the presence of a 5cm lump on Stephen's gallbladder. I remember very clearly this moment when everything changed and my world lurched from light to darkness, the domestic horror of it, leaning against a hot radiator, the clothes horse draped with a batch of laundry, music rising through the floorboards from the TV below, the noise of the kids' cheerful squabbling. I tried to grasp what Stephen was saying and my mind shied away from it. None of it was feasible. The doctors were not committing themselves as to exactly what this lump might be, only to say that it was 'in an awkward place'.

At the end of January, we were ushered into a seminar room at Lewisham hospital by a consultant gastroenterologist, a junior doctor and the Macmillan nurse. Their solemn faces and the two boxes of tissues set on the conference table did not bode well. The biopsy would need to be reanalysed by the team at King's, but the results were 'suspicious of carcinoma' (the consultant, standing in for the holidaying oncologist, apparently could not bring himself to deliver the news straight). The tumour could not be removed by surgery, entangled as it was in the bile ducts, and what's more the scans had picked up additional shadows on the abdomen that should not be there. Treatment could only be palliative, with the aim of prolonging life.

I asked about life expectancy, what 'prolonging life' actually meant, and the consultant told us that that this would depend on the type of biliary cancer, not yet determined, and the efficacy of the treatment. 'But he won't be gone in six months or anything like that, will he?' I said, expecting to be comforted with gentle ridicule, and the kind Macmillan nurse replied, 'We just don't know.' They left us alone to cry in each other's arms.

I keep thinking this is a dream, I wrote in my diary. *Surely it's a dream?* In my waking life I kept trying to wake myself up – it was the strangest feeling. I just could not believe this was really happening. I longed for that relief you get when you wake up from a nightmare and realise that it's all OK after all. For a long time, I carried on trying to wake myself up. Sometimes I still catch myself doing it now.

A few months after discovering that Stephen had incurable stage 4 gallbladder cancer, I began to write this book. I wanted to record how visiting, and thinking about, standing stones had helped me as I faced this greatest challenge of my life. I wanted to do something positive to distract myself from the constant overwhelming sadness. I wanted to explore what these amazing survivals from the past meant to me, and to other people. Standing stones had been part of the fun stuff we did with the kids since they were little – Sunday trips to the Medway megaliths (our closest stones), weekends at Avebury, holiday games of hide-and-seek around the Breton *allées couvertes* and the Cornish quoits – and that did not change when Stephen got sick. It seemed to me that there were certain insights I'd gained from being a stones enthusiast that also resonated in the situation I was in, facing the prospect of losing Stephen. These insights form the basis of this book's chapters, described along with the 'stone lands' that seem to embody them, from West Penwith to Avebury to Orkney. Of course, this is all highly subjective and every stones enthusiast will make their own meanings, but I want to offer up what they mean for me (as someone who is not an archaeologist, and who has never studied archaeology, but who has a boundless enthusiasm and love for these places). I believe that standing stones gain great potency from their association with ideas about endurance, survival, the past and memory, and that, if we let them, they will enchant our world with their folklore, mystery and magic. And I believe that these things can be helpful, whatever we are going through.

The first insight I had, brought on by the extreme shock of Stephen's diagnosis, was that *everything changes* – though our tendency is to believe it will not. My sense of security and stability dissolved, my future vanished, my faith in statistics and 'it won't happen to us' and basic causality (how could this climber-surfer-cyclist-wild swimmer who actively enjoyed bean salad and lentil stew have cancer?) was blown out of the water. It was a sort of enlightenment. I understood that my apparently solid everyday reality had simply been a construct of my incredibly powerful mind. There is no security. Everything changes all the time. Our lives are nothing but an illusion – a beautiful illusion, but an illusion nonetheless. Death is real. We are all skating on thin ice, all the time.

One of the central doctrines of Buddhism is that our human existence is characterised by impermanence. Having worked in mind-body-spirit publishing for most of my career, I've edited a fair few Buddhist and Buddhist-inspired books and I thought I knew all about impermanence and the idea that this world we see around us is just an illusion. Well, I didn't *really* know, but I do now. Stephen and I went into that January with a future stretching before us: we would move out of London, closer to the stones and the surf, we'd take the kids mountaineering, cycle across France, finally get up to Orkney, he'd finish his PhD, I'd write a novel, we'd both do less work for our respective employers and take more time for ourselves. We'd make the most of the decades we had left. We'd grow old together. Our kids would grow up with two parents.

Everything Changes, Even (Especially) Avebury

It is tempting to take a prehistoric landscape at face value and believe that it has always looked like that, just as it is easy to believe that life will always go on in the same way, that because something is as it is now, it will necessarily stay that way. But standing stone sites change just like anything else, and perhaps

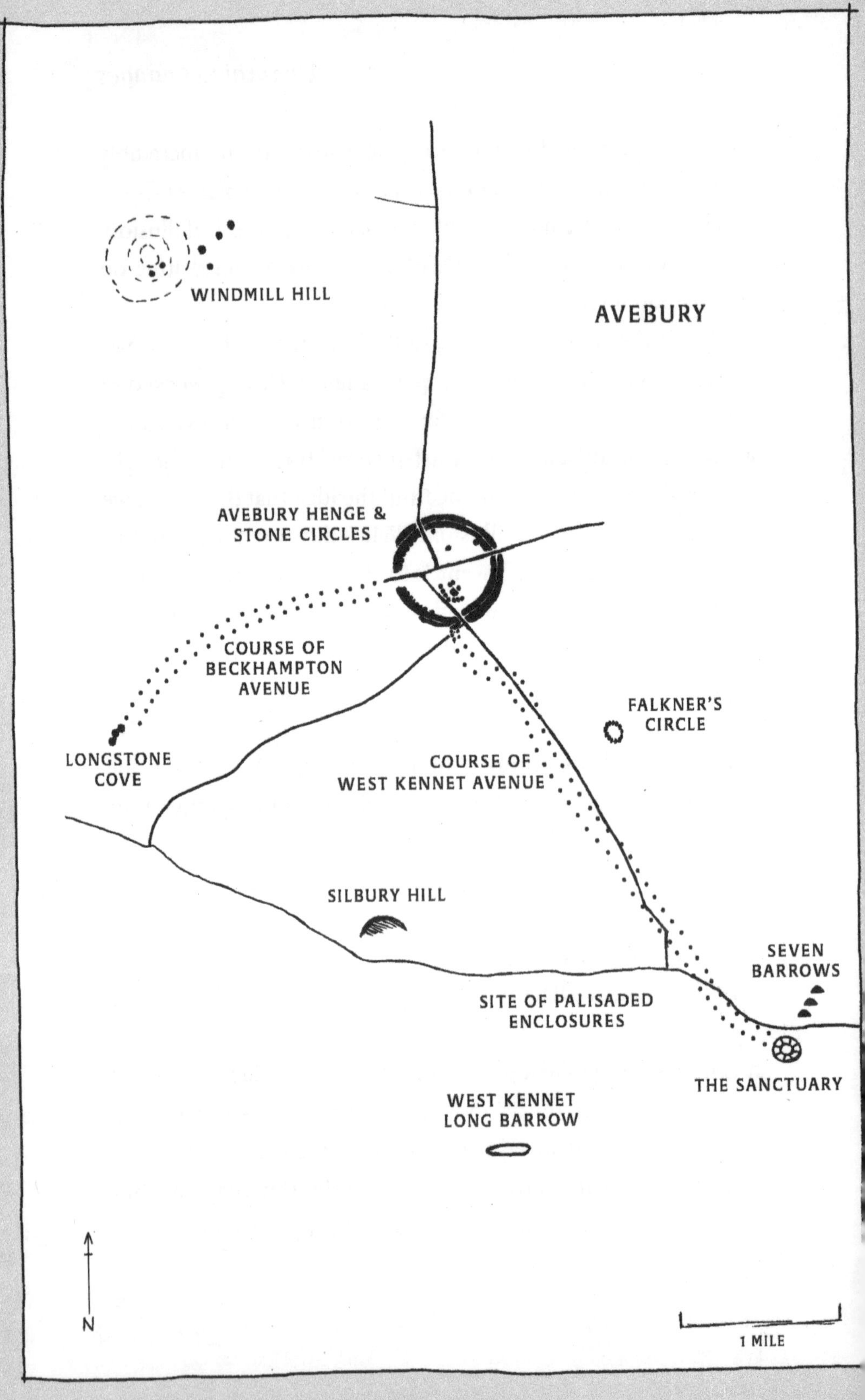

WINDMILL HILL
AVEBURY
AVEBURY HENGE &
STONE CIRCLES
COURSE OF
BECKHAMPTON
AVENUE
FALKNER'S
CIRCLE
LONGSTONE
COVE
COURSE OF
WEST KENNET AVENUE
SILBURY HILL
SEVEN
BARROWS
SITE OF PALISADED
ENCLOSURES
THE SANCTUARY
WEST KENNET
LONG BARROW
N
1 MILE

Everything Changes

nowhere demonstrates this better than Avebury. In and around this Wiltshire village are extraordinary ancient sites that have somehow made it through to the present day, and yet they do not represent an eternal landscape so much as a changing one, a succession of endings of traditions, which were perhaps experienced as painful by the people who lived through them. It is, indeed, a landscape characterised by loss, where the ghosts of stones stand alongside those that have survived.

Go back far enough through time and it's not stones that you'd see standing at Avebury but trees: oak and ash, yew and birch, hazel and hawthorn.[5] Among the trees, people came and went, making clearings, digging pits on Waden Hill and Windmill Hill. And then, in the early Neolithic *c.*3700 BCE, work started on a huge causewayed enclosure on top of Windmill Hill. This was Avebury's first monumental construction, a massive circuit of ditch and bank that entirely ringed the hilltop, apart from a series of uncut sections (causeways) left in the chalk, and which enclosed two further circuits of ditches, the whole structure taking an estimated 62,000 labour hours to construct. Today, this ancient hilltop just over a mile north-west of Avebury village is an evocative, lonely, windswept place, knee-deep in grasses and wildflowers in summer, and all the more attractive for being overlooked by most visitors. (It took us years of Avebury trips before we made it up Windmill Hill.) There's not much to see here now apart from the awesome views over the Wiltshire downs, and some dips and bumps in the ground that represent the remains of the Neolithic ditches and banks and the Bronze Age round barrows, yet in its time – before the stones – this was the most important gathering place in the region. Great numbers of people came together in certain seasons to feast in the enclosure, the scale of their ceremonies indicated by the thousands of animal bones found by archaeologists in the ditches, along with 20,000 pottery sherds and 100,000 pieces of worked flint.[6]

Around the same time as Windmill Hill was being constructed, early Neolithic people also built long barrows in the Avebury landscape, some of them just earth mounds, others with stone chambers containing human remains. West Kennet long barrow, set on a chalk ridge overlooking the Kennet valley a mile or so south of Avebury village, is the most spectacular of these. At the forefront of a mound 100 metres long, they built a passageway and five chambers from huge sarsen stones, with a roof high enough to allow people gathered for a ceremony to stand upright inside. Although the main phase of burials here seems to have been short, perhaps only 30 years, the barrow itself remained in use for over 1,000 years, the chambers gradually filled in with pottery, flint and animal and human bone. But then, at some time in the late third millennium BCE, the entrance was completely blocked by the huge stones that still stand in front of the long barrow today, closing off access to this ancient sacred space and ending for good whatever traditions had been observed there. And it might be that this closing of the long barrow, and the switch to new practices associated with the henge and the standing stones, was considered a shocking change, perhaps deeply upsetting for those who preferred the old ways.

Avebury's henge was constructed in stages from c.3000 BCE, the huge ditch and bank encircling ground where a small and presumably sacred wooden house had been built centuries

Everything Changes

earlier. At the same time, the work of raising Avebury's famous stone circles and avenues was in progress – a building project that would go on in phases until *c.*2200 BCE, transforming Avebury into a unified monumental landscape. The completed henge must have been an awe-inspiring sight, with a great, chalk-white ditch that dropped sheer for 10 metres and a massive encircling bank that could have been designed to screen off what was going on inside the henge or, alternatively, provide a grandstand for onlookers (or both). And what was inside the henge was stones – and lots of them. The ditch and bank enclosed a circle of about 100 stones, the largest stone circle ever built in Britain. This in turn enclosed two further stone circles, the northern and southern inner circles. Within these were yet more megaliths: in the northern inner circle stood the Cove, three enormous stones that may have been oriented on midsummer sunrise; in the southern inner circle, a square of megaliths surrounded the site of the ancient wooden house, and the long-vanished giant known as the Obelisk stood an awesome 6 metres high.

And there was more. Two very long stone avenues snaked across the landscape to link other monuments to the central henge: the paired stones of West Kennet Avenue ran south from the henge for 1½ miles to reach the concentric stone and timber circles of the Sanctuary on Overton Hill, while a second double stone row, Beckhampton Avenue, ran west from the henge for ¾ mile to the rectilinear arrangement of standing stones known as the Longstone Cove, and perhaps beyond.[7] Two enormous palisaded enclosures were constructed from oak posts by the River Kennet. And perhaps most inconceivably of all, an incredible

STONE LANDS

four million labour hours were spent building Silbury Hill, not far from West Kennet long barrow. This monumentally enigmatic heap of gravel, earth and chalk was gradually enlarged in size until it reached 39 metres high and 160 metres wide, the largest mound ever created in prehistoric Europe. Despite several excavations, no burial has been found inside Silbury Hill and its purpose remains unknown.

What survives today at Avebury seems awe-inspiring, magical, almost unbelievable, and yet it is a landscape that represents change and loss as much as it does survival. In the 14th century, some 40 of the prehistoric stones were buried, probably to clear land for farming. By the 17th century, the actual breaking up of stones was getting underway; in *Monumenta Britannica*, John Aubrey recorded how megaliths were destroyed for use as building material: 'Make a fire on that line of the stone, where you would have it crack; and after the stone is well heated, draw over a line with cold water, and immediately give a knock with a smith's sledge, and it will break'.[8] Aubrey recorded stones and even whole monuments that are now gone: the double stone ring at the Sanctuary, and the 'eight huge stones in a circle' in a lane 'from Kennet towards Marlborough' – likely a lost stone circle of which no other record remains.[9] He sketched the Cove, inside the northern inner circle, with its great third stone still present.

By the time Stukeley visited Avebury c.1718–24, the destruction was in full spate. Stukeley drew on local memory and the evidence of stone-holes to record megaliths that had been recently removed as well as those still present. He recorded the stones of the henge with fewer of them standing than when Aubrey had visited in the previous century. He plotted the path

Everything Changes

of West Kennet Avenue from the circle to the Sanctuary, showing many pairs of stones still standing, but also, now, many gaps. He described Beckhampton Avenue, its very existence doubted by modern archaeologists (whose trust in Stukeley was undermined by his obsession with seeing the hand of the Druids in every prehistoric site) until 1999, when excavations confirmed a second avenue had indeed run from Avebury henge to the Longstone Cove. According to Stukeley, the stones of Beckhampton Avenue once ran on beyond the Cove to Fox Covert, 'a most solemn and awful place'; archaeologists have so far found no evidence of this extension, but maybe one day they will.

In his *Abury* (published in 1743 but based on his researches of 20 years earlier), a furious Stukeley names and shames the destroyers of the stones, bitter that Avebury's 'stupendous' prehistoric monuments should have been sacrificed to 'wretched ignorance and avarice': Tom Robinson, who was 'particularly eminent for this kind of execution, and [...] very much glories in it'; Farmer Green, who took stones to build his house; John Fowler, who burned stones to build the White Hart alehouse; Walter Stretch, who used a broken-up megalith as building material for 'the dining-room end of the inn'; Farmer Griffin who ploughed up the Sanctuary in 1724, and 'that destroyer' Richard Fowler, who broke up stones at Beckhampton.[10]

By the 20th century, most of the surviving stones had fallen and the henge was overgrown with trees and shrubs, but this was far from being the end of Avebury's story. In the 1930s, the site was to undergo yet another dramatic change when Scottish archaeologist and marmalade heir Alexander Keiller bought the land on which the monuments stand and, with the help of a large team of locally hired workers, embarked on an ambitious restoration of the site. Today, the Avebury Papers project is painstakingly cataloguing and digitising thousands of photos, letters, diaries and other records from the Alexander Keiller Museum archive, with the aim of making them fully accessible online. When I visited the project's headquarters at Avebury Manor, Dr Fran Allfrey showed me some mind-bending before-and-after photographs of Keiller's restoration: the bank and ditch turned into a building site, trees blown up with dynamite and buildings bulldozed away, the henge recontoured, stripped back to its chalk bones and gleaming white – perhaps as it looked when it was first built all those millennia ago.

Or perhaps not. Archaeologist Stuart Piggott, who as a young man worked for Keiller at Avebury, described the restoration as 'megalithic landscape gardening'. And as Fran commented, 'It isn't standard archaeological practice to re-erect standing stones by sticking them back together and embedding them in concrete.' The photographs of megaliths being reset into the ground in the 1930s made me realise that the grass at Avebury must conceal a patchwork of concrete platforms. 'Keiller was so keen on fixing stones in concrete that he knocked down the Swindon Stone, which had never fallen, in order to re-erect it,' said Fran.

What's more, Keiller made decisions about the positioning of the stones based on the idea, current at the time, that they could be categorised as male (tall pillars) or female (triangular stones). He even changed the position of one stone in the West Kennet Avenue, which had been re-erected by his archaeological predecessor Maud Cunningham, because he believed she'd had it set up in the wrong place and upside-down.[11]

Not everyone loved the new Avebury. The artist Paul Nash wrote regretfully of his visit there in the last days before the restoration, when 'the great stones were in their wild state', half-hidden among crops and buried in undergrowth, 'wonderful and disquieting'.[12] For Nash, the restoration sterilised Avebury and left it as 'dead as a mammoth skeleton in the Natural History Museum'.[13] Nonetheless, there is something in those photographs of Avebury as building site that I find incredibly evocative. The methods of getting the stones upright – ropes, wooden stakes and a lot of manpower – were surely not that dissimilar to the ones used all those millennia ago. So when I read the surnames of the workers who reshaped the Avebury landscape in the 1930s, whose lives Fran and her colleagues are now trying to shine a light on – Ash, Ball, Bates, Blake, Bowsher, Bradley, Brindle, Buckingham, Bull, Butcher, Cable, Chivers, Dobson, Fishlock, Gale, Goddard, Griffiths, Hambridge, Harper, Horsell, Jones, King, Lanfear, Lovesey, Nash, Pearce, Pratt, Radbour, Rathband, Rogers, Salisbury, Sanderson, Strange, Tuck . . . .[14] – all noted in the archive as 'hands', I also think of the unnamed and for ever unknown Neolithic builders, whose hands first dug the ditch, built up the banks, raised all those stones.

STONE LANDS

Looking for Magic in the Landscape

I'm sure that if I, like Paul Nash, had first known Avebury in its wild, untouristed state, my mind blown by unexpected megaliths rearing up among the haystacks, I would have been heartbroken when, shortly afterwards, these picturesque ruins were taken to pieces, cleaned up and reassembled as a pristine restoration. But I have only ever known one Avebury and, to me, that Keiller managed to rescue so many buried and broken megaliths seems a kind of miracle, a turning back of the tide of history, a halting of the tendency to change and decay. It is not something that would be attempted now, but I'm glad it was done. And, in any case, almost a hundred years have passed since the restoration began, the concrete and chalk are long grassed over, the lichen has regrown on the scrubbed-up megaliths. Time has worked its illusion, making it all seem as if it has been this way for ever.

Visitors today find much magic and mystery in their wanderings around the Avebury monuments, and certainly do not experience them as sterile or dead. Since its 1930s restoration, Avebury has changed yet again and become something of a pilgrimage destination for alternative thinkers and spiritual seekers. Even when Stephen, Alex and Ava and I came at the bitter tail-end of winter (which we often did, for my birthday), the Henge Shop would be doing its usual brisk trade in crystals, oracle decks and hand-carved wands, and the stones would be as busy as ever with people wanting to commune with them in their various ways. The private rituals and public ceremonies conducted now may or may not bear any relation to what went on here thousands of years ago – and really, who cares? What matters is that people are still being drawn to this ancient place and giving it new life with their beliefs and practices.

An alluring web of mythology has been spun around Avebury by writers such as the visionary geographer Michael Dames, who was himself inspired by William Stukeley's conception of the stone monuments as a vast Druidic serpent temple extending over the whole landscape. In *The Silbury Treasure* (1976) and *The Avebury Cycle* (1977), Dames ties together monuments of different eras into a beautifully conceived myth cycle, suggesting that in prehistoric times sites such as West Kennet long barrow, Silbury Hill and Avebury henge were both stages for and symbolic participants in a year-long series of Goddess worship ceremonies to ensure the fertility of the fields and the return of the harvest. In Dames's scheme, the two avenues were serpents bringing the elemental life force of bride and groom to the henge for the May wedding festival of the Great Goddess and her consort, with the women of the community processing along West Kennet Avenue and the men along Beckhampton Avenue.[15] Silbury Hill is the Goddess herself and the place where the harvest is birthed at Lammas, the people gathering on the hill's summit terrace to watch the sun go down and the moon be reborn in the water surrounding the mound.[16]

Paul Nash believed that his 1934 painting *Landscape of the Megaliths* captured the energy and inner truth of the West Kennet Avenue, though entirely out of scale and geographically incorrect, in a way that the painstaking, tidy work of the archaeological restorers did not. It is only in his painting, he said, that

STONE LANDS

'Avebury seems to revive'. Nash's understanding of prehistory was not rooted in data and methodology, but rather in an attempt to intuit the unknown.[17] And in a way, megalith enthusiasts who come to Avebury today are confronted by the same problem and opportunity as Nash was. We can never, really, know what the Avebury monuments meant to the people who built them. All we can do is peer into the past, with whatever tools we have at our disposal, and see what intuition and imagination bring up.

For the broadcaster, writer and DJ Zakia Sewell, who has a passionate interest in exploring the folk culture of Britain and connecting with its ancient places, Avebury is 'still very magical and wild and free. There is something uncanny about the juxtaposition of these ancient stones and the ordinary village life around them. The connection to our ancient past feels somehow more direct there.'

She told me that her experience of the stones there is often a very meditative one. 'I like the idea that you can sort of tune in to the frequencies or traces of memory that are somehow embodied or left behind in these sites. I sit with the stones, meditate and let my imagination run wild, and try to get a sense of connection to the ancient people and whatever messages they may have for us in the present day. They're great places for reflection and contemplation. At the same time, there's something comical and silly and fun about the mystery of it all. There's something quite playful about Silbury Hill in particular!'

For Zakia, standing stones are a symbol of an alternative British story and identity: 'They're a way of making sense of my connection to Britain that has nothing to do with the dark legacies of empire or war. They're nothing to do with the stories and symbols that are rammed down our throats by the ruling classes. For me, these sites speak of another, subterranean spirit of Britain, something otherworldly and magical and mystical that really appeals to me not only because of its distance from those more troublesome histories, but also because of this magic. It is specific to particular landscapes and sites in Britain, but it's also a magic that's shared in lots of different places around the world.'

Zakia says that she is conscious sometimes of being the only person of colour at the sites she visits. 'It's quite common to have that feeling, walking through certain rural landscapes, that eyes are on you. I remember waiting one time at the bus stop to leave Avebury, and these two ladies walked past me and I was in that headspace of being a bit suspicious and self-conscious, wondering what they were thinking about me. And they just gave me a lovely smile and I smiled back, to counter that mental narrative. Then one of the ladies handed me a silver ring she'd just bought and she said, "You know, you gave me such a beautiful smile, I want to give you this gift."

'And that kind of confirmed the magic of Avebury for me, that there could be this exchange. This woman gave me a token as a memento of my time there and a reminder that this mental voice is not necessarily always telling the truth.'

In her BBC Radio 4 series *My Albion* and her book *Finding Albion*, Zakia is searching for stories through which we can connect to the land, to the deep past and to each other. Engaged in a parallel project, and coming at it from their own angle, are the creative collective Weird Walk, who publish zines and books and organise events based on finding re-enchantment via connection to ancient places. The three founders' collaboration was born out of a hike along the Ridgeway that inspired them to work creatively with the stories of the standing stones, burial chambers and earthworks they passed. They wanted 'to not just stretch the legs, but also get thinking and talking and creating around the land and its history, both real and imagined'.[18] Weird walking is both a physical and a psychic act, putting one foot in front of the other to leave the modern urban world behind and find a way back into the past, and so onward into re-enchantment and radical futures. The first-ever issue of their highly desirable zine (which alongside their book, also called *Weird Walk*, can be credited with raising the public profile of standing stones significantly in recent years) included, naturally, a guide to Avebury, rated as pre-eminent weird-walking territory: 'For us, there are few better places to explore on foot: this is England's Neolithic greatest hits set.'

Walking also inspires the artist known as the Man in the Woods, who makes 'artefacts that tell the story of strange, rural Britain' inspired by the walk he goes on each Friday, each time travelling by bus and/or train to the end point of the previous week's walk. In this way, the Man in the Wood's walks, which he shares with his followers on Instagram, add up to a single unbroken journey through the fields, woods and lanes of southern England. The walking, and his interest in prehistory, started when he lived in Salisbury in Wiltshire: 'The landscape around there, especially on Salisbury Plain and Cranborne Chase, is chock-a-block with hillforts, barrows, henges and cursuses. And it is relatively sparsely populated for the south of England, so you really get a sense of these monuments and their place in the landscape.'

He is particularly interested in Roman roads, which he's convinced are at least Iron Age, 'joining the dots between the hillforts', and probably much older. 'Following lines on OS maps and on the ground is a hobby of mine, tracing possible ancient paths along hedgerows and through modern housing estates. I'm always convinced that one day I'll realise I've accumulated all the pieces of a puzzle that I don't yet understand. Some sort of revelation, I suppose.'

I recognise this feeling of being offered partial insights into the meaning of an ancient landscape and the sense of imminent revelation. At Avebury, I am constantly being startled by new perspectives, by previously unnoticed sightlines from one site to another. Walking at Avebury I always feel wide awake, on the edge of understanding *something*, my senses sharpened by the conviction that there is mystery and significance here, if only I can grasp it. And at Avebury, where the ancient avenues and circular monuments themselves seem to lure you into movement, the revelation is surely to be gained by walking.

Whatever has altered here over time, the old sightlines remain, running from hill to monument and back again. Standing at the Sanctuary on top of Overton Hill, for example, where concentric circles of concrete blocks and posts mark where the stones and timber pillars once stood, and the traffic rushes past at motorway speeds on the Roman road now known as the A4, it's spine-tingling to scan the distant hillsides and pick out the old landmarks one by one: West Kennet Avenue snaking down from the little ridge that hides Avebury henge; Windmill Hill with its barrows on the horizon; Silbury Hill peeping balefully above the trees; West Kennet long barrow like a giant maggot in its field; and the tree-shrouded bump of inaccessible East Kennet long barrow, sinister as a setting from an M. R. James ghost story. All are still visible from here, as perhaps their builders meant them to be.

Today, Avebury draws people in ever-increasing numbers to celebrate the festivals of the Wheel of the Year, especially the key solar turning points of midsummer and midwinter. The Man in the Woods told me about his experience of waiting with a crowd of revellers within the henge for the sun to rise on the longest day. The previous evening, he'd walked in from Chippenham, a straightforward hike along a disused railway line that cleared his mind and prepared him for the all-nighter that lay ahead. 'By the time I got to Avebury I felt ready for it all. I like to be an observer, so I just wandered round, watching and taking it all in. I like the way these solstice events grow organically and are a real mix of things: Viking drinking horns, theatrical fire dancing and people who believe very sincerely in their neo-Pagan practice. They're a safe space to try an alternative way of connecting to the earth, the seasons and other people. I like that they're flexible and not proscriptive, and I like the sincerity as well as the comedy of it all.'

He continues: 'Staying up all night is a good way to lower your defences. It's difficult to overthink things when you're that tired, and I think it makes you feel everything much more keenly. We very rarely watch the sunrise and it is actually incredibly beautiful. The moving idea for me is that in a world full of distractions and buyable pleasure, so many people want to gather in a field and wait through the night to watch the sunrise. It means something different to everybody, but there is a kind of reverence present that feels very sweet and special. Perhaps even innocent. I can't imagine any other entertainment as simple as waiting to see the sun rise. And the idea that anybody still wants to do that now gives me hope.'

On our last morning in Avebury, I get up early, put on my running clothes and silently close the front door behind me, leaving Stephen and the children asleep. I especially do not want to wake Stephen, who has been more wrung out than he cared to admit by a day out in the wind and cold, and who, cancer or no cancer, is later today going to have to drive us all back to London.

Avebury is the same and yet not the same this February, and that in itself is very painful. We have come here because it was my fiftieth birthday a few days ago and we have to do something, but really we are just going through the motions. There is no joy in it. It is just over a month since Stephen fell ill and his chemo has not yet started; we don't have any answers, only this word 'incurable' that has changed everything. And that other word: 'palliative'. There's a constant sickening feeling of unease and dread, punctuated by overwhelming surges of sadness and despair.

And yet there are still beautiful moments, amid all this pain. We are still here, all together, in this wonderful ancient place that has been special to Stephen and me since we first met, and is probably special to the kids too, even if they wouldn't admit it. It is still possible (perhaps more possible than ever) to be moved by the incredible survival of these monuments now that life is falling apart.

STONE LANDS

As I exit the farm where we are staying, Silbury looms starkly, a slag heap against the steel-grey sky. To put some distance between me and the traffic hurtling along the A4, I run inside the fence along the field edge and it's hard going through the mud. But I'm making progress and eventually, after some clambering over fences, I'm in the meadow at the foot of the hill crowned by the West Kennet long barrow. The clear chalk-bottomed streams, fringed with crowfoot and starwort, are delightful and refreshing to see even on this dismal, drizzly day. Beyond the curve of a stream is a kind of nook tucked into the steeply rising ground, where the trees are hung with clooties, strings of beads and crystals. Here are the Swallowhead Springs, a source of the River Kennet, and much depleted since, according to William Stukeley, a fox spoiled them in the 18th century with its digging, disturbing the sacred nymphs who used to dwell there.[19] People have built up little dams of rocks to try to make more of the flow that remains.

Stukeley recorded that local people would hold a meeting on top of Silbury Hill every Palm Sunday, and take up cakes, figs, sugar and water from the springs and make merry. He noted that apium grew plentifully at this spring head, and that the country people had 'a particular regard for the herbs growing there, and a high opinion of their virtue'. It sounds like the spring water here may once have been thought to have healing properties.

I cross carefully on the slippery stepping stones and crouch down to the water. Feeling self-conscious, although no one is around, but determined to give this a go, I immerse the peridot ring recently given to me by my mum ('a healing stone', she'd called it, though she's not what you might describe as a crystals person). I pause for a moment with my fingers in the icy stream, letting the water ripple over the green stone of the ring, watching the raindrop circles spreading outwards, listening to the rustle of the clooties and twigs, the splash of rain, the hum of the A4. I don't have any clear idea of what I am going to achieve by this, only that I need to try everything and, judging by the offerings and tokens left here, I'm not the first to do so.

Despite the morning's gloom, I feel a lightening inside, a ray of hope. Avebury is working its magic on me. The peridot charged, I run back to Stephen.

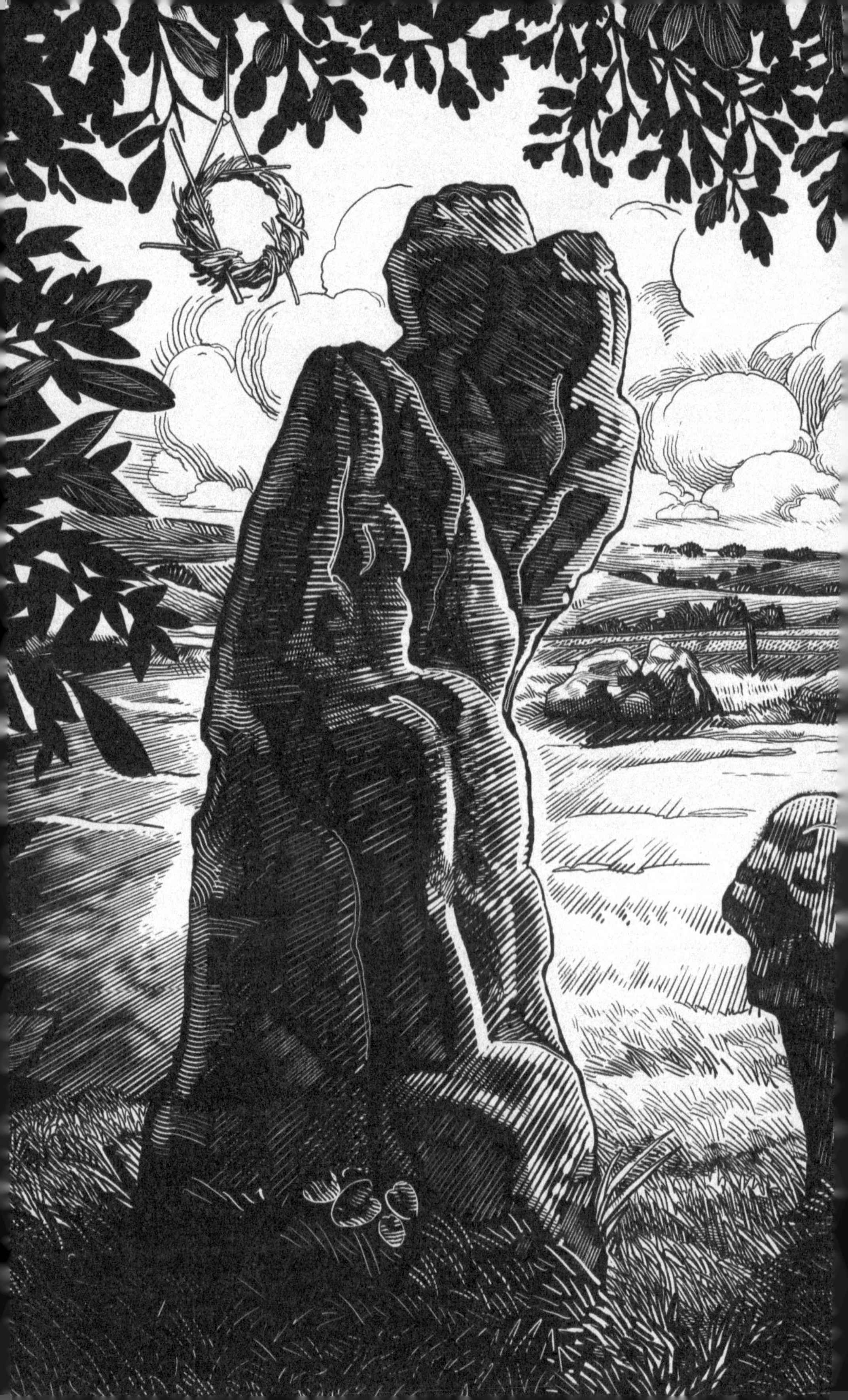

Chapter 2

THE STORIES WE TELL SHAPE OUR WORLD

- c.3800–3500 BCE: Whispering Knights built
- c.2500 BCE: King's Men built
- c.1500 BCE: King Stone raised

The Rollright Stones, OXFORDSHIRE

HERE'S AN OLD MEMORY, from a time long before I met Stephen. I'm lying on my back inside a close-set circle of jagged stones, like a ring of rotten teeth. The sky, deepening towards dusk, has a purplish tinge and the leaves of the trees that screen the stones from the lane are glowing an unnatural luminous green. People have been coming and going all afternoon, but now my companion and I have the stones to ourselves. We're sun-dazed, and hazy from the spliffs we've shared. Oxford, where I'm studying, seems a long way away. I'm struggling a bit at university, dealing with anxiety by drinking too much and at weekends escaping entirely, going off with my boyfriend in his car to explore the countryside.

Staring at the stones from my upside-down angle flat out on the grass, these gnarly, pitted and holed megaliths seem weirder than ever and it occurs to me there might be something

STONE LANDS

threatening about them. The King's Men are all around us and there's a tension in the air, a sense of expectancy. It's not that the stones are hostile, precisely, but they are sentient. They are watching – and waiting.

And then, something happens. A gust of wind brings the trees to life, leaves flashing green and silver like a shoal of fish. Just when you'd expect the breeze to die down it grows stronger, and then stronger again, the branches shaking fiercely as if the trees were in the grip of a giant determined to uproot them. This goes on for much longer than seems natural. I have the strangest sense that something important is about to happen, that something, or even *someone*, is about to burst through. The Green Man perhaps, or the witch who lives in these parts. If the stones are going to reanimate, then now ... *now* ... is the moment. I hold my breath and wait.

That first visit to the Rollright Stones, a mythic realm hidden in sedate Cotswold farmland, showed me how legend can enchant a landscape and create a portal to the otherworld that exists in parallel to our own. A world that looks much like ours, but where the old tales are real and anything can happen.

When I think about the Rollright Stones, I think about the stories: all those legends of stones that move, stones that whisper, stones that were once living, breathing people, of the tales of dancing fairies and malicious witches, of an ancient road frequented by ghosts, and of energy force fields radiating from the stones. It would be difficult, said Arthur J. Evans, the archaeologist who recorded many of the Rollright legends at the end of the 19th century, to find another site in which folklore lives on to the degree that it does here,[20] and this remains the case.

The Stories We Tell Shape Our World

We are still telling stories, still coming up with theories about this place.

I am thinking a lot about stories and storytelling these days, about how we constantly create and recreate our world through the tales we tell ourselves and others. On the last day of the last December of my 40s, I started a new diary. I seem always to have a few journals on the go; there's an everyday one with space for just a line or two per day, and another one just for holidays, and another for collecting writing ideas that I never get around to following up. This new diary was going to be an occasional stock-taking one, a place to work out what was going on for me and what I wanted to happen next. Because I was about to turn 50, and I wanted to make the most of the rest of my life. In this New Year's Eve entry, I listed all the things I'd been grateful for that year, finishing with the most important one of all: Stephen and the kids. *Such a privilege to have this love in my life*, I wrote.

A few weeks passed before I wrote in it again and by then everything had changed. *I never dreamed this is where we'd be a month later – a place where sadness is always close at hand and the future is very uncertain. Stephen has cancer and it probably can't be cured. We don't know what kind of cancer it is, or how fast-growing, or what treatment he can have or how long he will live.* I wrote all this down without really believing any it. *Am I really writing these words?* I wrote. *About us?*

We were being passed like a football between Lewisham and King's and Guy's, waiting for someone to confirm the diagnosis and the treatment plan, and the waiting was killing us and yet it was also a kind of reprieve, my first lesson in the efficacy of storytelling, of fixing your eyes on the hopeful stuff and blocking out the rest. Once they'd put in a temporary stent and got the bile duct draining again, and the jaundice subsided, it was possible to think, looking at Stephen as he set off on a bike ride or to meet a friend or to go to the library to read for his PhD (he was signed off work but filling his days in his usual energetic manner), that there was nothing wrong with him. Maybe his skin was somewhat yellowish and he was a shade thinner than before, but that was all. He was young, he was fit, he was positive, he was doing all the right things; if anyone had a fighting chance with this illness, it was him.

I'd always wondered how people managed to function with an appalling threat hanging over them. How can you motivate yourself to fold the laundry or meet work deadlines when you're living in the shadow of a terminal diagnosis? Well, as I discovered, it's actually quite straightforward: you do it by telling yourself stories. Something was obstructing the biliary tube and giving Stephen jaundice: it had to be gallstones. OK, so it wasn't gallstones . . . Then the lump surely was a benign cyst, or a lesion caused by undiagnosed hepatitis picked up while travelling in Asia. Whatever it was, it couldn't be *cancer*, or at least not a life-threatening form; how could this non-smoking, (mostly) moderate-drinking, super-healthy-eating, not-yet-50-year-old outdoors enthusiast have liver cancer? It just wasn't possible.

And as it turned out, it wasn't liver cancer. It was gallbladder cancer. So we found new stories to tell ourselves. We told ourselves that the dismal life expectancy associated with this rare cancer was only because it was typically found in patients 20 or 30 years older than Stephen and nearing the end of their

The Stories We Tell Shape Our World

natural lives (don't look at the internet, my friend Bob warned, offering to do the research for us so we wouldn't be frightened by the statistics). We told ourselves that we were lucky: if it had to happen, then thank goodness it happened when we were still living in London, close to multiple world-class cancer centres. We told ourselves cancer research was advancing in incredible strides and there were new treatments out there already that could cure the incurable, or at least, if they didn't exist now, we could confidently expect them to be developed in the next few years. It was just a case of holding on. We told ourselves stories about people living with stage 4 cancer, many of them still alive a decade or two or more after the initial diagnosis.

For the first time I properly understood the truth in the mind-body-spirit cliché 'change your thoughts to change your life'. In the office, I'd shut the meeting-room door and howl silently into my fists. Then I'd wash my face, go back to my desk and focus on my work, burrowing into the screen in front of me, shutting down the voices in my head. I caught my mind again and again in the act of shaping my world, turning it dark or light depending on the storyline, and I understood how our thoughts in a very real way create our lived experience. I saw exactly how my mind constructs reality by stitching a plausible illusion together, how it seamlessly weaves disparate bits of information into a convincing picture that you can't help but believe, a compelling fabrication that presents itself as the only reality possible – and then falls apart. One moment we are looking forward to the rest of our lives together (but the cancer is already there); the next, the illusion disintegrates and we are in an agony of fear and despair; the next, our minds are busy stitching our world back together again, because it's the illusion that makes living possible.

I'd always been someone who was quick to see the gloomy side, to blow up in a panic when something went wrong, but now that I was confronted with something really horrifically bad, I realised that we can, to some degree, choose the stories we tell ourselves. We can choose, even if we can only manage it for a short while at a time, to focus on love instead of fear. We can choose hope instead of despair. We can find moments of happiness in the midst of terrible worry. We can accept that our apparently solid reality is an illusion that cannot last and still find joy in focusing on all its wondrous details.

Stories that Enchant a Landscape

Rollright is one of those ancient places I keep getting drawn back to. I came back again a few months after Stephen's diagnosis, in a summer that was shadowed with darkness and all the more beautiful for being thrown into relief and for my new understanding that everything is finite. This time I was with the folklorist Neil Philip and his wife, the artist Emma Bradford. We talked about the legends associated with these stones, and they recommended Penelope Lively's *The Whispering Knights*, a magical book about this storied landscape that somehow I'd missed reading as a child. They'd invited me to lunch at their Cotswold home to celebrate sending the new edition of Neil's awesome collection of English folk tales to press, and very kindly drove me up to the Rollrights, because they knew I loved

The Stories We Tell Shape Our World

standing stones and they wanted to distract me from my worries back home. They had worries of their own: Neil's beloved Emma had been ill for a while and now she needed a wheelchair to get around. But she was determined to get up there, even if the Rollright paths were not that wheelchair friendly in practice, to see the stones again.

A combine harvester was working the field next to the King's Men stone circle that day and a cloud of dust hung over the wicker fairy who danced near by, like a visible manifestation of the potent energies some believe these stones emit. This place has a strong magical vibe. Pentagrams and wreaths dangle next to the rags and ribbons in the branches of the trees around the circle, and little offerings – tea lights, flower garlands, crystals, pebbles, coins, and the like – have been left around the stones and wedged in the crevices. A circular track, like a velodrome for the fairies who live in an underground hall here, has been worn in the dry grass by all the people walking round the stones; a couple are doing that when we arrive, touching each stone as they go.

There is something special about this place; that's the story that could have been told since as long ago as the early Neolithic. Around 3800–3500 BCE, the Whispering Knights portal tomb was built in what was then a clearing in woodland, its massive capstone (the flat stone forming the roof of the chamber) supported on large stone uprights. At least 1,000 years later, in the late Neolithic *c.*2500 BCE, the King's Men stone circle was constructed just 350 metres away from the portal tomb. And then, 1,000 years later still, *c.*1500 BCE (now in the Bronze Age), the standing stone known as the King Stone was erected a little way

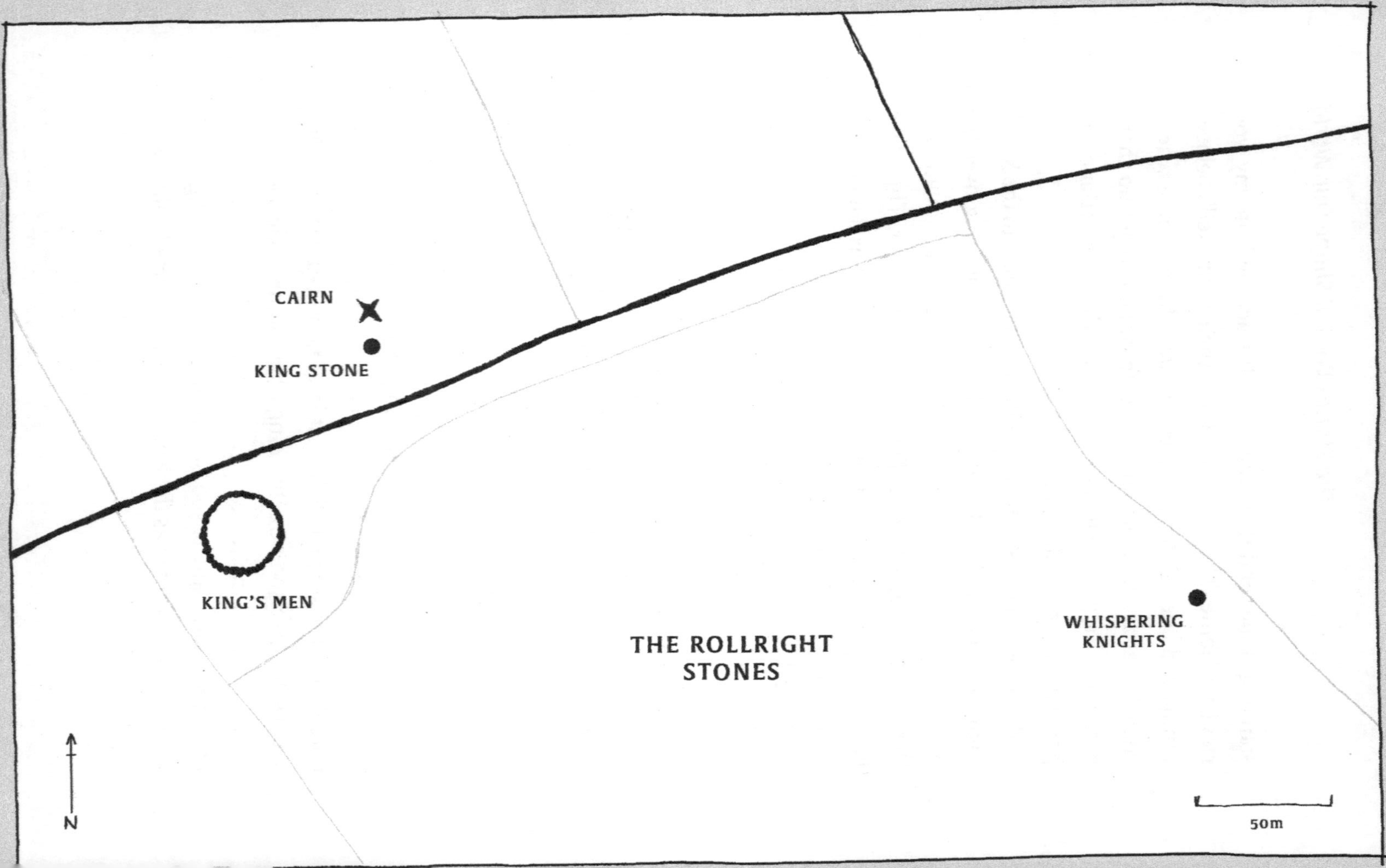
CAIRN
KING STONE
KING'S MEN
THE ROLLRIGHT STONES
WHISPERING KNIGHTS
N
50m

The Stories We Tell Shape Our World

north of the stone circle, probably to mark a burial ground. Though most of the prehistoric barrows have vanished, we know that many were built on the heath close to the stone monuments,[21] and the Saxons buried their dead here, too. Was the story that this was sacred ground handed down from generation to generation through the 2,000 years that separated the building of the Whispering Knights from the erection of the King Stone, and then on into medieval times and even beyond? In the Victorian era, Arthur J. Evans noted the 'curious kind of sanctity' that seemed to linger about the Rollright Stones, and he recorded the words of a farm worker who was asked where he was going one Good Friday: 'Why, I be a going to the King-stones, for there I shall be on holy ground.'[22]

The most famous Rollright story, of course, is the one about the witch, recorded by Arthur J. Evans in 1895. It goes like this. A would-be king of England led his soldiers onto land belonging to a witch. Just before he reached the top of the hill, the witch appeared and offered him a tempting bargain:

> Seven long strides shalt thou take, and if Long Compton
> thou canst see, King of England thou shalt be.

Confident of victory, the king-to-be takes the seven steps, but very unfortunately just as he reaches the top of the hill, a mound of earth rises up, blocking his view of Long Compton. The witch then calls down a curse on all of them (herself included):

> As Long Compton thou canst not see King of England thou
> shalt not be.

STONE LANDS

> Rise up, stick, and stand still, stone,
> For King of England thou shalt be none,
> Thou and thy men hoar stones shall be
> And I myself an eldern-tree.[23]

At that, everyone turns to stone except for the witch, who is transformed into an elder. One day, the legend concludes, the stones will change back to flesh and blood, and the king will defeat his enemies and rule over all the land.

This story is a powerful one because it's rooted in what's there on the ground; once you know the legend, it's hard to see the stones in any other way. Blink and the King's Men transform into a band of dusty, footsore, weather-beaten soldiers who've just marched up from Long Compton and are now slouching in a ring in the corner of the field. Look back at the Whispering Knights and see how the slabs of the portal tomb, slipped from their Neolithic position, are leaning in towards one another as if you've caught the treacherous counsellors in the act of conspiring to betray their leader. In the 19th century, it was thought possible to hear them whisper, if you put your ear to a crack in the rock. The girls bringing in the barley harvest would go there at dusk and listen, hoping to learn what their future held.[24]

Even the peculiar contorted shape of the King Stone seems to encapsulate perfectly the frustration of the Rollright legend – just three or four steps (that's all!) and he would have been King of England. Looking at this stone, it's as if we can see the trapped king bowing his head in anguish, although the distinctive curving outline was actually created by people chipping off pieces as good-luck charms or souvenirs (and this is why the protective railings were put up in the 1880s). What's more, just as the legend has it, Long Compton cannot be seen from the King Stone, because the view is blocked by a natural mound (with a grassed-over Bronze Age cairn set into its ridge). A few more strides and an epic view of Warwickshire, including the distant rooftops of Long Compton, opens up.

Under the King Stone, so one legend goes, is a cave where the cursed would-be king sleeps, like Arthur under Alderley Edge. Fairies live here too. Arthur J. Evans reported that one Will Hughes had actually seen them dancing around, 'little folk like girls to look at'. When Will's widow Betsy had been a child working in the hedgerows, she'd seen the very hole in the bank by the King Stone where the fairies came out to dance at night. She and her friends used to put a stone over the hole to keep the fairies in, and they'd always find it turned over the next morning.[25]

There are yet more tales. The stones of the King's Men circle can't be counted (this is true: I've never got the same number twice). Sometimes they go down the hill at midnight to drink from a spring, and a gap in the bushes has been worn by their passing. Any attempt to steal the dislodged capstone of the Whispering Knights always leads to trouble. In one version of the story, 20 horses and a great deal of effort were required to drag the stone down to Little Rollright and haul it across the stream to make a bridge. In the night the stone flipped itself onto the river bank, so the next day the people tried again, only to find it on the bank yet again the following morning. After the third failed attempt, they realised the stone would have to be returned, and a single horse sufficed to take it back up the hill.[26]

There are still elder trees growing around the King's Men, but it's not obvious which is the witch. In fact, it's only relatively recently that the witch became so prominent in Rollright folklore. She's not mentioned in the earliest surviving version of the legend in William Camden's *Britannia* (1586), nor in the one recorded by Dr Robert Plot in his *Natural History of Oxfordshire* (1677). In an early 18th-century version of the Rollright rhyme, it's a Danish general who wishes to become King of England, and a Saxon general who frustrates him.[27] A mid-1800s version of the story refers to a 'great magician'.[28] It's only at the end of the 19th century that the Rollright witch appears in recorded legend, and by this time Long Compton and its surroundings had a reputation as a haunt of witches. One of the many local stories gathered by folklorists in the early 20th century tells of Dolly Henderson, who lived down the hill from the Rollright Stones and bewitched a woman named Ann Hulver and a boy. Ann wasted away until she looked like a skeleton, but she and the boy were saved when the boy's brother threw a thorn stick at Dolly and made her arm bleed, breaking the spell.[29] This echoes an old Rollright tale recorded by Arthur J. Evans: on Midsummer's Eve, the people would come to the King Stone, gather in a circle and cut the blossoming elder to release its sap – the witch's blood. As the witch bled, the king would move his head, the blood-letting ritual having weakened the witch's power enough to lift for a while the curse that kept him frozen in stone form.

It's not clear if the other Warwickshire witch stories were inspired by the Rollright legend, or if the Rollright legend had changed because of them. Either way, the tales of malevolent local witches cast a shadow over Long Compton in 1874, when James Haywood killed his elderly neighbour Ann Tennant with a pitchfork because he believed her to be just one of many witches plaguing their village. In the same year as the Long Compton murder, a witch-hunting mob elsewhere in Warwickshire stormed into Tysoe to attack another woman, stabbing her in the hand with a corking pin to draw her blood.[30] Stories shape our world for good or ill, and the idea that a witch's curse can be broken by making her bleed can be a dangerous one.

A further twist in the story of the Rollright witch came in 2015, when a metal detectorist discovered an ancient burial close to the King Stone. Archaeologists uncovered the grave of a high-status woman from the 7th century, who had been buried with several possessions including a mysterious ritual tool – a long-handled skillet decorated with a silver disc inlaid with a garnet.[31] It was this skillet, thought to be a rare artefact used in ceremonial, perhaps even magical practice, that led to the newspapers announcing that the original witch – Rita of Rollright, they called her – had been identified at last.

Telling Stories about Stones (and Ourselves)

Throughout the 20th century, lurid stories of blood rites and Satan worship swirled around the Rollrights, but although several people told me that they knew someone who'd found evidence of animal sacrifice at the stones, I think it's been a long while since anyone tried anything like that there. (Although the feeling that these stones in particular have a dark side does seem to persist.) These days, the word 'witch' is no longer an insult but an identity cherished by many, and witchcraft is widely embraced as a benevolent nature-oriented spirituality. The eight festivals of the Wiccan Wheel of the Year – Imbolc, Ostara (spring equinox), Beltane, Litha (summer solstice), Lughnasadh, Mabon (autumn equinox), Samhain and Yule (winter solstice) – are observed by many outside the organised Pagan communities as well as those within. And it makes sense to me that people should be drawn to celebrate the changing seasons at a stone circle, which evokes in its very form not only the sun but also the idea of a year that rolls ever on, turning each ending into a new beginning.

Interfaith Minister Rev Helen James and the energy worker and crystal healing teacher Kelly Peacey are friends who conduct Wheel of the Year ceremonies at the Rollright Stones and other ancient sites. For 30 years, Helen worked in TV, news-reporting and presenting for ITV Yorkshire/Meridian, then running her own video production company promoting some of Britain's best-loved dramas, including *Endeavour*, *Poldark* and *Midsomer Murders*. All the while, she was feeling drawn in a spiritual direction, which led her to train as a Reiki Master and in 2021 become an ordained Interfaith Minister. These two strands of her life now come together in her *Sacred Journeys* video series, which explores the visits she and Kelly make to sites across Britain, and which Helen films, directs and edits.

Helen describes what happens when the group exit their cars with their gongs and bells in the Rollright lay-by: 'People who are out walking their dogs want to join in. Once, some ladies had come from Oxford having felt an intuitive call to visit the stones. When they saw us they said, "*Now* we know why we've come. We want to be with you!" Then suddenly there's 25 extra people taking part – and that's so wonderful. Children join in too, scattering rose petals and counting the stones. We gather outside the circle, so the stones are free for those who don't want to be a part of our ceremony.'

They meditate, connect with the stones, share their experiences and invite each other to let go of the things that no longer serve them. They express their love and gratitude for the land, and leave offerings – only things that will disintegrate, such as cookies or seasonal flowers. And then they have something to eat, sharing whatever people have brought with them: different curries and bakes, a little glass of mead.

Kelly adds, 'The nature of the rock used at ancient sites is really interesting. I see standing stones as extra-large healing stones and I believe the builders of the Rollright Stones understood the subtle electrical and magnetic properties of the oolitic limestone they choose to use there, which includes quartz, calcite and traces of iron. Quartz is one of the most abundant stones on the planet and it's found in most everyday electronic devices, including your mobile phone. It's clearly there not just for us to revere but also for us to make use of, to amplify our thoughts and our intentions. I believe the people who built Rollright placed each stone with great precision to interact with the subtle energies of the land.'

Alison Merry is an artist, as well as an archaeologist by training and a Morris dancer. One evening she went with her side, the Miserden Morris, and their friends the Boss Morris (the side that Merry's daughter Alex leads) to the Rollright Stones. Their intention was to meet just for the joy of it, not to draw a crowd of onlookers, but to enjoy dancing with each other at this special place and to celebrate a couple of birthdays. She describes the event, which sounds like a huge amount of fun: 'One of Boss was having a birthday and decided it was to be elf-themed so, as we're always looking for an excuse to dress up, gnome hats and false beards were bought. We read some poetry at the stones and ate cake and just celebrated being there. It really was an eccentric evening and not, I hasten to add, entirely typical of a Morris dance-out – but it was joyful to all be together and to dance around the ancient stones in our uninhibited way. I think we can presume that ceremony of some sort took place there in prehistory, so there was a sense of continuity in us using the space for dance.'

When Alison showed me the lines that they read by the King Stone that elfin evening (by Damian Walford Davies, taken from the introduction to his book *Megalith* and delivered as a poem or a sort of incantation), I was struck by how they beautifully capture the way we project our human preoccupations onto the stones and are forever telling stories about them in order to tell stories about ourselves:

> In their lichened, faceted faces we see our lineaments; in their solitariness, our loneliness, or our need to be alone; in their gregariousness, our congregational temper; in their alignment, our deviousness; in their poised mass, our fragility; in their rootedness, our deracination; in their age, our ephemerality; and in their naked outfacing of time and the elements, a valuable lesson in patient dissent.[32]

The Stories We Tell Shape Our World

'It was very special and moving to stand there and hear those words about the stones,' Alison says. 'I think we all share a sense of their mystery, romance, antiquity, power and beauty. And many sites have legends, but the Rollrights have a richer stock than most.'

Alison has painted the King Stone and King's Men at the moment of transformation, when they are simultaneously human and rock. She let the shape of the megaliths reveal the man within: 'My starting point was with the stones themselves, drawing an outline of each one. Then I looked for a human form as best I could and imagined it as the contorted shape of a soldier mid-petrification, reacting with surprise and terror as their body turned to stone! My young children – as they were back then – loved watching them materialise.'

Whenever Stephen and the children and I have come to the Rollright Stones, it has been on our way back to London from somewhere else – Oxford or the Malverns or Wales. And whenever we've come, I've always been reminded of my very first visit and the feeling that I'd stumbled upon a portal to a parallel world where the hills and fields and streets might look the same as ours, but where an elder tree could be an enchanted witch, and a circle of stones might at any moment turn back to human form. A world where magic is real.

This July noon, as the combine harvester prowls up and down, and the dust cloud swirls, and I talk with Neil Philip and Emma Bradford about folklore and legend, the Cotswold fields seem busy with shadowy figures: all those soldiers and a witch and the standing stones that just won't stay still. I look out for ghosts on

STONE LANDS

the fast country lane that you have to cross to get from the stone circle to the King Stone, an ancient road (part of a medieval saltway and very possibly much older) that happens to mark the Oxfordshire–Warwickshire border and was described by energy-researcher Paul Devereux of the Dragon Project as the 'spook road' because of the paranormal visions some of his group experienced there.[33]

I catch the echoes of my own past too, of the visits Stephen, Alex, Ava and I have made here. I see a tiny girl in a pink cardigan with a determined expression on her face and a hand on the railings surrounding the King Stone, clearly plotting to somehow get in and climb it. I see a serious-looking, perfectly composed boy listing the canon *Star Wars* films in order and refusing to be tricked into enthusiasm about this ancient site by the information that the Tom Baker *Doctor Who* episode 'Stones of Blood' was filmed here (with the addition of a large polystyrene dolmen). I see a tall, thin, athletic man crossing the field to the Whispering Knights, running ahead of his children, drawing them on, laughing at the youngest one, who is hiding her face in her coat and expressing extreme displeasure at being made to walk around these stupid stones while trying to suppress her giggles. I see him scooping her up in his arms and putting her on his shoulders, which is what she wanted all along. I see the four of us playing games of hide-and-seek, trying to fit our bodies behind too-small stones. Jumping out at each other and playing chase, pretending to be the witch.

There is a last time for everything, though when that happens we rarely know it for what it is – and so we should approach each thing as if we'll never have a chance to experience it again. Remembering always that happiness is one of those things that's clearest seen when looking back.

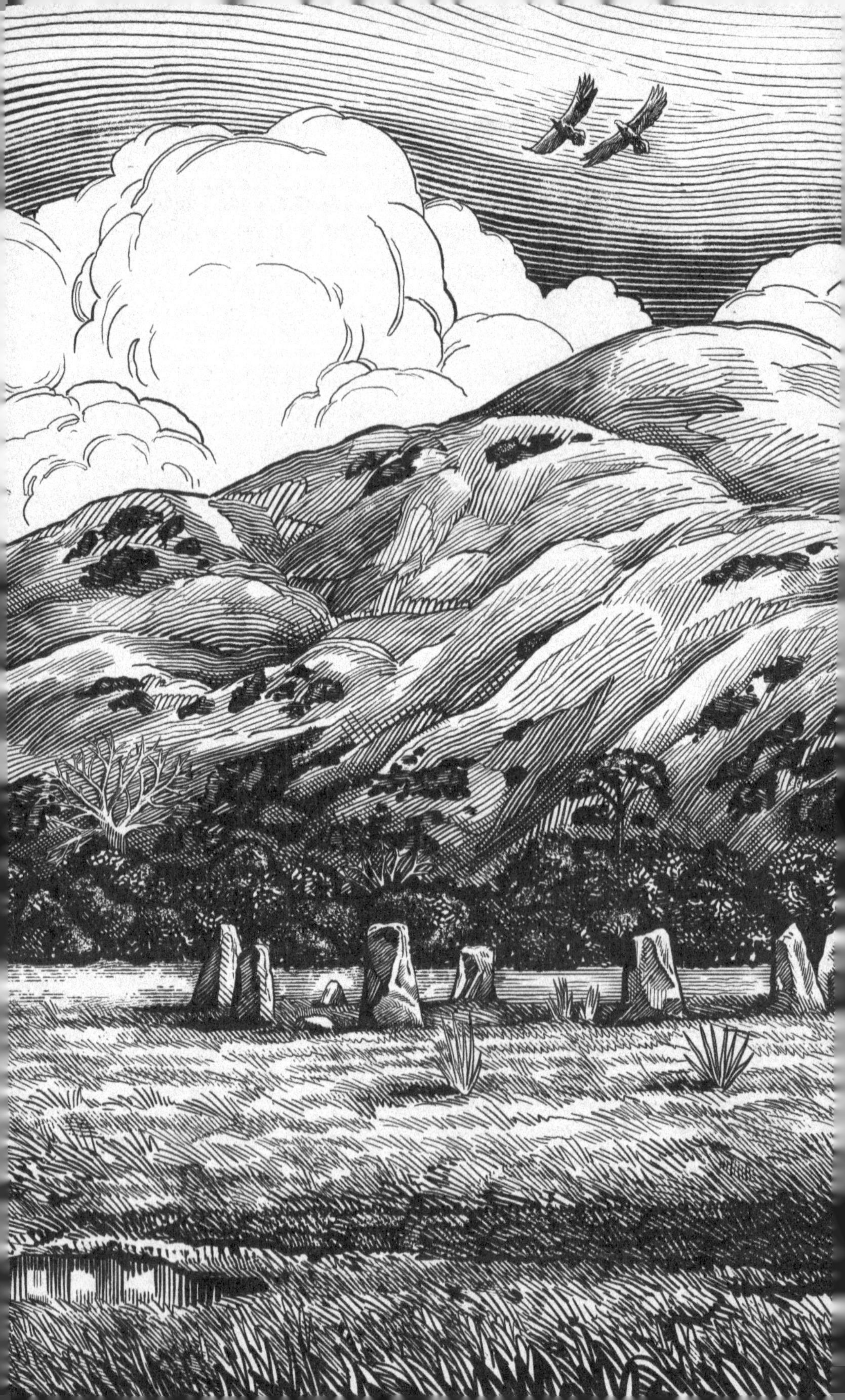

Chapter 3

THE THING IS TO KEEP GOING

Stones of the Isle of Mull

I'M PICKING MY WAY across the pasture, following the trail of white stones as the sign by the parking place instructed. If the golden eagles surfing the air currents high above the flanks of Ben Buie have any interest in the tiny figure of a human far below, they might be curious as to why I'm taking this winding route and making such slow progress across the field. On the ground the reason is obvious – bog. The weather has been especially wet this year and the cows that graze this field have churned up the soil so much that now to some considerable depth it's more liquid than solid, the consistency of a very loose cowpat. Unfortunately, my wellies are 520 miles away, so I'm hopping from tussock to tussock, trying to find a path through the mire.

I'm only grateful that the cows themselves are nowhere to be seen, probably drying off their shaggy coats in a nice cosy barn somewhere. The presence of multiple fresh cowpats adds an extra edge to the situation. Highland cows look cute, with their floppy over-the-forehead fringes and curving horns, sweetly bullish like a shy teenage boy. But I prefer them behind a fence and if a herd of them were to come wallowing over to investigate me right now, it would be impossible to retreat with any speed.

Black clouds are gathering and the light has dimmed. It's hard to make out the white marker stones in the gloom, especially as most of them are almost submerged. Logs and planks have been laid across the worst bits but these are often unreachable, marooned in deep mud. My leg sinks in over the top of my hiking boot and I manage to tug it out again, the bog clinging to my calf as if it's trying to suck me in. There are now no white stones to be seen at all, in any direction. I have the alarming sense that the entire ground has become unstable and any minute now is going to swallow me up. I've been working slowly across this field for almost an hour and I can still see the car, but a boggy labyrinth lies between me and it, and I'm not quite sure how I'm going to find my way back.

And then my heart leaps – the stones! There they are, away across the pasture: the ghostly shapes of the megaliths of Lochbuie circle. The electricity that has been low-level humming through my veins all the while I was hopping through the mire now flares up in a burst of excitement: it's them! That moment of sighting stones for the first time, seeing them standing upright as they've stood for several thousand years, never fails to thrill me. There's a moment of recognition – ah yes, I know you! – as if the form of a standing stone is hardwired into my psyche and I feel

The Thing is to Keep Going

immediate connection with each of its individual manifestations. The stones always seem so *alive*, on the verge of movement, and I can understand all those legends of people turned to stone because that's exactly what they look like when you catch your first glimpse of them across the moor or over a hedge. They look human.

As I peer excitedly into the murky distance, one of the stones does actually move, and then another. And then another. I realise I am looking not at distant stones but at deer. The rain is getting heavier. I've lost the path. It is past the kids' lunchtime and I know they will be staging a riot in the car, and that Stephen will have had enough of eagle-watching by now. And, frankly, I'm scared of this bog, of its loneliness and unpredictability. I turn back.

This fail really bothered me. I'd had my heart set on getting to Lochbuie, the remote stone circle on the southern shore of the Inner Hebridean island of Mull, off the west coast of Scotland. Getting from London to Lochbuie is no small undertaking: a two-day journey via car and ferry to Tobermory, and then a somewhat hairy drive, once you leave the main (albeit just single-track) Tobermory–Fionnphort road, for eight long miles down a bumpy lane that winds through gnarly woodland and tunnels of rhododendrons, and alongside a glittering sea loch. Stephen was driving, as always; my contribution as a non-driver was to peer ahead to give warning of oncoming cars and try, with enthusiastic commentary on the surroundings (Look at the loch! Look at the eagle!), to distract the children from fighting in the back seat and complaining about how long it was all taking.

STONE LANDS

I had a list of excuses for not getting to the Lochbuie circle (inappropriate footwear, kids, weather) and repeated them frequently to myself and others, but I didn't convince anyone, least of all myself. What it boiled down to was that I'd come close to an enchanted place and let myself be foiled by a bit of mud. This really rankled. It was just so *disappointing* . . . and all the more so as I'd let quite a few people know that I was going to these stones, and then had to explain shamefacedly that I hadn't managed it after all.

So the following spring we did it all again, setting off on another stones pilgrimage: the two-day journey to Mull, the hairy drive to Lochbuie, the bog. This time we were prepared with wellies, snacks and a more determined attitude, and the four of us took on the mud together. Alex and Ava, at that time aged seven and four, turned out to be natural bog trotters, balancing trustfully on submerged logs, leaping nimbly from grassy tuft to tuft, squelching happily through knee-deep mud.

There are stations on the way to the Lochbuie circle, letting you know you're on the right path. First a single standing stone, a flat slab scarred with a map-like pattern of cracks. Then a ruined kerb-cairn in a clump of trees, the surviving stones giving a sense of the outer kerb that once ringed the (now disappeared) cairn. Then, in the field of the circle, the brutally truncated stump of a stone, struck by lightning perhaps. Then, as you get close to the circle, two tall outliers, one of them a tapering, jagged monolith, its top like an index finger pointing up to the hills.

And then at last, standing before a fringe of rhododendrons and with the head and shoulders of Ben Buie offering an awe-

The Thing is to Keep Going

inspiring backdrop, the nine megaliths of Lochbuie circle! They are all ancient and original apart from one small boulder that marks the spot of a missing stone. Mossy, fissured and sturdy pillars these, no giants but like Highland cows obstinately holding their own, persisting in the face of bad weather and the passing of millennia. In their triangular-ish forms, they seem to echo the shape of Ben Buie rising above. As we approach, the clouds draw apart and sun lights up the water-sodden grass, as if in celebration of our arrival, turning it into a glittering field of the cloth of gold. The eagles sweep over the flanks of Ben Buie, their shadows racing each other across the moorland hundreds of feet below. We take possession of the circle at last and I walk sunwise around the nine stones, touching them one by one. The wind shakes the trees and brings the sound of rushing water from the sea loch. It is a glorious and unforgettable moment – for the adults, at least. The kids are hungry again and moaning.

If at First You Don't Succeed . . .

Stone fails are a part of the megalith hunter's life, and for every spectacular shot on my camera of granite pillars soaring dramatically against a blue sky, there's a lame image taken from behind a barbed-wire fence of a distant jumble of rocks defended by a herd of cows.

The novelist Jackie Fraser (author of *The Bookshop of Second Chances* and *The Beginning of Everything*) had trouble with the Lochbuie bog, too. I initially connected with her through the #dailymegalith she used to post on Twitter, then ended up

STONE LANDS

getting her involved in the writing and editing of *The Old Stones* (the brilliant guide to Britain's prehistoric sites by Andy Burnham of The Megalithic Portal, which I commissioned when I was an editor at Watkins). Jackie is a dedicated stones enthusiast who's spent decades working her way through pretty much all the standing stone sites of Britain. She has her own approach to traversing boggy ground which I wish I'd been brave enough to try: 'It was extremely wet at Lochbuie, wet enough that after a short time I took my shoes off altogether and went barefoot across the bog, water squeezing between my toes. Cautiously, because farmland is full of sheep shit and rusty metal and risk of tetanus and goodness knows what else. It was a good feeling though – primal. It felt significant.'

Though she didn't fail Lochbuie, other sites have eluded her: 'I always feel that if a site has been given a signpost, any cows there should be reasonably friendly, but we've failed a number of places because of them. We failed Llech Golman and Hendrefor burial chambers on Anglesey (twice). Sheldon recumbent circle in Aberdeenshire is quite close to the road, so was tantalisingly visible from the gate but surrounded by cows and therefore inaccessible. At Ardlair in Aberdeenshire we were foiled by cattle on the first visit but managed to see it the second time.'

I agree with Jackie that a visit doesn't really count if you can't actually touch the stones. It turns out her second trip to Ardlair was 12 years after that initial fail – sometimes it's just not possible to let something go. I know the feeling. And as a city dweller, I also get that thing about cows. I hesitate to enter a field with a herd in it, even when the field also contains a standing stone. And while usually I find, having plucked up the courage to climb

The Thing is to Keep Going

over the stile, that the cows do no more than lift their heads while carrying on chomping in situ, I've twice had to run out of a field as the herd started to gallop en masse in my direction. No doubt they were being curious . . . but you just never know. (I once failed a stone site – Gwern-y-Cleppa, on the edge of Stephen's hometown of Newport, South Wales – for cows when the cows were *on the other side of the fence*, which surely represents the height of cowardice. I blame the children, of course. The way the bullocks were behaving – pawing the ground, running at the fence, even *leaping* – was more than a little disconcerting for us all. And the fence really didn't seem that substantial. That's my excuse, anyway.)

A megalith hunter can waste a lot of time fruitlessly battling through gorse and brambles when in fact the stone in question is a hundred feet higher up the hill and easily accessible by a footpath. If instinct tells you you're on a hiding to nothing, then you probably are. One of my proudest moments as a stones enthusiast took place at Gruline in central Mull, on the neck of land between Lochs na Keal and Bà. There are two stones here known on The Megalithic Portal app* by the imaginative names Gruline 1 and Gruline 2. Stephen was, as ever, obligingly driving me around so I could tick off the sites. Gruline 1 was easy enough to find if not to approach: over 2 metres high and standing proud in the middle of a big field that also contains horses (in some years, a bull) east of the Salen–Craignure road. Gruline 2, on the other hand, is buried in featureless rhododendron jungle west of the

---

* This iPhone app, called 'Pocket Guide – Megaliths', is an invaluable tool for tracking down standing stones.

STONE LANDS

road. Although it's marked on the OS map, on the ground you're faced with impenetrable thicket and no real indication of where the stone actually is. Stephen parked up in what seemed vaguely like the right place, and got out his binoculars to see what the birds were up to, hoping for a glimpse of sea eagles and to keep the kids in the back seat placated by feeding them biscuits (needless to say they did not wish to accompany me on the stone quest). I marched along, looking for the river that the road apparently crossed to orient myself, noting the various openings into the undergrowth. And then . . . I had a feeling. That was all it was really – my inner megalith sensor going off. More or less at random I plunged into the bushes, pushing my way through branches (eyes shut to stop them being poked by twigs), clambering over mossy hillocks, forcing my way through rhododendrons, birch and bracken, excitement building and heart thumping because I was sure now I was on the right track, I had the scent of the stone . . . and yes, there it was! A pointed grey head poking out of rhododendron foliage like a hiding troll. When I got up close I found a magnificent leaning slab, well over 2 metres high, so regular and sharp-edged that it looked more like a piece of cladding from a tower block than a prehistoric standing stone. I was pretty pleased with myself for sniffing it out.

Keeping Going

Megalith geeks are characterised by their perseverance and so, I discover, are cancer patients. Only how much more so,

The Thing is to Keep Going

because wanting to visit every standing stone on Mull will never have the same motivational urgency as wanting not to die. And more than wanting not to die, Stephen wanted to *live*, to get the best out of life even as he got sicker.

'I'm going to make the most of being ill,' he said. 'I haven't had a proper break from work for decades. I'll spend more time with the kids, help you out with the school pick-ups and make some progress on my PhD. Get a hammock so I can lie in the sun after chemo and listen to music. Sort out stuff in the house like our horrible bathroom. Bake more bread and really get into the meditation. Concentrate on project managing the illness.'

The way he put it, it sounded like a staycation – apart from the bit about project managing the cancer. It was very typical of Stephen to have in mind a list of interesting improvements (to our home, to our lives) and to look on his diagnosis as an opportunity to put them in action. It was also typical that he would take responsibility for exploring every aspect of his illness, as thoroughly and carefully as he would a telecoms research project at work, or an important purchase such as a tent or a bike. Neither he nor I had any idea then what lay ahead and how much keeping going he'd have to do, through all the appointments with consultants, nutritionists, physios, district nurses; through the bloods taken so often that bruises ran down his inner arms from elbow to wrist; through chemotherapy, as he sat patiently in the ward, reading academic papers for his PhD or listening through his headphones to Talking Heads or Wagner, Ali Farka Touré or Can, as the toxic chemicals were injected into his body. He hated the sensation of poison flooding into his veins, and was so scared before the first session that his body would revolt in a massive allergic reaction that he thought he was going to have a panic attack and had to ask the nurse to pause the drip, but he endured it because it was, the doctors assured us, the treatment with the best results for his type of cancer. He kept going through all the nausea and the chemo-induced peripheral neuropathy that had him lying every night on his back on the bedroom floor with his legs propped up on the wardrobe, trying to calm the twitching in his muscles so he could get back to sleep.

He could no longer manage his old Ashtanga yoga routine, so he signed up to a beginners' class and then to a cancer patients' class. He started to take a serious interest in meditation, practising every day alone or with others online. He read books on Buddhist approaches to pain management, grief and consciousness, such as Martin Aylward's book on embodied awareness *Awake Where You Are*, trying to go deeper into his body to inhabit his senses more completely, to experience this beautiful life to the full. He kept cycling, 'pootling about on the bike' as he put it now that his favourite but very steep 'hills of South London' route was too much for him. He got a season ticket to Brockwell Lido and found that swimming outdoors still gave him a massive life-affirming boost, coming home from these swims fizzing with energy and excitement, even if he needed a wetsuit now and couldn't stay in for as long as he used to.

He went with his friends Jon and Bethan to see the Steam Down Collective at the Albany in Deptford, and returned fired up by the music, the range of non-alcoholic beers on offer these days and the fact that going out to gigs was possible even with stage 4 cancer, if there's somewhere to sit down for a bit. We saw Eliza Carthy at the Union Chapel, and LCD Soundsystem at Brixton Academy. We saw Mark Rylance's awesome revival of *Jerusalem*, a play that had blown us away 13 years earlier and now moved us deeply because Rylance, as a visibly older yet still incredibly athletic and powerful Rooster Byron, seemed to be raising two fingers to ageing and death on our behalf. Stephen met his friend Tom to watch the Tour de France at the Look Mum No Hands café, as was their yearly tradition. We finally got around to watching *The Sopranos*, and held hands while avoiding looking at each other when the cancer storyline came up. We planned a camping holiday in Scilly, just as we had for the past three summers. We kept going.

And, of course, we kept going to stones. We came back to Lochbuie the spring after Stephen was diagnosed, two days before we were due to get married on Iona. This was our fourth visit to Mull and Iona, and it is said that if you go to Iona once, you'll go three times – so a fourth trip seemed like abundance, a blessing, and also as if the good things might be coming to an end.

It had taken us a long time to get married: almost 19 years had passed since we first met on Wednesday 4 June 2003 in the bar of The Social on Little Portland Street. I still remember the moment when Stephen appeared in the doorway next to my friend Meirion (my former manager in the fiction department at Hatchards bookshop), and I sized him up from the other end of the long, narrow bar – a cute-looking, tall, skinny man with sticky-up hair and specs – and I thought, *He looks nice*, and also, *I bet he's Meirion's new boyfriend*. Then he came to sit next to me on one of the brown leatherette banquettes and we circled each other in a tentative conversation about saunas designed to establish whether he was gay or not. It turned out that he wasn't – he was an old school friend of Meirion's from Newport. We had our first date, meeting outside the NFT bar on the Southbank, just two days later.

I remember waking up hungover at first light the morning after the Social (it was June so this was very early) and not being able to get back to sleep for thinking, *I've found him at last*. I'd been looking for 'the one' for a long time. I knew Stephen was right for me from the very start, from the way we got on so easily without any (or many) of the misunderstandings, clashes and irritations I typically experienced (no doubt caused) in a relationship. We got each other straightaway. There was an instant and massive sexual click but the connection was much deeper than that. We were just really, really *interested* in each other. He wanted to find out about all about me, to hear about my travels in India and the books and films I loved, to look at the little objects I'd acquired (the first and only person ever to express an interest in my collection of pebbles from the different beaches of my life). I loved hearing his stories about riding a horse, even though he couldn't ride, in Mongolia when he was delirious with malaria, and going to the World Scout jamboree in Australia as a teenager, and flirting with Kim Deal backstage at a Pixies gig when he was a student at Manchester Uni. We'd both just come back from travelling on our own for a year; we were both planning to do an MA. We'd read or wanted to read the same books. In a letter written not long after our walk along the Ridgeway to

The Thing is to Keep Going

Avebury, he mentioned looking through my books: *They all seem familiar to me, like we've both been visiting a secret garden for years but always at different times and now I've caught a glimpse of you there. Now we can go there together and show each other the hidden pathways and sunny glades and spiders' webs.*

Basically, we were in love. I expect we were quite annoying to be around. We moved in together the year after we met, but for some reason we didn't bother getting married, even when we had kids. Maybe it was the thought of having certain members of our families in the same room at the same time. We were coming up to our 19th anniversary and tentatively planning a tiny wedding on Iona when Stephen was diagnosed with cancer.

The path to the stones at Lochbuie was much drier that year we came back to get married, and I'm pretty sure the route had changed, running along the field edge instead of following a Hansel and Gretel trail of white stones through the bog. Less exciting but easier, which was, all things considered, just as well. That year the four of us had no difficulty at all in navigating to the stone circle, only Stephen, three months on from his cancer diagnosis, was walking more slowly than he used to, stopping to take deep breaths, and we didn't need to chivvy the kids along. Aged 12 and nine now, they kept up with us easily – and perhaps, that year, they didn't want to drop behind.

I set up my phone on one of the standing stones to take a picture of the four of us within the circle, and looking at it now I can see how tightly Stephen is gripping my hand, and how closely we are holding the children to us. All the while I was inside that circle with him, I was asking the stones to heal him.

I didn't know if they had any power, but it was worth a shot, I thought.

A Pilgrimage to Iona

The Iona wedding was to be just us, the children, Veronica the registrar and her two Fionnphort neighbours as witnesses. We were to stay in a cottage outside Fionnphort, within striking distance of Lochbuie, and hop over to Iona for a couple of nights to get married. 'I think going to Iona will help me,' Stephen said, and I eagerly shot back, 'I think it will too.' He'd articulated the secret desire I'd been nursing in my heart: that somehow going to Iona, a place of pilgrimage for so many, would cure him of this incurable disease. Indeed, I was thinking of our whole journey as a sort of pilgrimage, first to the stones of Lochbuie and then on to Iona. It was by no means certain that we'd be able to go; weakened by the chemotherapy, Stephen had already been admitted to hospital several times with an infection. When I was emailing with Veronica about the arrangements, I warned her that we might not be able to come at all. But she expressed her belief that we would make it, and we did.

I've always been drawn to the idea of pilgrimage, of reaching a sacred place via a long and challenging journey that is as transformative as the destination itself. The island of Iona, where St Columba set up his abbey in 563 CE, has been a pilgrimage site since the 7th century and it remains so today, renowned as the birthplace of Celtic Christianity and as a 'thin place', where the spiritual realm is said to be within touching distance. On previous trips, Stephen had driven us all the way from London to Mull via the Oban ferry; this year that sort of exhausting haulage wasn't going to be possible for him, and I was still in the very early stages of trying to relearn driving, so we took the train to Glasgow and picked up a hire car there. If our journey was a pilgrimage, then the Glasgow Premier Inn was a pilgrim's shelter, in the shadow of the motorway overpass and in no way beautiful but somehow pure, a place where life was stripped back to just being together. All the worries about work and health left behind, and the four of us asleep in a row by 10.30 p.m. and awake at 7, by far the longest and deepest sleep I'd had since the diagnosis.

To get to Iona – now as in previous centuries – you have to cross Mull to its south-westernmost point at Fionnphort. At the start of the 19th century, eight ancient stones were still standing alongside Loch Scridain on the road through the Ross of Mull to Fionnphort, half a mile apart and in sight of each other. The stones were believed to be part of a series that once extended across the whole island of Mull to guide pilgrims to Iona.[34] Several of those eight stones have since disappeared – toppled by a would-be treasure hunter in the 19th century and broken up by quarrying – but at least three survive on what is still the road to Iona, and we passed them on our way to the cottage. Stephen stopped the car so I could hop out to pay my respects at each stone, as I always did on the way to Iona. Taoslin stone stands in a small sloping field above the road just before Bunessan. The Tirghoil stone is west of Bunessan, a splendid monolith of pink granite on pastureland full of nervously bleating sheep, with an astounding view across Loch Scridain to the layer-cake lava flows of the Ardmeanach peninsula. The farmer granted me access to the field with a cheery 'Nay problem', which is the usual response to stone-viewing permission requests in these friendly parts. And then there's the slightly underwhelming stone randomly sited on the gravel driveway of Achaban House on the outskirts of Fionnphort.

Canmore (the online catalogue of Scotland's archaeology) classifies all three stones as prehistoric while also acknowledging the possibility that they might actually be medieval route markers. To my completely untrained eye they look pretty prehistoric – surely far too big and heavy to have been practical for use as signposts in medieval times? Whatever their true age, it is easy to imagine long-ago pilgrims looking out for them as they battled through the mud and the Hebridean weather, and taking the appearance of each one looming up on the horizon as welcome confirmation that they were making progress to the Iona boat.

In addition to these uncertain albeit impressive stones, there are eight (possibly nine) bona fide prehistoric short stone rows on Mull, which is quite a lot for one island, and over the years Stephen, Alex, Ava and I have visited most of them. These very ancient rows, all in the northern half of the island, are also, like the Loch Scridain way-markers, associated for me with ideas of pilgrimage, of taking offerings to a sacred site. For one thing, there's something about the way we came back year after year to seek them out (religiously, you might say) that has the flavour of a pilgrimage about it. For another, there is the quartz.

In the 1980s and '90s, Roger Martlew and Clive Ruggles's North Mull Project investigated the stone rows of Mull, looking in particular at whether the rows could have been oriented towards the horizon in order to mark key points in the cycle of the moon. Two of the rows they excavated are at Ardnacross on the north-eastern coast, where Ava and I once nervously sneaked past a herd of dairy cows to climb to the hillside terrace where the stones are set. When we got there, we found most of the stones were fallen and overgrown, and the cairns so ruinous as to be almost invisible, but the views soaring over the water to the mainland's remote Morvern and Ardnamurchan peninsulas were incredible, and the one properly upright stone had a delightful lichen heart at its base. The archaeologists couldn't work out exactly where on the horizon the rows would have pointed, so could not form any definite conclusions about their lunar alignment, but what they did find was lots of fragments of white and transparent quartz, which had been brought to the site from elsewhere and scattered around the standing stones and built into the kerb-cairns.[35]

At the Glengorm stone row, in the grounds of a stately home close to the north coast of Mull, three tall, elegant pillars stand on a knoll within a natural grassy amphitheatre that opens grandly to the seaward hills. The first time we came, the Highland cows grazing around the stones freaked six-year-old Alex out and he was deeply irritated by Ava sitting unbothered among the stones like one of the Sìth (in a pink cardigan and minus the mono-nostril that the fairies of Mull are said to sport), apparently intent on staying in this cow-threatened spot all afternoon – 'Come on, we need to get out *now*!' These stones are set in a sort of semicircle, having been inauthentically re-erected in recent centuries, but they once stood in a row and

STONE LANDS

here too excavation uncovered quartz chippings left in ancient times. Martlew and Ruggles said that the practice of bringing quartz to these stone rows could have gone on for centuries, and perhaps represented a key part of ceremonies linked to the observation of the moon.

The Mull stone row that I've visited most often is the one at Baliscate, because it's easy to access on a run from the youth hostel at Tobermory harbour, where we stayed every trip apart from the wedding year. I once (in his younger, more malleable years) managed to persuade Alex to run with me (panting dramatically but not complaining too much) all the way up the hill to Baliscate. The path that leads from the pottery to the stones turned out to be lined with scallop shells – the symbol that is associated more than any other with pilgrimage, with those who journeyed to the tomb of St James at Santiago de Compostela. When we reached the field where the stones stand, we performed a peculiar ritual of our own, a series of ballet moves induced by having to leap across the boggy bits to reach the stones. As at Ardnacross, the wide-ranging view across the Sound of Mull is awesome and exhilarating, and perhaps one of the reasons the stones were raised here in the first place. Significant quantities of quartz pieces were found at Baliscate, too.

Quartz has long been linked to the idea of pilgrimage on Mull and Iona. When local archaeologist Dr Clare Ellis excavated a medieval chapel site at Baliscate,[36] not far from the prehistoric stone row, the team found hundreds of white quartz pebbles, which she believes could have been left as offerings

The Thing is to Keep Going

by pilgrims in memory of healing miracles performed by St Columba of Iona using white stones from the riverbed. Clare told me that 'quartz seems to have been used through time, and in the Neolithic and Bronze Ages appears to be largely associated with the dead, so its optical properties probably carried some special significance'. We can get some sense of what quartz meant to prehistoric people from the example of places such as Newgrange, in the Boyne valley in Ireland; the circular façade* of this passage tomb set in its huge grassy mound was coated in quartz that would have had to be transported to the site in massive quantities. Why did Neolithic people associate quartz, which above all encapsulates the qualities of light, with a place of burial, of metaphorical and actual darkness? It is interesting that Newgrange was built to allow the rays of the rising sun to penetrate its passage and chamber at winter solstice, marking the moment when the light begins to grow again. Archaeologist Timothy Darvill has suggested that quartz could have symbolised the soul and a gateway to the spirit world, and that the early Christian Church deliberately adopted the symbolic use of quartz to provide continuity with the Pagan past.[37]

I think of the prehistoric people of Mull collecting pieces of quartz and taking them, perhaps a long way, to the stone rows,

---

* Or platform. Professor Josh Pollard told me that archaeologists are suspicious of the modern reconstruction of the Newgrange façade. 'It's much more likely that the quartz and granodiorite were used as part of a platform at the base of the mound. The effect would have been similar.' He points out that, at Knowth, pebbles of different geologies were used in circular settings outside the tomb's entrances, 'creating an amazing aesthetic'.

STONE LANDS

and I wonder what drew them to do this. Taking quartz to standing stones is something that people still do (or have started doing again) today; you will often come across lumps of quartz at standing stone sites, as well as shells, coins, candles, flowers, pieces of fruit, etc. – offerings of a sort in our modern context.

Columba and his 12 companions came to Iona by boat from Ireland, and 1,500 years later boat is still the only way to get there. As the little ferry nears the island and the abbey on the headland lurches into sharp focus, there is a strong sense of approaching somewhere special, even sacred. The island itself seems a living thing, like a monster St Brendan might have encountered on his *peregrinatio* in his oarless boat: a green humpbacked sea creature floating in a turquoise sea. At any moment it might decide to rear up and shake the abbey off its back.

For such a small island, just three miles long and less than two wide, Iona is intensely varied in its landscape, with its beaches of multicoloured sea-smoothed pebbles and dazzling strands of crushed white shell, its moors of springy heather and waterlogged moss, its rippling sand dunes and wind-raked machair, its one great hill – Dùn I – and its endlessly shifting lightscape, as restless as the ocean. There is something Tardis-like about the place. The first year we came, Stephen, the kids and I tramped around the whole perimeter in one day, and while sometimes it felt like only a few steps were needed to cross from one side of the island to the other, at other times we lost our way in a maze of moorland hillocks, gullies and bogs.

The 1,000 high stone crosses that are reputed to have once stood on Iona are almost all gone, and there are no prehistoric standing stones anywhere on the island, or at least not now. Thomas Pennant, who visited the island as part of his Scottish tour of 1772, recorded a small circle of stones surrounding a cairn on top of Cnoc nan Aingeal, the Hill of Angels, close to the Bay at the Back of the Ocean on the western side of the island, but no trace of what sounds like a prehistoric kerb-cairn remains today. Pennant reported that 'the natives were accustomed to bring their horses to this circle at the feast of St Michael, and to course around it'.[38] The Hill of Angels is where Columba is said to have debated with a heavenly being soon after his arrival on Iona; today this smooth green knoll is more often referred to as Sithean Mòr, or the big fairy mound. Across the track is the little fairy mound, Sithean Beg. Perhaps fairies and angels have always been the same thing.

I had the strangest feeling, when we came to Iona for the very first time, that the compacted layers of my past and personality were shifting and lifting, that my skull had been opened and light and air were being let into the dusty corners of my psyche. That there were signs here to be read, if only I could understand them. Once, when the four of us were on the beach at the top end of the island, the evening sky was split by a line of brilliant white dashes – white birds flying north-west. Wild swans: a good omen, we thought. At night the honking of geese was like the plaintive bellowing of a sea monster stranded on the shore. Stephen spotted dolphins out to sea and possibly a whale.

One night in the Iona youth hostel, close to the beach where Stephen and I would get married six years later, I woke from a vivid dream thinking that I'd done something terrible, and for a

STONE LANDS

long time I couldn't shake the guilt and fear, rummaging through my memory for whatever it was I'd done and forgotten. The feeling was deeply uncomfortable but at the same time I sensed that Iona was doing me good, working on me as a gardener digs up clay-heavy soil and mixes it with air and sand, making me face up to anxieties suppressed deep inside. I wonder now if those feelings of dread and guilt related not to the past but to the future, and that somehow I had intuited what was to come. And maybe Iona was preparing me for it.

We arrived on Mull a few days before the wedding. That evening, the four of us walked from our cottage outside Fionnphort to Kintra, where there's a little bay fringed by a row of 18th-century cottages and a wonderful rockscape: rounded boulders heaped up like balls in a soft-play pit, sloping fissured slabs perfect for leaping from one to the other, and rocky outcrops shrugging off their grassy coats. The low, soft light brought out the pink in the granite, and across a cobalt sea there was Iona, waiting for us, Dùn I rising at its heart. We climbed the biggest outcrop together, dislodging some sheep in the process who rattled down out of our way, then we sat looking out over Iona and the Dutchman's Cap and the other islets, Stephen peering through his binoculars and occasionally exclaiming and drawing our attention to oystercatchers, gannets, terns. We climbed down onto the pebbly shore and I splashed my face with water from the Sound of Iona. Then we came to a place where to make progress you had to jump from one rock to another, and the kids and Stephen all did it with no problem, but for some reason I was overcome with fear and couldn't bring myself to jump. An inner voice was telling me not to and I just couldn't, so I climbed down

The Thing is to Keep Going

instead, to the accompaniment of much jeering. Well, I needed to be able to walk to our marriage ceremony, right? Still, I was a little ashamed of myself.

We were married in a hollow in the machair above the white sands and turquoise-sapphire shallows of Iona's North End, on a bright, breezy day just before Easter. The registrar spoke of the good times and the hard ones that lay ahead, as Stephen and I blinked back our tears. She bound our hands with a strip of Iona tartan. Stephen didn't look ill, a little thin, perhaps, but that just meant he carried off his tweed suit with extreme elegance. The children hopped about in their party clothes and looked on with a mix of mortification and, mostly, tolerance for this latest of Mum and Dad's weird schemes. It felt like a miracle that we'd managed to get there. And a miracle, given that this was the Hebrides, that it didn't rain.

Just below the summit plateau on Dùn I, the highest point on Iona, is a natural shrine: an inky black pool, its perfect stillness set in contrast to the ever-tossing and turning ocean all around. This is the Well of Eternal Youth, said to be visited and blessed by St Brigid at midnight on the summer solstice, its waters offering healing and rejuvenation. I went up there on the morning of our marriage ceremony. I'd wanted Stephen to come with me but it was clear that he wasn't up to the climb. I dipped my head in the pool on his behalf, thinking that maybe I could transport the healing properties of the water back down to him. The cold felt like an iron band squeezing my head, but I had an intuition that this improvised ritual, painful and potent, would somehow help us both. If a miracle was going to happen anywhere, it would be on Iona.

STONE LANDS

Stephen had taken his wetsuit to Iona hoping for an invigorating immersion in the crystalline waters, but he was already feeling shivery on the afternoon of the wedding, and though we made it over to the western coves, his very favourite part of the island and where he'd planned to have a dip, he didn't get in. By the end of the next day he was back in Oban, in hospital on an antibiotic drip, laid low by another infection. I stayed behind in the Mull cottage with the kids, trying to keep things jolly while going insane with worry.

Eventually, he emerged from hospital, his temperature gone, and we carried on with the holiday. One afternoon I went looking for the Poit Na H-i stone, which you get to from the main road by following a very private-seeming track through farmland. I encountered a stern-faced granny in a buggy, clearly the landowner, who thought my nervous wave was me trying to flag her down, although that was the very opposite of my intention as she looked so scary; but she grinned when I explained that I was only waving to say hello and that I was going after this stone, and motioned me to carry on. Poit Na H-i turned out to be a fine twisting, tapering megalith well over 2 metres high and set in a wide-open landscape between sea and hills. When I got back to the cottage, flushed with this stone-bagging triumph, Alex insisted that the two of us return to Kintra and try the rock leap again. Nervously I agreed and he was incredibly patient through what must have been a really tiresome 45 minutes as I repeatedly approached the edge and shied away, urging, 'Come on, Mum, you can do it,' over and over again with barely any note of irritation in his voice, gracefully demonstrating the move for me (once with his eyes shut).

Eventually I did it. 'Right, very well done; now come on, let's get back and have a nice evening,' Alex said. That afternoon, I could see how he was becoming in some ways very like his dad.

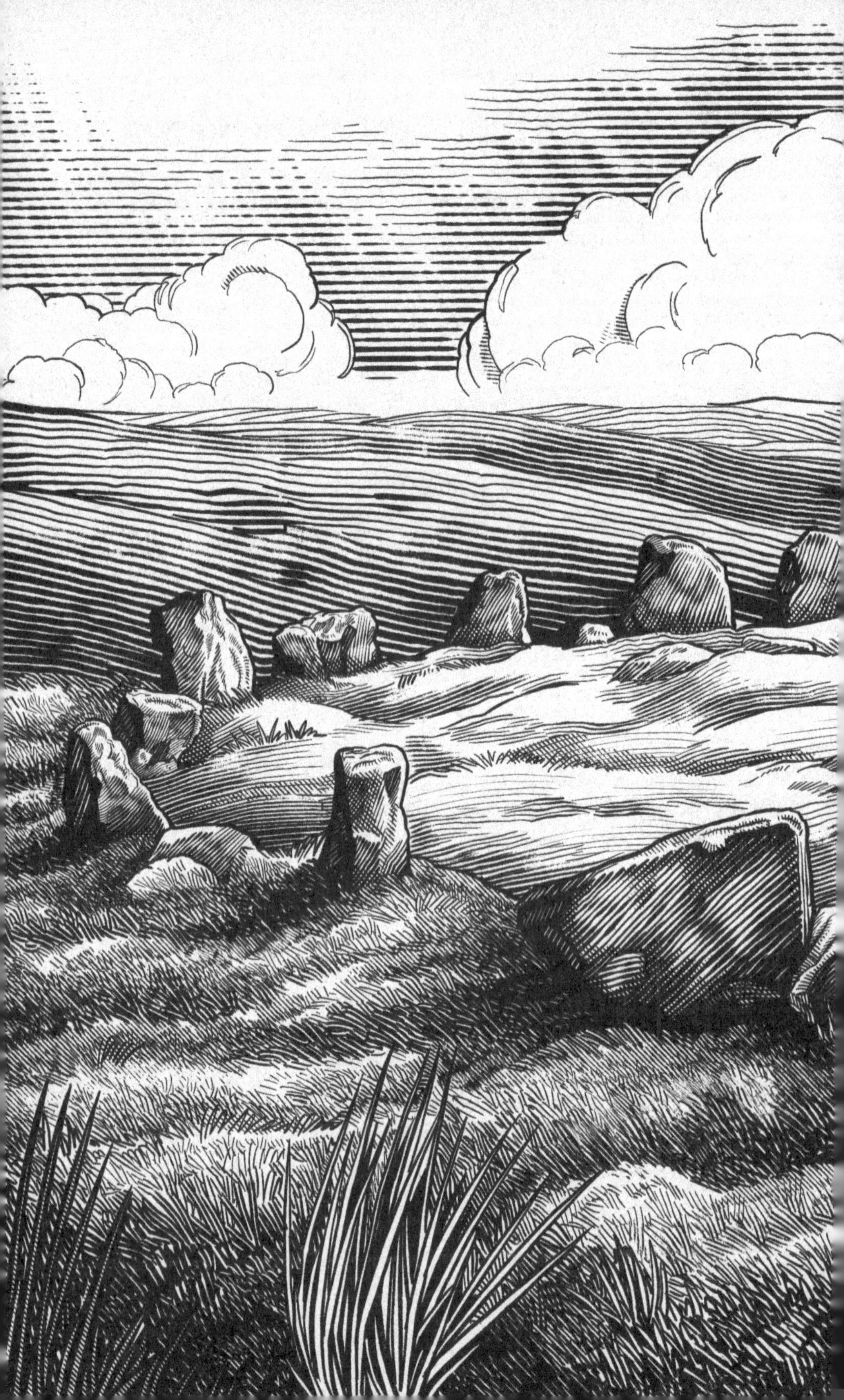

Chapter 4
HOPE IS THE MOST HUMAN QUALITY

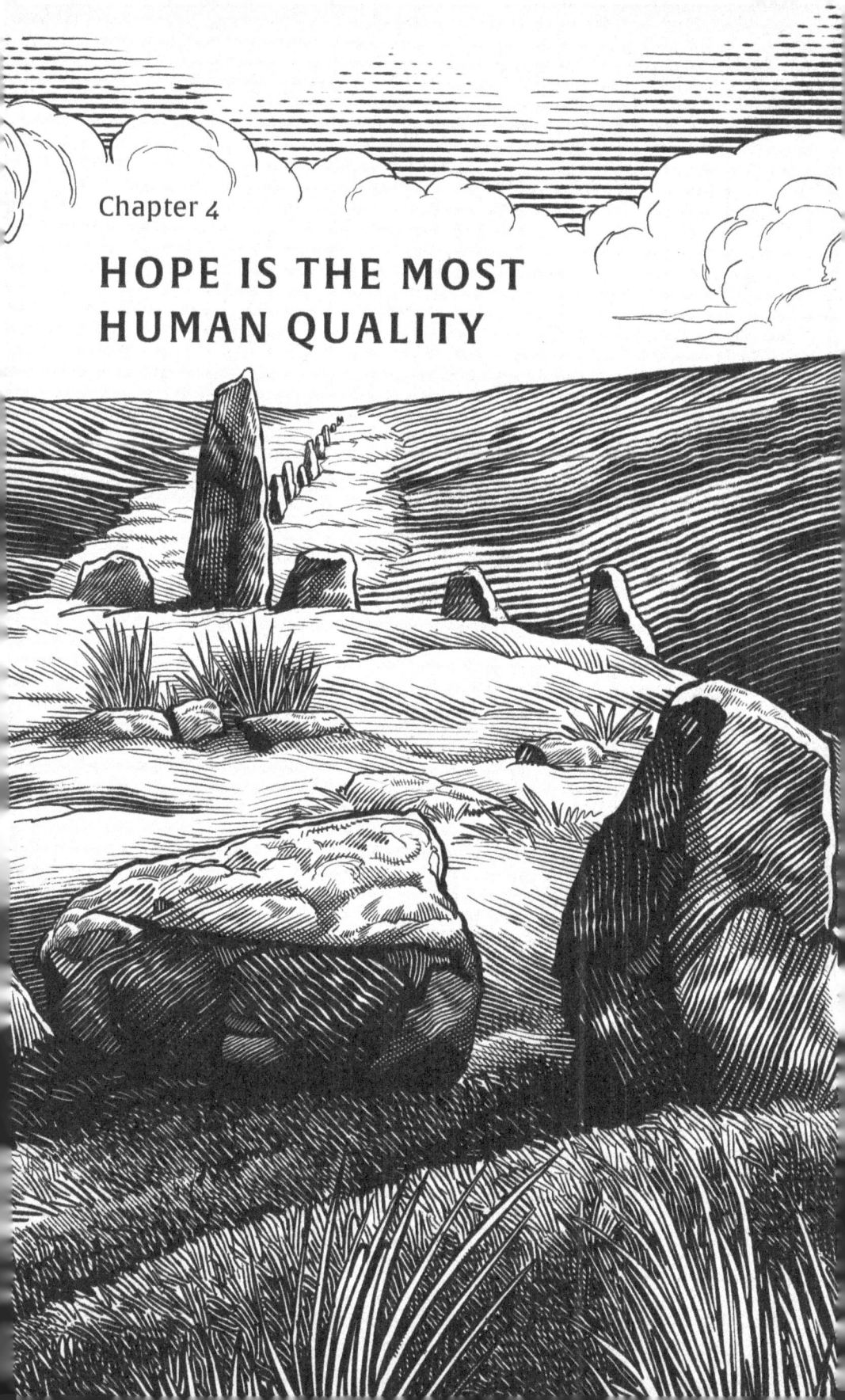

Stones of Dartmoor, DEVON

THERE'S A LITTLE BLACK notebook that Stephen has been writing in for a long time. On the opening page he's jotted down some terms relating to his PhD on the German media theorist Friedrich Kittler: *the historical model, the relation to the signifier, the changing symbolic* – concepts that I have still, after almost two decades of Stephen talking about them, not managed to get my head around. There are lots of these notebooks, in drawers all over the house, full of tiny scribbles about his academic research, notes from work meetings on telecoms strategy and fixed-mobile convergence, indecipherable passwords, dates of people's birthdays, and list after list of books, films, music and places that he hoped, sooner or later, to explore.

This particular little black book, though, is different. On the second page is another note: *Heidegger's prescription was a turn to the poetic.* And then the rest of the notebook is about birds.

STONE LANDS

> **JULY 11TH, Elmlea, Isle of Sheppey:** *several marsh harriers hovering over the reeds. Ringed plover playing next to the island. Black-legged godwits on the shoreline. Oystercatchers in flight over the sea wall.*

> **SEPTEMBER 6TH, Rainham Marshes:** *Dry, sunny & warm. Flocks of goldfinches feasting on thistles, darting around and then wheeling away showing light under-feathers. Two spotted flycatchers in the bushes. A sedge warbler or whinchat. Chiffchaff on the reedbed. Several marsh harriers overhead. Kestrel on the ground in a field with prey.*

On it goes, through the months and years of our life together.

> **MARCH 27TH, Calgary Bay, Mull:** *Heavy showers & bright spells. White-tailed sea eagles over the crag. A few buzzards on the smaller crag, chased off by hooded crows.*

> **MARCH 29TH, Lochbuie** [this must be the date of my first, failed attempt on the stone circle there]: *Black-throated divers. Lots of chaffinch in the bushes near the Post Office hut. Oystercatchers in the bay. A few cormorants standing on posts in the water. Greylag geese in pairs, possible barnacle goose. Two golden eagles soaring over Ben Buie.*

Eventually we get to the year Stephen fell ill and there's a page with just two words: *Post-diagnosis*. Around them he's drawn a jaggedy circle, a sort of star-burst.

Hope is the Most Human Quality

More notes follow about birds spotted on our April wedding trip to Mull and Iona, and by the end of May we're on Dartmoor.

Kingfisher! Flying upriver. Viewed from the steam train to Totnes. Quite a distance away but very clear and could see for good few seconds.

I remember the moment Stephen glimpsed this kingfisher from the window of the wood-panelled steam train. He cried out with delight at the flash of marine blue and orange – an actual kingfisher! – then his eyes filled with tears, and he turned his face away to hide them from the children. Later we had lunch in an old-fashioned tea rooms at Buckfastleigh, with Union Jack bunting outside and rose-patterned teacups and lace doilies inside, and I had to leave the table mid-meal and hide myself in the loo until I'd managed to stop crying. Then I splashed my face until the redness diminished and returned to the table and tried to think of something cheery to say.

Walking a Dartmoor Stone Row

Things are looking brighter the next day as we take the stony path from the car park at the north-east end of Burrator Reservoir. We are on our way to the Down Tor stone row and cairn-circle, and the weather is on our side: there's no wind and the sky is a dome of hard blue, with only the lightest of cirrus veils draped over the horizon. The world is bright, alive and

STONE LANDS

pleasing on this May morning, each thing more intensely itself than usual and just *right*: the grass thick and lush underfoot, the branches laden with masses of fresh young leaves, the path made poignant by mossy old stone walls and the ruins of farms that saw unbroken habitation from medieval times until the early 20th century. At Middleworth Farm, three eerie doorways in a row inspire Alex to explain the Monty Hall probability problem.* We speculate about the people who once lived in these ruins, we stop to refuel with biscuits and chocolate, we joke and laugh and chivvy the kids along. I'm excited because the Down Tor stones look incredible in the pictures I've seen online and because Stephen is feeling strong today; he will make it to the stones. The words of the oncologist at Guy's, spoken not two weeks ago, are still ringing in my ears: the primary tumour has not grown, the tiny tumours in the abdomen have completely gone. The chemo is working. *In palliative terms*, she added, but it feels, this bright, hope-filled morning, that it's possible to put worry to one side, to believe that one day we really might be able to find our way back to normal.

Then we're out on the moor, the ground is steepening and Stephen is falling behind. I drop back to see if he wants to rest. I offer him a biscuit, but that isn't going to do the trick. 'You go on with the kids,' he urges. 'I don't think I can make it.' Now we're out of the tree shadows I can see his face in full sunlight,

---

* The one based on the US game show *Let's Make a Deal*, hosted by Monty Hall. Monty offers contestants a choice of three doors, one hiding a car and the other two goats. If you choose a door and one of the other doors is opened to reveal a goat, will changing your choice of door increase the likelihood of getting the car? Apparently it will, but I still don't really understand why.

Hope is the Most Human Quality

and he no longer looks at all well – how could I have thought that he did? – his face pinched, his cheeks sunken, his skin yellowish. Fear reaches into my chest and squeezes my heart and the familiar nauseous sinking feeling is back, a freefall terror induced by the sudden withdrawal of hope. 'No, no, don't worry, it's fine,' he reassures me. He touches my hand. 'I just don't want to tire myself out and risk getting another infection. I'm fed up with hospitals and would quite like to stay out of them from now on.' He indicates through the gap in the moorland wall up to the jumble of boulders cresting the hill like a ruined castle – the rocky outcrop of Down Tor. 'I'll go as high as I can up there and do a spot of birdwatching.' He has his binoculars with him, as usual.

Alex and Ava sense an opportunity to abort the stones trip, but I'm not having any of it, and neither is Stephen, who knows from experience that birdwatching and shouty kids don't mix. I crack the whip, and the children and I are on our way, heading up to the horizon through broken-down sections of moorland wall. Somehow Stephen's inability to reach the stones has made me all the more determined to get the kids there, and I deliberately force the fear and worry out of my head by focusing on powering on up through a confusing scatter of boulders and through the moaning that escalates as Ava stubs her toe on a rock ('I've broken my toe! I can't walk *any more*! You're *literally killing* me!') and Alex becomes enraged at my inability to navigate ('You've made us walk all this way for *nothing*! You don't even know where we *are*!'). I sense mutiny is close. 'Chill, guys,' I say, feigning nonchalance while resorting to the fount of all knowledge, The Megalithic Portal app, striding confidently across the grassland and hoping against hope that the blue dot really is moving closer to the stone-row icon – and not, in fact, further away (as is my usual experience with the blue dot).

I look up and there's something suspiciously grey and pillar-like poking out of a fold in the moor. 'Hey, that's a stone!' I exclaim, and Alex says, 'I know, I saw it ages ago.' (*You might have mentioned it*, is what I think but I'm too busy making for the stones to bother saying so.)

And what an awesome site this is! I've never seen anything quite like this combination of a stone circle and a long stone row before. An ocean of grass rises and falls in waves, rushing unbroken up to the horizon. Before us, on a low, green knoll, is a circle of stones set around a stone-lined cavity in the ground, the remains of a ransacked prehistoric cairn. Just outside the stone circle stands an imposing four-sided pillar, the leader of an army of stones that have marched here in single file across hundreds of metres of moor.

This stone row stretching into the sea of grass calls me to walk it, as it must have summoned a great many others over its thousands of years of existence. (The children, apparently entirely deaf to its ancient summons, stay behind eating biscuits at the cairn-circle.) I follow the path of stones, touching each one as I go, as the row curves down the hillside and then starts to climb again. Some stones are so small that I have to crouch down to touch them and soon my fingers are stained with mud and cow poo. The black earth is delightfully firm to walk on, the grassy tufts springy under foot. As I walk, I think, over and over again: *The little tumours have gone. The primary tumour has not grown. He can get well – please let him get well.*

Hope is the Most Human Quality

The lichened granite is rough under my hand, the sun warm on my head, the onward motion of one step after another feels calming and potent.

At the eastern end of the row is another terminus stone, about half the height of the giant at the western end, but still taller than most of the others and definitively marking a stopping point. From here I can see the whole row running up to the cairn-circle at the other end of the monument, like a silver necklace thrown onto the moor, its pendant resting some way below the top of Hingston Hill.

Birds scatter across the sky and I wonder what the stone row looks like to them and whether they understand its geometry and flowing energy as a part of nature, as right and inevitable as the sweeping lines of the moor and the eruption of tors along the horizon.

The Courage to Hope

It's the taking away of hope that makes you understand how much we need it to function. Night had fallen by the time we emerged from Lewisham hospital after that terrible meeting in which I'd heard spoken aloud for the first time words such as 'incurable' and 'palliative' and 'life expectancy'. Stephen and I said a painful goodbye and I went to find my bike, fumbling with the lock for several minutes in the dismal sodium glare, my hands shaking. I just couldn't seem to remember how to get it open. I tried to cycle off and the wheel twisted under me.

I gave up on trying to ride the bike. I was clearly not up to it and in any case I was in no rush to get home and face the children, who still didn't know what horror was hanging over them. As I pushed the bike through the darkened park behind the hospital, preferring to take my chance with any dodgy characters lurking there than have to face the crowds on the main road, I waved up at the row of yellow rectangles on the top floor, one of which marked the window by Stephen's bed. And then I called Sarah, who had been my friend since we both worked at Foyles bookshop on the Charing Cross Road in the 1990s. She answered, her voice full of worry and concern. And then I lost it completely, my sobs choking my attempts to explain.

In that moment of despair, I knew with devastating clarity what was coming. I was going to lose my love, my soulmate, my anchor, my partner in parenting and adventure and boring household stuff. Alex and Ava were going to lose their dad, the only one who loved them as completely as I did. Our magical carefree holidays, blissful escapes from reality, were over. No more driving down to Cornwall or up to Mull in search of megaliths (or anywhere else, for that matter, given that I couldn't drive). No more boozy barbecues in the back garden. No more late-night dancing in the living room taking turns to choose the tune. This life, which I'd confidently assumed would go on for ever, or at least until we were both old and decrepit, was already over.

'Fi,' Sarah said, 'you haven't lost anything yet. This isn't the time to despair. It's premature. You can't know what will happen; there are so many new cancer treatments out there. You have to hope. You have to fight for Stephen as you've never

Hope is the Most Human Quality

fought for anything before. And you have to keep fighting. It's going to be the hardest thing you've ever done but you of all people can do this. Stephen's *so lucky* to have you fighting for him.' Sarah has always believed, much more than I do myself, in my ability to get things done.

There were more people to ring and tell bad news to: Stephen's mum and my own mum, Stephen's brother Chris and his wife Tracy, my brother Duncan and his wife Lisa. I wanted to curl up in a ball on the ground and never speak to anyone again, but I kept going through the dark park, putting one foot in front of the other, making one call after another. And though I didn't have any hope, everyone I spoke to did. They told me I had to be strong, to keep going, to have faith, for my sake and the children's and Stephen's, that he'd get through this. They told me that the situation was worrying but by no means hopeless. Not one of them believed he would die. He was young and fit, and the doctors were going to throw everything they had at this (and there was a lot to throw).

And they were right to tell me to hope. Hope is what motivates us to keep going, to dare to want something that will hurt us if we don't get it, to try to stop the unstoppable, reach the unreachable and cure the incurable. Hope is why we make ourselves vulnerable by loving another person, even though we will be parted from them in the end – because a parting, one day, is inevitable. Hope is why people put their hearts on the line and try to have children, despite infertility and miscarriage, and though the children, if they come, will grow up and leave us. After Stephen's diagnosis, I came to realise that courage can simply mean hoping, wholeheartedly and with confidence, for a positive outcome and taking one step after another to try to get there, even when there are no solid grounds for hoping. Yes, it takes courage to hope, but it can also take a few words spoken with emphasis – *so lucky to have you fighting for him* – to give you courage.

Standing stones, by virtue of the essential hardness of rock and the fact they remain with us several thousand years after they were erected, are symbols of endurance, longevity and survival. I would also suggest that they are symbols of hope. By setting up these stones and changing the landscape in such a remarkable and lasting way, people were making manifest their hopes and dreams, investing their resources and reputations in this work, putting their stamp on the land, staking their claim on the future.

In Britain, monument building began around 4000 BCE, apparently part of a set of Neolithic practices that arrived in south-east England from continental Europe, such as making pottery and polished stone tools, growing crops and domesticating animals. Over the next few hundred years, this 'Neolithic package', including the building of earthworks and stone monuments, gradually spread until it was established across much of Britain and Ireland.[39] People were then to continue creating monuments using megaliths for some 3,000 years more: from the chambered tombs and passage graves to the stone circles and rows and then on to the individual standing stones, which were still being set up in the late Bronze Age, *c*.1000 BCE. While there's a clear practical rationale for practices such as making pots and axes, growing wheat and barley, and keeping pigs and sheep, the incredible effort involved in building a massive

Hope is the Most Human Quality

dolmen with an 80-tonne monster capstone raised on uprights like the one at Garn Turne in Pembrokeshire, or in constructing a megalithic complex that spreads for miles across the landscape as at Avebury, or in moving an entire stone circle's worth of bluestones from the Preseli Hills all the way to Salisbury Plain, does not offer the same obvious benefits. What did the prehistoric monument builders hope to achieve?

Perhaps they were motivated by the hope that marking the darkest and lightest moments of the year, as was done at Stonehenge by aligning the monument to midwinter sunset and midsummer sunrise, would ensure the return of light and warmth each year. Or the hope that through the agency of the monuments the land could be made fertile and a good harvest ensured, as Michael Dames speculated about Avebury. Or the hope that death could be cheated and the memory of individuals or the renown of the tribe be made to last for ever. Or the hope that by transporting megaliths with great trouble from a distant land, a migrating group might stake a claim to a new home.

Of all the prehistoric monuments, there is something that seems especially hopeful about a stone row, especially one that stretches for hundreds of metres, as Down Tor and many other Dartmoor alignments do. I think it's the way a stone row takes you from A to B, inviting you to progress across the landscape from one point to the other, implying a sense of purpose and a reasonable certainty of achieving it.

The Dartmoor stone rows are on the whole rather enigmatic, with little known for sure about them – even their date is uncertain (usually assumed to be Bronze Age, although peat lying above and below fallen stones at Cut Hill has been carbon-dated back to the Neolithic[40]). The person who knows more than anyone else about them is Dr Sandy Gerrard. He worked for English Heritage for just over 20 years and in his academic research focused mainly on the early tin industry in Devon and Cornwall, but what he's best known for, among megalith enthusiasts at least, is his work on stone rows. In 2012, a wind farm was being built at Bancbryn near Sandy's home in Carmarthenshire and his neighbours, concerned that due process was not being followed, asked Sandy and his wife Helen to survey the site for archaeological remains. Amazingly, within a few minutes they had identified what appeared to be a prehistoric stone row snaking for several hundred metres through the development site. The small stones had previously been obscured by vegetation but had been completely revealed by a fire and now they stood out clearly against the scorched moor. When he surveyed the row, he found that it extended for 700 metres and included at least 173 stones.[41]

Work on the wind farm had already started, and Sandy was unable to get official recognition that his discovery was a genuine prehistoric stone row. 'In my opinion the row would have been treated more favourably if it had been found earlier,' he says. He points out that Bancbryn has a cairn at its upper end and is set in a wider context of cairn cemeteries and associated 'landscape treats' (visual links to distant points such as the sea and distinctive hilltops) – all elements that he has identified at many other prehistoric long stone rows.

After discovering the row at Bancbryn, he set out to visit every surviving stone row in Britain in order to get proper fieldwork-based data to support his claims. 'I dread to think

Hope is the Most Human Quality

how far I drove and walked!' he told me. 'The existing data was patchy, so I set about trying to provide a degree of consistency. To do this I needed to visit every surviving site and between 2013 and 2018 I managed to visit all but a couple, which I mopped up in 2019. Subsequently a few more sites have been brought to my attention and I have visited those. There are still a couple on my to-do list but this is the nature of things and I guess they will keep coming.'

He surveyed all the rows with a compass and measuring device, and logged the data on his website, The Stone Rows of Great Britain (stonerows.wordpress.com). This website is a thing of wonder, the only online resource dedicated to exploring all the known surviving and destroyed prehistoric stone rows in Britain – 292 of the former and 20 of the latter. The website reveals that there are more ancient stone alignments on Dartmoor than anywhere else: 84 of them known and most still surviving. On the page for the Down Tor (Hingston Hill) row, a series of photographs analyses how the tors seem to appear and disappear as you walk westwards towards the cairn-circle. At certain points, as you walk along the row and the ground swallows up the hills leaving only a rocky tip visible on the horizon, some of the tors come to resemble prehistoric cairns, heaps of stone which are often found in the vicinity of stone rows (often at their end) and are associated with burial and death.[42] Sandy thinks all this could have been deliberate, a conscious ritual interaction with the landscape, and he believes that the views you experience when you walk along a stone row, especially when it terminates in a cairn, are key to understanding the ancient stone alignments. 'These monuments appear to bridge the gap between life and death, giving us a glimpse into what was seen as significant in prehistoric society.'

Rebecca Lambert is an archaeologist and artist who lived for a while on Dartmoor. She remembers vividly coming across Down Tor for the first time: 'I was taking an early-morning stroll and the mist was still lurking, refusing to release its grasp. I could hear ponies calling out to each other ahead of me, so I decided to follow their calls. Something began to appear on the horizon; at first I wasn't sure whether it was people, or animals, or something else. As I got closer, I realised I'd reached Down Tor.

'My first thought was *Wow*, quickly followed by a rush of awe, wonder and joy. I felt immense peace while I was with those stones and a sense of being connected to the people who had erected them; outside of time and wrapped up in the folds of the landscape. The atmosphere was so charged that if I'd reached out my hand, I would not have been surprised if I'd felt fingertips connect with my own.

'I've visited Down Tor many times since, in both a professional and a personal capacity, but that first meeting is the one that will always remain with me.'

Rebecca reflects on Dr Kenneth Brophy's research into stone rows, which approaches them as memorials radiating away from the central burial of a person considered important in the group (at Down Tor this original burial would have been in the cairn-circle), with subsequent deaths marked by the erection of another stone in the row. The terminus stone could mark the closing of the monument when the last members of the group died or moved away. Rebecca speculates, 'Perhaps we can see a stone

Hope is the Most Human Quality

row as a kind of megalithic family tree, a permanent memorial for the living to see. If this is the case, it would tie in with Mike Parker Pearson's theory that during this period, stone was used [at Stonehenge, for example] to represent the dead.'

She adds: 'I was living on Dartmoor during a really difficult period in my life. I'd begun my career in archaeology but had been forced to step away from it, and I was experiencing conflicting emotions about the landscape, prehistory and myself. This encounter with Down Tor began my journey back towards prehistory – and back to who I truly am.'

I find this idea of a stone row commemorating the lives of those who died thousands of years ago very poignant. The memory of these people has long faded, but their stones mark the landscape still. They prompt us who are here today to think of those who raised the stones and of those who the rows commemorate. They make us reach out our hands in the mist. In this, perhaps, the hopes of their builders are in some way fulfilled.

The Guardian of Merrivale

It's a Dartmoor kind of day today: the sky is grimy grey, forbidding clouds hang low over the moor and the rain is pattering loudly into the waterlogged grass. My waterproofs aren't really up to the job: my jeans are sodden, my arms are soaked up to the elbows and there's water trickling down my back. The kids, fed up with the rain, are heading back to the car after a bit of leaping over the leat (the 19th-century water channel) and a few desultory attempts to push each other in.

STONE LANDS

It's only a short walk to Merrivale from the lay-by on the Tavistock road, so we'd been sure Stephen would get to these stones at least, but the rain came on relentlessly and after a few steps he decided that it wouldn't be a great idea to get drenched and cold. I didn't want to leave him in the car for too long but he pressed me to go on and have a proper look around, so now I'm exploring this incredible place with its hut circles, its stone rows (no fewer than six of them), its marvellous cist – a stone box with a cracked lid like something from an Arthurian fable – and its circle of low stones set next to a towering monolith 3 metres high. The larks, chirruping joyfully, don't seem bothered by the weather, and neither am I.

Only, I'm not quite alone. I want to take a video of Row 2, an impressively long double row of stones stretching into the misty moor, but there's a man at the far end, somewhat marring the view. As I wait by the triangular terminus stone for him to finish whatever he's doing, I imagine what it must have been like for the country people during the plague of 1625, coming to this spooky ancient place to drop off supplies for disease-stricken and locked-down Tavistock. The townsfolk picked up the food at the stones and left money in payment,[43] and the farmers must have been keen during this coming-and-going to avoid encounters with potential carriers of pestilence. Maybe it had even been like this: a sighting of a distant figure in the gloom, a longing for them to hurry up and go away.

He doesn't seem to want to leave so in the end I give up and take the video anyway, walking slowly down the row between the two lines of stones, my boots squelching in the puddles, the rain dripping relentlessly, the larks still going crazy. Crouching

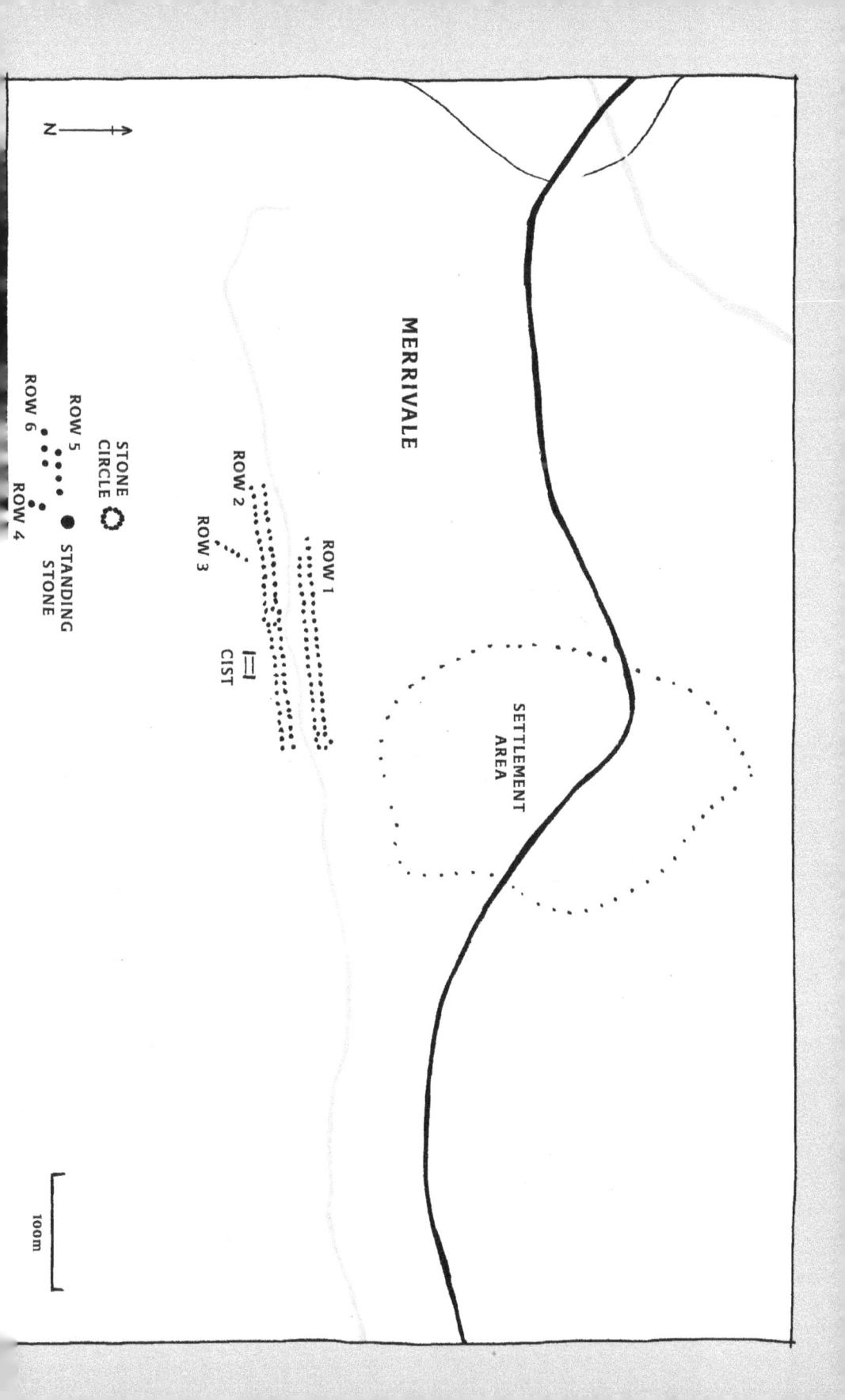

STONE LANDS

down in his dark anorak, he's not unlike one of Merrivale's granite megaliths himself. As I get closer, I can see he's doing something around the base of the stones with a trowel. It looks like he's gardening.

When I get to the end of the row, we exchange cautious greetings. He is elderly, with a look of determination and concentration on the lined face that pokes out of the anorak hood. I comment on his trowel and the rain. 'Ah, I'm out here in all weathers, a bit of wet doesn't bother me,' he says. 'I'm the spiritual guardian of Merrivale.'

He adds: 'I'm tidying the place up. Visitors make such a mess walking up and down the rows, tramping the turf into mud and damaging the stones.' He eyes me sharply and I guiltily hope I haven't contributed to the damage. 'There's no funding nowadays and if I didn't keep this site tidy, no one would.'

He wanders off to another row, a small, intent figure in the murk. Phone in my pocket, the filming and photographing done, and Merrivale's Guardian out of sight somewhere behind me, I am free to walk the avenue again with full focus, touching each stone in a ritual of hope. There is something about walking in this space defined by two lines of prehistoric stones that feels incredibly potent, as if this particular formation of stones is drawing me, as it must have done many thousands of people before me, into the performance of an ancient magic. Unknowingly we may repeat the old rituals, though to ends of our own.

How can you see an avenue like this and not want to walk along it? With the Guardian's words in mind, I take extra-special care in the placing of my feet as I go. When I reach the triangle at the eastern end, I lay both hands on the cold, damp granite and,

Hope is the Most Human Quality

shutting my eyes for a moment, tune in to the larks. Their chatter seems to intensify, as if they're trying to give me a message and I have a feeling that something has changed. It feels, right now, that it is possible to achieve the impossible, through simply wanting it enough.

The Power of Hope

The Cornwood Maidens stride across Stalldown Hill, visible for many miles around as a group of willowy if unusually tall hikers making determined progress along the ridge. These four granite pillars, each well over 2 metres high, head up the Stalldown stone row, which stretches for 859 metres across the moor, the tallest and most dramatic alignment of megaliths on Dartmoor. The easiest way to visit this magnificent ancient row used to be to drive to New Waste and walk up onto the moor, but in 2014 the car park here was closed by the landowner Alexander Darwall.[44] A petition was got up to demand restoration of road access to the high southern moor, especially on behalf of young families, the disabled and elderly, but the car park remains shut.

The protest about the closure of the car park was muted in comparison with the controversy that erupted in 2022 in response to Darwall's decision to launch a legal battle to overturn what was widely held as the public right to wild camping on Dartmoor. For 40 years, since the Dartmoor Commons Act established the right to open-air recreation, Dartmoor had been the only place in England where backpack camping without having to ask the landowner's permission was considered legal, so long as no damage was caused. Darwall argued that some campers were causing harm to livestock and the environment and creating a fire risk. In January 2023, he took his case against the Dartmoor National Park Authority to the High Court and won. The judge ruled that the right to wild camping did not exist, had never existed, and that Darwall did not have to tolerate the pitching of tents without permission on his land.[45]

I've never wild camped on Dartmoor but we are a camping family through and through, and I've done my share of wild camping. I felt a sharp sense of loss when I heard the news – for myself, for my children and for all the people who were now sharing, in the press and on social media, their memories of expeditions into the wilds of Dartmoor and their sadness that these were never to be repeated. It felt like some of the magic had gone out of life. Our horizons had narrowed again, and some more of the hope for our future had gone.

And, it turned out, people weren't going to take that lying down. After the High Court ruling, the campaigning organisation Right to Roam, who are demanding a law giving full public access to the downlands, woodlands, rivers and other wild places of England, experienced a massive surge in membership. Right to Roam argue that the countryside should be accessible to all, that our right to the health and wellbeing benefits of being in nature outweigh the landowners' right to exclude, and that, so long as each person observes their responsibilities to respect the ecology and agriculture of the countryside, they should have a

Hope is the Most Human Quality

right to explore these open spaces, to walk, kayak, cycle and swim there, to watch the stars and sleep there too.[46]

On a bright winter's day not long after the High Court ruling in Darwall v. Dartmoor, some 3,000 people walked onto Stall Moor near Cornwood to make their voices heard. Beating drums, shaking tambourines, blowing horns, bearing banners with slogans such as 'Nature is for all, not the few', 'Wild camping is cheaper than therapy' and 'Defend Dartmoor', they invoked the spirt of Old Crockern, the fearsome folkloric guardian spirit of Dartmoor, to protect the land and their right to wild camp there. 'We are Crockern,' they chanted together.

The day after the Cornwood protest, fell-running champion and Dartmoor resident Ceri Rees took a group of runners to the stone row on Stalldown Hill. 'There aren't many parts of Dartmoor that are truly isolated like this. Up on that ridge, it's like another world. After you've dropped down over the River Erne, there's a sharp ascent and you never know what you're going to get at the top – the weather is so unpredictable. Even if it was clear at the bottom, when you get up there those incredible stones might be reaching out of thick mist.

'The runners I took up to the Stalldown stones after the protest all had a similar feeling: this wow factor of being connected with our ancestors in a vivid way. Whether you believe the folklore or not, just seeing them is a very visceral experience.' He adds: 'The prehistoric stones up there also help runners and walkers with navigation. I've used the Hillson's House cairn as a refuge in bad weather. The Stalldown stones are good waymarkers because they're oriented broadly north–south, pointing to the sea.'

At the end of July 2023, the campaigners triumphed when the Court of Appeal overturned the High Court's decision and ruled that open-air recreation on Dartmoor did, after all, include the right to wild camp.[47] Cue much rejoicing – but Right to Roam's campaigning is far from done. They point out that, despite the 2000 Countryside and Rights of Way Act that delivered a limited Right to Roam, in England and Wales we still do not have legal access to 92 per cent of the countryside and 97 per cent of the rivers. Their hope for the future is a full Right to Roam, like the one that exists in Scotland.[48] Darwall, meanwhile, is currently seeking to overturn the Court of Appeal's ruling, and the Supreme Court has granted leave to appeal.

Ceri supports Right to Roam because his business, Wild Running, requires access to Dartmoor that now can't be taken for granted. 'Standing stones are part of our common heritage and they shouldn't be owned by any individual. You can still get up to the Stalldown row, but since the New Waste car park was shut it's harder for young families like mine to visit them. When an individual who owns huge swathes of land goes to court to stop access, what that's saying is that we should question whether we have a right to be there at all. We should question our attitude to the place we call home. I run there, I walk there, I take my family there. For me, that land is home.'

You Can Breathe Up There

The ancient sites of Dartmoor feel like home for Rebecca Holley, too. An artist creating textiles inspired by the moor's

Hope is the Most Human Quality

standing stones, she uses a traditional rag-rug technique working entirely with strips of reclaimed fabrics – old curtains, worn-out T-shirts, vintage nylon nighties – drawn through a hessian board with a hook. When I talk to her via video call, she shows me two textiles that she's made inspired by the stone circle at Froggymead (also called Fernworthy), as well as a work-in-progress on the prehistoric complex at Shovel Down. She holds up the finished Froggymead textiles and I can see, even through the computer screen, how they shimmer and flicker as the light interacts with the different materials, as if sunlight and cloud shadows were passing over the stones. Her enthusiasm and delight in her work and in the stones shine through, too.

'Shovel Down, with its avenues of stones, is really special, one of my favourite places. I go there for big life events, like my 50th birthday, to walk the avenues. You walk up between the stones and only as you get to the end do you see a large standing stone. It feels significant. I think it was built for rites of passage – birthdays, marriages, whatever.'

How does Rebecca capture the essence of the stones in her art? At the site, she sketches, draws in pastels and takes photographs; back in the studio she researches the history and folklore of the stones; she feeds all this material into the final design, which she creates on paper first, then recreates using fabric strips. She's been interested in ancient sites ever since her parents used to take her stone hunting as a child.

Her textiles are intensely bright, a cascade of tropical colours. People often ask where all that colour comes from, given that the landscapes of north Dartmoor are so stark. 'I don't

STONE LANDS

know,' she says. 'Maybe the colours just reflect that it's a really happy place and you feel like you can breathe up there. There's something incredibly special about sites like Froggymead and Shovel Down. You can feel the presence of the people who created them. They give me goosebumps. It's like going into a beautiful old church. Just talking about it now gives me goosebumps.'

I'm so interested in how these prehistoric places that survive in our modern world continue to inspire us. Beckie Burr is a photographer engaged in a long-term project to capture the magic and mystery of ancient sites. When I ask her if she has a favourite standing stone site, she says it would have to be the Dartmoor row Assycombe, where two long lines of stones climb through woodland to culminate in a majestic pillar and a cairn. She tells me, 'The past feels closer at Assycombe than anywhere else I've visited on Dartmoor. The dark pine trees that surround the stones radiate a deep, knowing silence, and there's often an eerie stillness there. For me, nothing makes the veil of time feel thinner than being able to follow the processional route of a stone row, walking in the footsteps of the site's creators and the many people that have come afterwards.'

She often photographs standing stones at night and finds visiting them in darkness a completely different experience to going in the day. 'At night, the stones seem to take on different shapes and my imagination goes into overdrive. I often wonder if my presence is welcome – I hope that it is.'

Beckie has photographed many megalithic sites on Dartmoor, from Merrivale to Drizzlecombe to Stalldown. Before she gets out her camera, she tries consciously to soak up the energy of the stones and imagine the ceremonies that may have taken place there. 'Although my ideas are probably far from what actually happened, it helps to bring these places to life in my mind. I believe that standing stones all have their own unique personality. There's an energy and a memory that comes with every stone and I try to capture this through my photographs, to tell a part of humanity's story that we'll never fully understand.'

Looking for Stalldown, she once found herself enveloped in a fog so dense she could hardly see her own feet. 'It felt like I was lost for hours and then the row suddenly emerged before me, the stones rising up from the hillside like ghostly figures, guardians of the moor. Stalldown has an eerie energy.' She feels strongly about the Right to Roam protests and the need to ensure access to the land where these stones stand: 'I've had some wonderful experiences wild camping out on the moors near the sites I photograph. I hope one day that England will follow in Scotland's footsteps in having a proper Right to Roam law.'

Thinking about the ancient places of Dartmoor gives me goosebumps, too. Even when I'm in a city hundreds of miles away, it's as if the special moments there, like walking the Down Tor stone row, live on inside me, offering me sustenance when I need it, a way to escape my everyday life. It's so important for us to be able to access these wild and lonely landscapes, to connect with the past through the archaeology that survives best in remote places, to feel our hearts expand with the freedom of a vast open horizon, to listen, in the quiet of the moor, to the

STONE LANDS

larks and to our own feelings. To let our troubles dissolve, if only for a moment. To breathe freely.

In the afternoon of the Down Tor day, after a pub lunch at the Royal Oak at Meavy, Stephen said he was feeling much better and that he thought we should go to see the Brisworthy circle. 'Are you sure?' I asked, a surge of hope lifting my spirits high, and he said, 'Yes! Let's do it. That chicken and chips has sorted me out and I need to see *some* stones on this trip.' The weather was still as fine as it could be, and it wasn't far to drive through the lanes to Brisworthy Farm. So we went.

It's supposed to be a 15-minute walk from the farm to the stone circle, but we took a lot longer that day. There's a photo of Stephen climbing over a stile; I took it because I wanted to record him in that magical landscape, the moor running into the far distance to meet the sky, and in the foreground, growing out of a broken-down stone wall, a solitary wind-battered hawthorn – a fairy tree. But what strikes me most about that photograph now is the awkward care with which Stephen is navigating the stile. He is leaning slightly forward with his hands firmly on the post and both boots on the same step, as if he is consciously keeping his balance and willing himself to complete the move. This is not how he would have crossed a stile five months before.

When we reached Brisworthy circle, he lay down on the grass just outside the stones, his head resting on his backpack, and breathed deeply in relief. I was anxious that he was worn out, but he was smiling as he took in the wide ring of stones, the two spreading hawthorn trees – this circle's guardians – and the encircling bowl of moorland that rose on all sides, crowned to the east by Legis Tor. 'This is a lovely one,' he said.

There's an entry in Stephen's notebook about Down Tor, where earlier that day he had birdwatched while Alex, Ava and I were exploring the stone row – another moment of avian-induced delight:

Cuckoo!

Good clear view of cuckoo flying – quite distinctive, like small raptor but not quite, with odd wingstroke and no neck. Plenty of cuckoo calls from trees. Come back some time.

He has underlined the words *Come back some time*, and drawn an asterisk next to them. There are always more birds to see, more tors to climb, more stones to find. He knew he would come back to Dartmoor. This was his hope and it was a certain one.

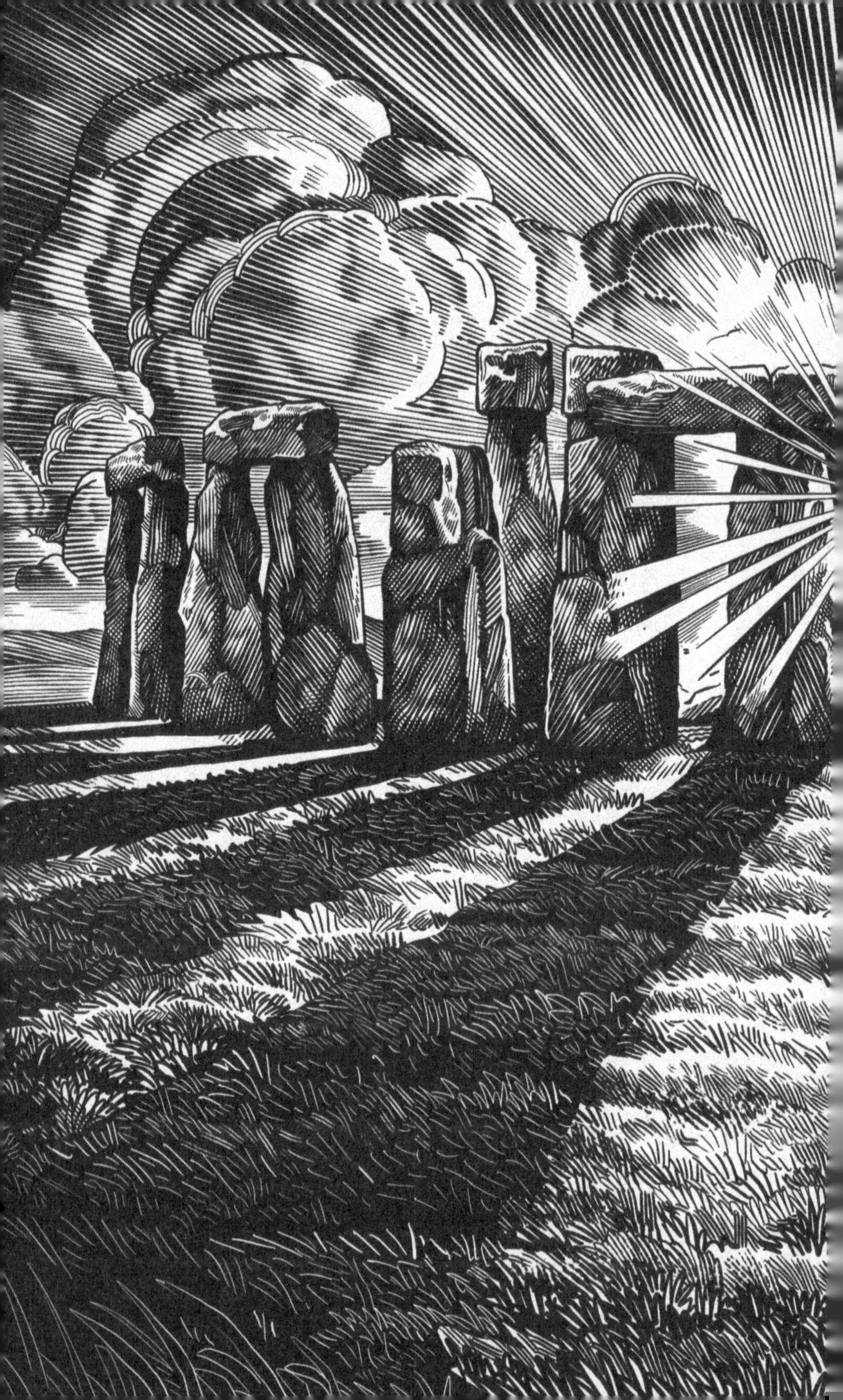

Chapter 5

ANYTHING IS POSSIBLE

- c.8820 BCE: earliest date for a Stonehenge car-park pit

- c.3400–3000 BCE: Waun Mawn built and dismantled

- c.3080–2950 BCE: Stonehenge ditch dug and bluestones from Preseli set up in Aubrey Holes

- c.2620–2480 BCE: sarsen trilithon horseshoe, double bluestone circle and outer sarsen circle built at Stonehenge

- c.2280–2020 BCE: further bluestone settings built/rearranged at Stonehenge

Stones of Preseli, PEMBROKESHIRE
Stonehenge, WILTSHIRE

I AM LYING WITHIN Bedd Arthur, 'Arthur's Grave', an oval of smallish sharp-edged bluestones that lean as if the wind has raked them into submission, as if even rock can be moved by air if you blow often and hard enough. It does feel like these Preseli Hills have been created by the clash of elements, the grass tussocks bleached white by the unforgiving sun, the earth pummelled and rolled out like pastry by the storms, and scarred in the high places by eruptions of igneous rock from which gigantic pillars and monstrous building blocks have been hacked by millennia of freeze and thaw.

The sweeping lines of the hilltop opposite are interrupted by a series of such rocky outcrops, a sprawling settlement of giants. This is Carn Menyn, once thought to be the source of the Stonehenge bluestones, those megaliths of not especially blue-looking spotted dolerite that were transported in prehistory from Wales

STONE LANDS

to Salisbury Plain. It has been pointed out that the shape, size and orientation of Bedd Arthur is so similar to the bluestone oval at the heart of Stonehenge that one must surely have been inspired by the other, that perhaps they were even built by the same people.[49]

In the far distance is a plain of green fields where people go about their daily lives and the blue horizon that signifies the rest of the world, but these stark Preseli uplands are another realm. There's something that feels transgressive about lying here on the ground, within Arthur's Grave. I should be marching through, one boot in front of the other, eyes on the map, mind on the weather forecast, but instead I am prone on the bristly turf, absorbing the healing energy of the earth, letting it fix whatever bits of me need fixing.

It is early summer in the year before Stephen is diagnosed and there is no special reason, at this point, for healing to be on my mind, except that I've been reading about archaeologist Timothy Darvill's theory that Stonehenge might have been a temple to which sick people travelled in the hope of a cure, and that the bluestones might have been transported to Salisbury Plain from these Preseli Hills, home of the gods or the ancestors, because of their perceived magical and medicinal qualities.[50]

I lay my head back on the rough grass, close my eyes and try to sink beneath the skin of the present and catch the echoes of the past. Almost immediately a cuckoo calls and then, as if heralded by its song, the wind picks up. I can hear it rushing towards me from a long way away, drumming on the ground like horses' hooves. Closer and louder the hoof beats come: it is King Arthur and his knights, riding out of the *Mabinogion* in pursuit of the ferocious boar Twrch Trwyth! At last the wind swarms over me, picking up my skirt, and I jump up like a puppet on a string to smooth it down again, a ludicrous performance that causes Ava, who has just raced down from the ridge, to burst into fits of giggles. She crouches down behind one of the stones so that she's entirely hidden apart from her arms sticking out on either side, and utters gnomic messages in a squeaky voice. The effect is strangely convincing: the stone has come to life.

Wind forward an hour or so and we are approaching Carn Menyn. Even the children are silent now, subdued by the effort of climbing and by the grandeur of the massive rocks that loom above us, a dark fortress hewn from the earth by giants. There is something unsettling, even menacing, about them, as if the giants built a castle and then angrily tore it down, ripping away life's beautiful illusion to reveal the inner workings of the world, the uncompromising building blocks on which our existence rests. One day, it will all return to this.

We shake off our sense of foreboding. The kids are moaning – it's too hot, too hard, too boring. To cheer them up, Stephen leads them in scrambling over boulder heaps and up rock stacks. Like him, Alex and Ava climb lightly and easily, balancing above long drops with not a care in the world. My heart beats faster and sweat prickles on my palms and scalp as I watch, and I only just manage to restrain myself from calling out tiresome warnings. Luckily The Megalithic Portal app gives me something to look at instead of my children on the verge of serious of injury and/or death.

STONE LANDS

If this place was hewn from the earth by giants, there is evidence of actual human hewing on Carn Menyn too. It was identified as a potential source of the bluestones as long ago as the late 19th century, although the most recent thinking is that other Preseli outcrops, such as Carn Goedog (just a mile away from Carn Menyn) and Craig Rhos-y-felin are the sites of the quarries that supplied Stonehenge.[51] On the slope below the outcrop is a large, ruinous prehistoric chambered tomb, its capstone collapsed onto the cairn and one stone standing upright like a signpost left for passing megalith enthusiasts. One or two other stones on the scree-littered slopes also appear to have been deliberately raised, perhaps as way-markers, whether in ancient times or much more recently.

Close to the tomb I find a bone, picked clean and lying on the grass like an offering, startlingly white in this landscape of ominous greys and greens. The leg bone of a sheep, perhaps. It seems to speak of the transience of all living things and the enigmatic messages we leave for those who come after. Of what lies beneath the skin: the dolerite bones of Preseli and our bones of calcium and collagen.

How to Control the Uncontrollable

It was our first trip to Pembrokeshire and I was enchanted by this region of stones and stories, and pleased to discover that the name 'Pembrokeshire' derives from the Welsh for 'end of the land', setting it alongside those other magical and similarly named western places Finisterre and Land's End. I wrote in my diary, *We have seven full days here and I've resolved to enjoy each one. No arguments. No looking at work emails. Minimal social media. No ruminations.* In my diary, I obsessively catalogued the details of the days, as if I were both conscious of our great good fortune and scared that we might lose it. Little things like the hedgerows frothing with hawthorn flowers, cow parsley, foxgloves, pink campion and bluebells, which I ran between early one morning on my way to the early Neolithic burial chamber Carreg Samson. Two donkeys in a buttercup field. Two paths diverging in a wood. The bulge in one of the dolmen's uprights, worn smooth by all the hands that have touched it over the years. How I put my finger into a hole in one of the upright stones and found a coin wedged there.

Each day I noted in my diary how far through the trip we were, how many full days were still to go. Our last but one day in Pembrokeshire was 4 June, the anniversary of the night Stephen and I had met at The Social 18 years earlier. We had a low-key celebration: I cooked a chilli and he got some (megalithically appropriate) Bluestone Brewery ales and a bottle of fizz from the local Spar. We drank in the chimney corner of our holiday cottage, looking out at the pink-grey dusk and the outcrop shaped like a witch's hat on the horizon near St David's Head, just chatting and enjoying the moment. The day we left, I wrote that I was feeling heartbroken to be going, though I didn't really know why – the whole summer still lay ahead.

Something, it seems, was making me count my blessings. We had another seven months before he would be diagnosed. The cancer had probably already started to grow.

Before Stephen became sick, I thought a diagnosis of incurable illness would be the worst thing in the world, impossible to endure. I had already thought of it, you see, in the bleak insomniac hours when all catastrophic outcomes seem possible and even likely. Stephen's dad, Philip, had died at the age of 58 from motor neurone disease. Abbi, the first wife of Stephen's brother Chris, had died at 34 from a brain tumour, when their children were aged just five and three. It must be the worst thing in the world, I used to think; how can you carry on, knowing that someone you love will die soon? How can you carry on, knowing that *you* will die soon? But as it turns out, it *is* possible to live with a terminal diagnosis and even go forward with hope by focusing on taking small steps towards achievable positive outcomes. Because anything is possible and that includes the chance that small steps, if we take enough of them, will lead us out of horror.

And in truth we are *all* living with a terminal diagnosis: we all know that we will die and none of us know when that will be. Maybe your time will be up in 40 years or in ten, or maybe it will be tomorrow, this afternoon, in five minutes... or NOW. Here it is: The End. The goodbye to this world that's coming to us all. And we're not dead until we're dead, right?

I am not religious but in the months after Stephen's diagnosis I prayed a lot, talking to a God in whom I did not really believe (maybe a bit) to ask for help. I went to Westminster Cathedral in London to petition the relics of St Bernadette of Lourdes for a cure, a strangely Catholic thing to do for an agnostic brought up in the United Reformed Church. And I wasn't the only one. In the heart of what may be the most secular city on earth, thousands of people were queuing to come into the presence of the ornate golden reliquary housing fragments of the ribs, knees and thigh of a young woman from the Pyrenees who once saw a vision of the Virgin Mary in a cave. Each of us wrote our request on the paper supplied and deposited it in a special postbox from where the petition would be taken to Lourdes. The tour of Bernadette's relics had been arranged because Covid had prevented pilgrims from travelling to Lourdes; if they could not go to Lourdes, then Lourdes would come to them. As I wrote out my heart's desire I promised this: if Stephen could be cured, which would amount to a miracle even in the eyes of modern science, I would make public my petition and its result.

It's thought around 50,000 people passed through the doors of Westminster Cathedral to visit the relics – that is a lot of petitions. I hoped Bernadette could manage that many.

We put our faith in modern science, too, in the clinical trials that are producing new life-saving cancer treatments all the time. My friend Bob, a devout Christian who took me to Westminster Cathedral to see St Bernadette, also ceaselessly trawled the internet looking for medical solutions and attended a cancer conference on our behalf, refusing to accept the word 'incurable' (he's an independent-minded kind of person). One work colleague told me of a relative, her body riddled with cancer and given weeks to live, who now, after a course of immunotherapy, was incredibly – miraculously – cancer free. Another told me of her mother, diagnosed with throat cancer and still

STONE LANDS

going strong years after the doctors issued a dire prognosis. We had meetings with hepato-pancreatic-biliary specialists, who gave us guidance on how to access medical trials and biomarker testing, and with a herbalist, who prescribed juicing and powdered food supplements in nigh-on unmanageable quantities (we did our best).

I attended an alternative healing conference and picked up a bagful of pamphlets on probiotics and antioxidants, mistletoe and turmeric, reflexology and matrix re-imprinting. I read books about people who'd healed themselves from cancer by going vegan, cutting out sugar and removing mould from their home.

I juiced a lot of kale. We tried to cover all the bases.

A Prehistoric Lourdes?

Stonehenge is, of course, the most famous standing stone site in Britain by far, its enormous trilithons – pairs of massive sarsen uprights joined by a stone lintel – instantly recognisable all over the world. This is the one standing stone site absolutely everyone has heard of even if they don't know anything else about stones. Megalith enthusiasts are often a bit sniffy about the place, deploring the commercialisation and the crowds, the high ticket price, the untouchability of the stones and, on the rare occasions that any other standing stone site*[52] is covered in

---

* Or indeed any prehistoric site with astronomical associations, such as Goseck, the 'German Stonehenge' – which has no stones at all!

Anything is Possible

the press, its invariable description as 'the Stonehenge of the North' (or wherever) even if it looks nothing like Stonehenge, which is always the case.

If, however, we can only purge our mind of all the clichés and look straight at this place as if we'd never seen it before, it has to be acknowledged that Stonehenge is, in fact, pretty awesome. Imagine what it must have been like, in the days before fences and security guards and the visitors' centre, when the A303 was just a muddy track and it was possible to wander across Salisbury Plain on a moonless night and happen by chance upon these stones, as Tess and Angel do at the end of *Tess of the d'Urbervilles*. They feel their way in the blackness among the massive uprights as the wind plays an eerie booming tune upon the stone edifice. What is this place, they wonder, which seems to be all doors and pillars, with architraves high above and yet no roof? It is a Temple of the Winds, says Angel.

And that is what Stonehenge still looks like from a traffic jam on the A303 – the view enjoyed for free by thousands every day – some kind of sanctuary from the Classical world, impossibly ancient and massive, incongruous on the Wiltshire downland. On the plain on either side of the road and often unremarked by those driving past, prehistoric barrows swell out of the earth, themselves very ancient and indicating that the wider landscape has been considered sacred for millennia.

As the A303 drops down and takes you right by the monument, the incredible prehistoric architecture is silhouetted on the skyline, with some of the massive stone lintels that were (uniquely for a stone circle) installed using mortise-and-tenon

STONE LANDS

jointing still in their original places. The fringe of ant-like human visitors makes the enormous sarsens seem all the more impressive. Isolated some distance to the east is the Heel Stone, a bulky, unshaped megalith that looks, in contrast to the neatly sculpted pillars of the circle, like an oversized priest in flowing robes conducting the ceremonies. From the perspective of the A303, it seems like the Heel Stone could hold the key to at least some of the meaning of Stonehenge, standing apart from the circle as it does (it probably once had a companion, but the stone that stood close by has long since vanished).

I wonder whether the homophone *heel/heal* bears any relation to the Heel Stone. It's been said since at least the 12th century that the stones of Stonehenge have healing powers. In Geoffrey of Monmouth's legend of the Arthurian age, *The History of the Kings of Britain*, Merlin is discussing with Aurelius Ambrosius, the Romano-British leader and uncle of King Arthur, how to build a monument to commemorate the Britons slain by the Saxons. Send for the Giant's Ring on Mount Killaraus in Ireland, advises Merlin; these stones were brought from Africa to Ireland by the giants and possess valuable medicinal properties. The giants would pour water over the stones and catch the water in baths in which the sick would be cured. The stone-infused water was also mixed with herbs and used to heal wounds. There isn't one of these stones that doesn't have some medicinal power, Merlin concludes. His argument persuaded the Britons to travel to Ireland to steal the stones, though the megaliths were so huge the men needed Merlin's magic to take them down and get them on the boat and over to Salisbury Plain.[53]

Anything is Possible

Timothy Darvill argued that legends like this support his theory that Stonehenge could once have been a healing shrine; and he wondered if the 'spherical temple' of Apollo in the land of the Hyperboreans, mentioned by the historian Hecataeus of Abdera in *c.*330 BCE, had actually been a description of Stonehenge.[54] Apollo was the god not just of the sun (and Stonehenge is famously a monument that marks the sun's solstice extremes), but also of divination, music and *healing*. Darvill suggested that there was archaeological evidence of sick people travelling in prehistoric times to the Stonehenge area from far away: the Amesbury Archer, for example, who was buried 3 miles from Stonehenge *c.*2300 BCE, had grown up in central Europe and suffered from a seriously damaged knee as well as what would have been a very painful jaw abscess. In short, he was a pilgrim, said Darvill, to a sort of prehistoric Lourdes,[55] its renown spread across Europe via networks of exchange of goods and ideas.

Many archaeologists are unconvinced by the 'prehistoric Lourdes' theory, pointing out that only three, at most, burials of unwell people have been found at Stonehenge,[56] and yet it's an appealing one when you think of the way many people relate to standing stones today. When I started to write this book, I posted on social media asking about people's unusual experiences at standing stone sites, and I was amazed and excited to be sent over a hundred responses to this one enquiry. I was struck by the number of people who believed that standing stones had some kind of beneficial powers, whether that be to heal, to make fertile, to give energy, to grant a wish. So many of us, it seems, are prepared to entertain the belief that individual standing stones have a character, even a consciousness of their own, that it is possible to interact with them, to learn and receive gifts from them. I understand this. It's something I've always felt myself. It's what prompted me, after Stephen was diagnosed, to touch every stone in every circle or row that I visited and wish for him to get better. I never failed to do this. Because if anything is possible, you have to try everything.

Here are some of the things people told me. One of my respondents, an academic working in the heritage sector, described a powerful experience she'd had at the Ring of Brodgar of interacting with non-human beings who granted her wish to give up smoking (she asked me not to identify her as she felt that going public wouldn't be viewed positively by her colleagues!). Two fathers described being overcome, one at the Clava Cairns and the other at Beaghmore, with a knowing that they would be able to have children, despite previous struggles with miscarriage and worries about infertility. One respondent said that resting his forehead on a stone at Avebury had taken away a migraine; another that she'd experienced a feeling of deep peace and wellbeing at the Rollright Stones, an untangling of the knot of anxiety that she usually carried with her. One woman described how, 'though not generally a hippy-dippy cosmic-type person', she experienced both times she was pregnant an overwhelming desire to go and hug the stones at Avebury. Many people said touching the stones helped them to feel calm and grounded, because the stones have been there for so long or because of their special energetic properties. Another of my respondents described seeing a gaunt-looking woman with a scarf wrapped around her head walking inside the King's Men circle at Rollright; she'd come there, not for the first time, to draw support from the stones in her cancer treatment. A woman shared that her mother now made a pilgrimage to Avebury each year following her successful recovery from stage 3 cancer.

Those who manage to get into Stonehenge on a private tour, or who visit at solstice when the public is allowed inside the circle (and for free), find that it's possible to have an intense, exciting experience with the stones, even at this most commercialised and touristed of sites. Maria J. Pérez Cuervo, the founding editor of *Hellebore*, a magazine devoted to folklore, magic and the occult in Britain, says the popularity of Stonehenge prevents the 'instinctive, personal connection with the site' that she's always seeking. However, she was twice lucky enough to experience being within the inner circle at dawn, in a very small group: 'both times it's been radically different from a regular visit – the closeness, the silence, the overwhelming mystery.'

For her, standing stones are an icon of Britain, but not in a nationalist way. 'They represent the essence of Britain and the magic in its landscape. They are monumental in an essential way, without refinement, as a sketch can sometimes be more powerful than a finished idea.' She believes the mysteries surrounding the stones' original function and the tales of enchantment and wonder are key to their appeal. 'Whenever I visit a stone circle, that great mystery – time, our existence, our identity – is immediately manifest.'

STONE LANDS

I got to know the Seed Sistas – Fiona Heckels and Kaz Goodweather – through working with them on their two books and their beautiful plant oracle cards, and I knew that they liked to hang out at standing stones. These herbalists, performance artists, witches and eco-activists are also old friends whose two families come together to celebrate the winter solstice, often at Stonehenge. It's an intergenerational thing, with kids and dogs and grandparents in attendance. 'We try to make it fun for everyone,' says Kaz. Added fun for the adults comes from flasks containing a brew of hot chocolate and magic mushrooms, shared before dawn.

For Kaz, Stonehenge is very different from all other stone circles. 'There's a lot of fizzy, exciting energy at Stonehenge. I think it's because there's been so much conflict, with the Travellers and the Battle of the Beanfield and the way English Heritage controlled the stones, and now with all the opposition to the road tunnel. Wherever there's conflict, there's a kind of energy; and wherever there's oppression, creativity rises up to meet it. If you come at solstice, you're met with fences and security guards in high vis trying to contain all the chaos. And that can be very exciting.'

'We'll often have a moan about Stonehenge,' says Fiona. 'But when we go, we always end up thinking of it as a place that generates energy and excitement even.'

The last time they celebrated winter solstice at Stonehenge, they stayed in local B&Bs and walked up to the site in darkness. 'There was a sense of pilgrimage, walking up to the stones,' Fiona says.

'We always end up learning something there,' adds Kaz. 'Last year, there was this incredible Chinese woman with a traditional stringed musical instrument, I think it was 400 years old, and she was playing the sounds of the constellations. She was an astrologer and a musician who explored the vibrational tones of Chinese music. I was just blown away by this music from the stars.'

Fiona says, 'It makes so much sense to be celebrating together at winter solstice, having come through the dark time when the days are getting shorter and reached the turning point. The mushrooms do help to enhance the collective hilarity and bring a real sense of joy, fun and playfulness. We often do the hokey-cokey as a massive group and get everyone else to come and join in, and we'll bring a rounders bat. We also take wreaths and light candles in them to reflect on the year and bring any loved ones who have passed over into the mix.'

'On mushrooms you can communicate with the stones,' says Kaz. 'They become animate in a way that's hard to articulate.' She adds: 'Solstice at Stonehenge is exciting because we're given this short time in which we have some freedom among the stones, we're allowed to go in and play. And then when it's all over and we're leaving, all the tourists who've paid the entrance fee start arriving for the day.'

STONE LANDS

Marking the Solstices on Salisbury Plain

My own earliest memory of Stonehenge is not of stones but of the car park. I was in my late teens and, tolerated by the stewards, my then boyfriend and I had put up a tent on the grass strip on the edge of the car park, next to some slightly aloof Swedish tourists with much flashier camping gear than ours. This was the old car park, where three white circles on the tarmac marked the positions of prehistoric pits discovered when the parking area was extended in 1966. Thirty years after this discovery, the pine charcoal found inside the pits was carbon-dated and archaeologists were astounded to learn that it dated back an incredible 10,000 years. These pits were dug, perhaps to hold totem-style wooden poles, *5,000 years before any stones were raised here.*[57]

At the time of this first remembered visit, in the early 1990s, I didn't even notice the white discs in the car park. I was less interested in archaeology, then, than in the Stonehenge Free Festivals and the 1985 Battle of the Beanfield (when police in riot gear beat up a convoy of New Age Travellers and put an end to the summer parties at the stones) and in the subsequent struggles of Druids and Travellers for admittance at solstice. We must have seen the stones that day and now we were back by the tent, the shadows lengthening and the car park mostly emptied out. We were enjoying a spliff prior to heating up our baked beans, when the sleepy summer evening was disrupted by the roar of an engine. A truck veered into the car park and screeched to a halt. A bloke jumped out, grabbed two large

Anything is Possible

canisters from outside the stewards' hut, yelled something indecipherable to his mate, leaped back into the truck and off they zoomed again.

It was all over in a flash. We blinked, not quite sure what had happened. I discreetly stubbed out the joint as the steward approached us, chuckling to himself. 'Well, they won't get far with that,' he said. 'That's lawn-mower fuel! I'll be looking out for them sat on the verge on my way home . . .'

This episode has stuck in my mind. I find it strange but perhaps fitting that if an archaeologist could dig into the layers of my memories of Stonehenge, it would be the car park they'd find at the bottom.

What was it that drew people to mark this chalk upland, in the Mesolithic, with pits and (perhaps) wooden poles, and then in the Neolithic, several millennia later, with stone? If you stand at the heart of Stonehenge at midwinter, you will see the setting sun sinking between the uprights of the Great Trilithon; if you stand there at midsummer, facing in the opposite direction, you will see, through the main entrance of the henge, the sun rising behind the Heel Stone. Beyond the Heel Stone, the parallel banks and ditches of the earthwork known as the Avenue continued the alignment north-eastward for 500 metres, towards the summer solstice rising sun.

Amazingly, it turns out that this part of the Avenue is in fact mostly natural in origin – two ridges separating parallel strips of sediment-filled gullies and chalk bedrock, which would have been highly visible to prehistoric people as stripes on the grassland. By a crazy coincidence, these natural stripes happen to be

STONE LANDS

aligned on the solstice axis, inscribing the yearly northernmost and southernmost positions of the sun – the extremes of light and darkness – into the very ground, marking it out as a cosmologically significant place. Mike Parker Pearson and his excavation team argue that this, surely, is why a stone circle was built here, its north-eastern entrance positioned at the end of the parallel stripes, and why the ridges were enhanced with ditches dug alongside them and soil piled on top to create banks. This solstice-aligned landscape phenomenon explains the orientation of the stone circle to midwinter sunset and midsummer sunrise, and could also be why, 5,000 years earlier, pits had been dug in line with the north-east end of the stripes, under what was many millennia later to become the first Stonehenge car park.[58]

In the early 1990s, the car park was out of bounds on a summer solstice eve (a four-mile exclusion zone having been imposed around Stonehenge at solstice since the Battle of the Beanfield to keep away Druids, Travellers and other would-be revellers), so my companion and I parked up on a side road and waited for it to get dark, with the intention of somehow sneaking into the site around midnight. We had the following plan: to down a couple of bottles of Merrydown cider, so if the police found us, they would be unable to send us away as we'd be over the limit and that would constitute an incitement to drunk driving by the police themselves. A cunning plan indeed.

We started on the Merrydown and not long afterwards the police turned up and sent us away. Without needing to confer, it occurred to both of us simultaneously when faced with actual police that maybe it wouldn't be a good idea to try the 'but we're over the legal limit' argument, so that was the end of our solstice celebration. As we drove away looking for somewhere to stop and get some sleep, hoping that we weren't actually over the limit, we passed a Druid walking through the darkness alongside the A303 like a ghostly visitation from the far-distant past: stately, white-robed, calmly intent on reaching the stones. I wonder now if this was Arthur Uther Pendragon himself, known as King Arthur though born John Timothy Rothwell, the Stonehenge access campaigner and Battle Chieftain of the Council of British Druid Orders, who between 1985 and 2000 was arrested every year for breaching the exclusion zone at summer solstice.[59] In 2000, English Heritage relented and restored public access to the Stonehenge stones at solstice. Now, Druids, and anyone else who wishes to do so (and every midsummer some 15,000 people do), may stand within the stones and watch the sun rise on the longest and shortest days of the year.

Anything is Possible – Even Moving a Stone Circle

Stonehenge has changed a lot over its long history. After its ditch was first dug, c.2950 BCE, a circle of bluestones stood just inside the ditch in the stone-holes known as the Aubrey Holes (after their discoverer John Aubrey) – their position is shown on the ground today with concrete markers. At some point this first stone circle was taken down. Up to half a millennium after the digging of the ditch, a horseshoe of massive trilithons of

SARSEN TRILITHON
HORSESHOE

BLUESTONES

SARSEN
STONES

ALTAR
STONE

SARSEN
STONES

BLUESTONES

SARSEN TRILITHON
HORSESHOE

STONEHENGE
CENTRAL MONUMENT

N

10m

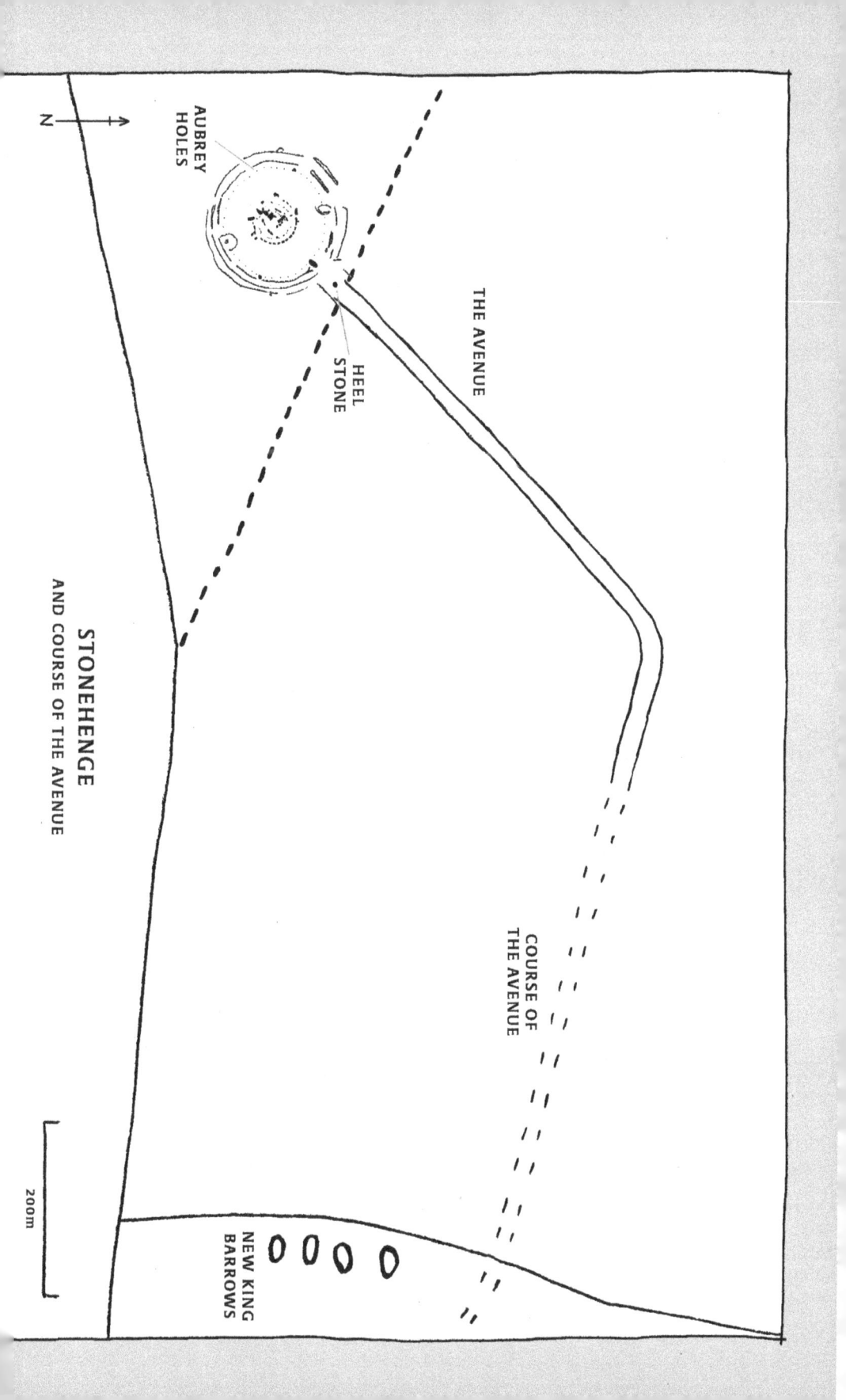

STONEHENGE
AND COURSE OF THE AVENUE

AUBREY HOLES

HEEL STONE

THE AVENUE

COURSE OF THE AVENUE

NEW KING BARROWS

N

200m

sarsen stone was set up, surrounded by a double circle of bluestones (presumably including the original outer circle in new positions), of which only a few now remain. The horseshoe of sarsen trilithons and the double bluestone circle were then surrounded by a final ring of great sarsen standing stones linked together by lintels.[60]

The source of the different types of Stonehenge stone – sarsens and bluestones – has been much debated. Geochemical analysis has shown that 50 of the 52 Stonehenge sarsens that survive (out of a probable 80 originals) share a common chemistry, implying that they came from the same place, which, the report suggests, is West Woods, Wiltshire, about 15½ miles north of Stonehenge and not far from Avebury. Even the massive Heel Stone, long thought to have been a natural sarsen found on Salisbury Plain and perhaps the first stone to be raised on the site, is now believed to have been taken from West Woods.[61] What's more, recent research has revealed that the Altar Stone, a sandstone (though not sarsen) megalith previously thought to originate from southern Wales, does not come from Wales at all, but from somewhere in north-east Scotland (Mainland Orkney has been ruled out), at least 460 miles away from where it now rests at the ceremonial heart of Stonehenge.[62] That's a long way to drag a 6-tonne stone, which makes it likely that it was transported south by sea.

Also pretty mind-blowing is the journey that around 80 bluestones took from the Preseli Hills, some 140 miles away as the crow flies and on the ground or via water probably a lot further. The bluestones are much smaller than the sarsen giants, weighing 2–5 tonnes as opposed to 10–30 tonnes, but still: their journey, whether it took place by land, sea, or both, would have required an almost inconceivable effort from the people of that long-ago era.

A few months before we visited Preseli, the bluestones hit the headlines with the spectacular revelation that there might actually be some truth in Geoffrey of Monmouth's legend of the origins of Stonehenge. A stone circle *was* brought to Wiltshire from the west, said Mike Parker Pearson and his co-researchers, but from Pembrokeshire rather than Ireland. The archaeologists posited that the bluestones transported from Wales to Salisbury Plain had once stood in a circle at Waun Mawn in the Preseli Hills, not far from the rock outcrops now thought to be their original source. The team said they had unearthed the stone-holes of the dismantled Waun Mawn circle, and pointed out the remarkable similarity between that site and Stonehenge: both circles were oriented on summer solstice sunrise, and the Waun Mawn circle would have had a diameter that was identical to that of the enclosing ditch of Stonehenge.

There was yet more evidence to tie Waun Mawn and Stonehenge together. In Waun Mawn's stone-hole 91, an unusual pentagonal imprint, left in the earth by the stone that once stood there, closely matched the turf-line profile of Stonehenge's Stone 62. Dating of wood charcoal and sediment from the stone-holes put Waun Mawn's construction and dismantling before 3000 BCE, so before the bluestones were set up in their original positions in the Aubrey Holes at Stonehenge. What's more, isotope analysis of cremation burials at Stonehenge found that four out

STONE LANDS

of 25 sets of remains tested belonged to people who lived the last decades of their lives in south-west Wales, an area that includes Preseli.

The theory of Parker Pearson and his team was that Neolithic migrants from Wales had taken down the stone circle at Waun Mawn, transported the bluestones with immense effort to Wiltshire, and then set them up again on Salisbury Plain. Perhaps these stones represented the migrants' ancestors and so were an essential part of the group's identity, in which case bringing them along could have been as crucial as transporting their family and their animals.[63]

The idea that the Stonehenge bluestones had once stood in a kind of proto-Stonehenge at Waun Mawn was highly thought-provoking and intriguing, but (sadly) has since been more or less disproved by geological analysis.*[64] Even so, the fact remains that 5,000 years ago around 80 very heavy megaliths were somehow transported from the Preseli Hills to Salisbury Plain – and that alone is an astounding feat.

When I get to see Waun Mawn for myself, I do so with the mind-boggling Stonehenge theory at the forefront of my mind. As we approach the site of the dismantled circle, I'm enjoying the thought that the faint track we are following across the

---

* There is no geological match between the remaining stones at Waun Mawn and the surviving Stonehenge bluestones, making it unlikely that the latter ever stood in the Waun Mawn circle, although they definitely originated in the Preseli Hills. However, it's been speculated that the unfinished then dismantled stone circle at Waun Mawn (which interestingly appears to have been constructed around a large tree, perhaps an oak, with a hearth set below it) may have provided a kind of blueprint for Stonehenge.

moor was probably created by archaeologists, and also the idea that we might be walking in the much (much) older footsteps of the people who built a stone circle here and of those who hauled the stones away again. We rise up the moor towards the ridgeline, anticipation growing, and then in a moment of high drama as we crest the hill, the wide-rimmed bowl where the circle once stood is revealed below, the land generously offering itself up to the sky and to us. I try to imagine how it would have felt in ancient times to catch sight of the monument below, a navel in the belly of the hills, the source of sacredness. Today, only one small stone still stands here with three megaliths that have fallen, the four of them marking out an arc which, if taken to completion, would describe the perimeter of a great circle. The surviving stones are made more potent by Parker Pearson's ideas and by the shades of their vanished companions, but really it is the landscape that offers a sense of theatre rather than the stones themselves. Cloud shadows play over the hills like actors on an immense stage miming out the story – if only we could understand it – of what actually happened here.

A party of walkers approaches. They're clearly on some kind of guided tour, as one of them is pointing and explaining, while the others assume a respectful listening stance. This obscure corner of the Preseli Hills, with its prehistoric remains that are quite insignificant in comparison with many ancient sites that survive in Pembrokeshire, has been touched with the glamour of Stonehenge.

We retreat in the face of this unconscionable intrusion, back over the ridge and down to a pair of standing stones and

STONE LANDS

a solitary megalith known on The Megalithic Portal as 'Waun Mawn W' (as opposed to 'Waun Mawn NE', which is the remains of the circle). I take a video of the single standing stone, which at over 2 metres high is the finest individual stone here; a futile act, perhaps, to film a rock, but I want to capture the trill of lark song, the hissing of the wind in the tough moor grasses, the way the stone is gilded by sunlight and lichen, the beautiful curve of the hillside set against a heartbreakingly blue sky. I want to capture this place, this day, this moment.

Later that afternoon, we walk through a tangled witches' wood with a wonderful climbing tree with low-trailing limbs like a ladder, and a stream that rushes and tumbles over boulders, clinking rocks in its eagerness, racing us down to Aber Rhigian cove. When we get to the beach, we plunge into water that stabs us with icy needles and is totally exhilarating, my whole body fizzing and tingling. The water is insanely clear, golden diamonds rippling on the seabed, lumps of quartz exerting a luminous appeal. The waves throw a dazzling, dancing veil of sunlight onto the wall of a cave, a magical grotto where the sea fairies live. White gulls rest on the water, observing us, and once we are all back on the beach, they come ashore by the grotto, like a band of enchanted princes.

From among the sparkling lumps of quartz on the beach, I choose an oval white stone that's less showy but delightfully smooth and cool against my skin. A Druid's egg. On one side of the oval is an arc of holes that made me think of the stone-holes of Waun Mawn. These tiny holes, like windows into a glittering fairy cavern, reveal the stone's inner crystalline nature. I carry it

Anything is Possible

across the little bridge over the stream, up through the witches' wood and back to the cottage. This Druid's egg holds within its perfect, smooth, oval form the memory of that day, and I have it with me still.

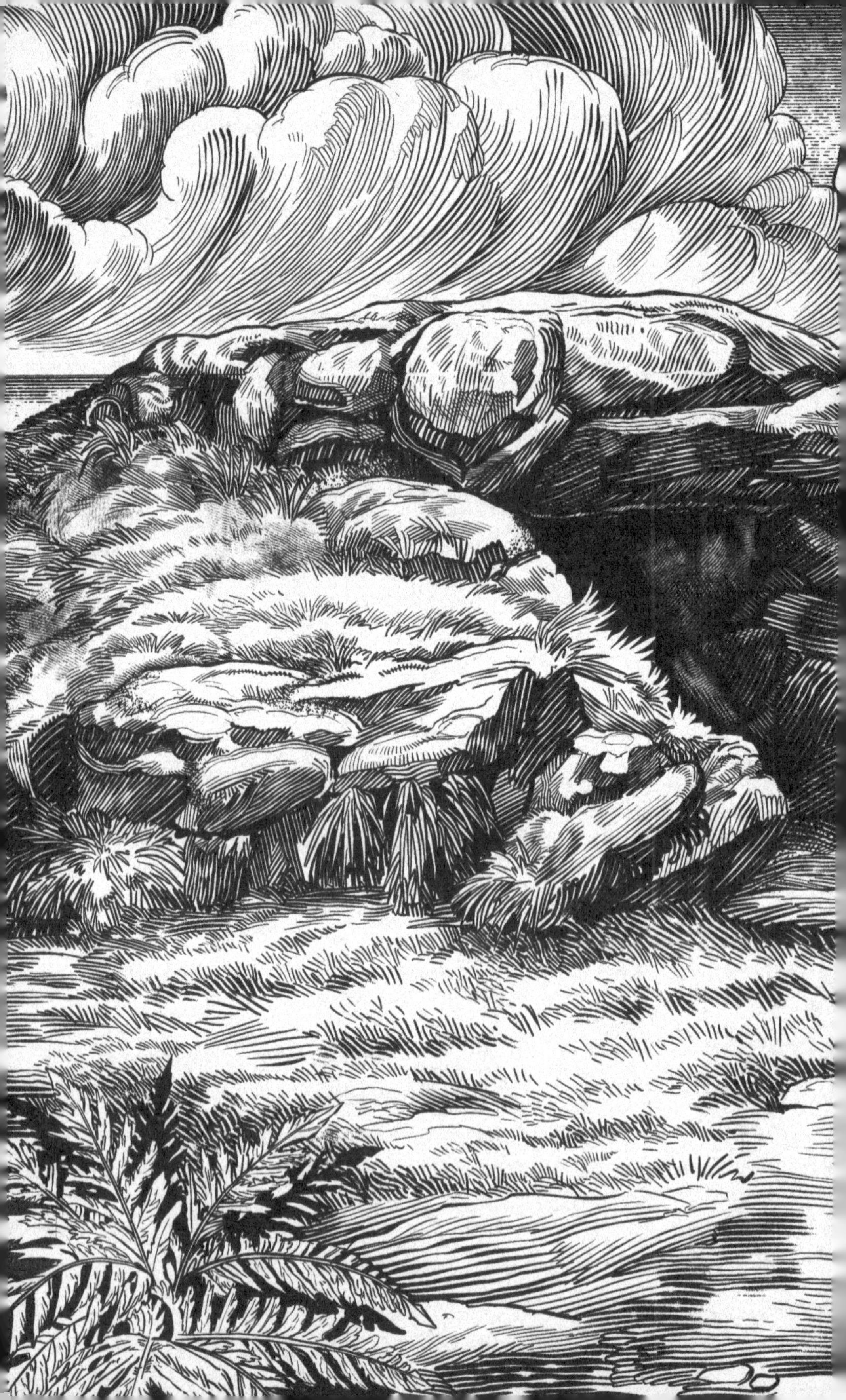

Chapter 6

WE CANNOT HOLD BACK THE TURNING WHEEL

Stones of the Isles of Scilly

THE SUN IS NOT long set and Alex, Ava and I are lying on a springy bed of heather next to a prehistoric burial mound on Shipman Head Down. For the fourth summer in a row we are camping on Bryher, the most beautiful (in our opinion) of the Scilly Isles. We are watching the stars as one by one they burn a hole through the firmament and take up their positions in the sky. We work out that the lights below us must belong to the Hell Bay Hotel; that other lights must be ships on the horizon, a lighthouse, the houses on St Mary's. We speculate about who might be buried in the mound beside us – King Arthur himself, perhaps – and wonder if the bones are still there, or if they've been dissolved by the acid in the soil, and if there's any chance that a shadow might spill out from under the capstone and swell into a ghostly form that creeps up on us, spectral sword in hand. The pale heather roots grip the soil like bleached

STONE LANDS

finger bones, while the sea drums an endless funeral dirge for the thousands of sailors lost around Scilly's shores. On this wild heathland, high above the churning Atlantic, there are at least 134 prehistoric cairns and what seem to be the remnants of prehistoric stone walls, perhaps even stone rows. It is a spooky place even in daylight and now, in darkness, the down seems to reach into emptiness for an immeasurable distance, as if offering not just a route to the northernmost point of the island but a way into the past. Somewhere in the dark over there, beyond the rising heath, are two lines of boulders that mark the ramparts of an Iron Age hillfort. In winter, I tell the children, the waves in Hell Bay are so massive that they fly right over Shipman Head Down and fall on the heads of people on the sheltered, Tresco-facing side of the island.

Later I sit outside the tent with Stephen, who despite the clemency of this August night is wrapped in a thick jacket and a blanket and wearing the woolly hat and scarf he bought on Iona. We tip back in our chairs, awestruck by the stars that grow brighter and nearer every second. Our old friends – the Great Bear, the Little Bear, Lyra and Cygnus, the 'W' of Cassiopeia – come now to remind us of the many times we have star-gazed together, of that summer in France when Ava was still a baby and we saw, from the garden of our cottage in the middle of nowhere, the Perseids streaking through the sky, an incredible abundance of shooting stars, a fireworks display for the solar system, a celebration of our happiness and a blessing on our future.

Tonight is our last night on Bryher and the Milky Way is revealing itself to the two of us one more time, a path of wonder across the heavens, a reminder of our human insignificance compared to the galactic-scale mechanics in which our own planet is just one small cog. It is heart-stopping.

The Lost Land of Lyonesse

At the start of *Exploration of a Drowned Landscape*, Charles Thomas writes about the sense of strangeness and mystery that arises in a traveller approaching Scilly by air: 'the very existence of so many isles, large and small, miles out from the Land's End, can strike you for the first time as preposterous.'[65] I can imagine this is so, but we have always come by boat. And (at the time of writing) there is only one boat: the *Scillonian III* ferry, which has been transporting passengers between Penzance and St Mary's since 1977.* If it breaks down, as it did when we were on Bryher in 2019, there's no option if you are burdened with a large quantity of camping gear, but to wait until it's fixed . . . a happy accident that gave us the perfect excuse for not turning up at work on the Monday and two precious extra days on the island. Built to navigate the shallow waters around St Mary's, *Scillonian III* is an especially flat-bottomed vessel and prone, once past Penlee Point near Mousehole, to heaving and rocking in the most unsettling fashion. I've seen the lower decks strewn like a field hospital with blanket-wrapped bodies, every face green, the upper deck awash with vomit as stricken passengers stagger for the railings and fail to make it;

---

* Her successor, *Scillonian IV*, will come into service in 2026. A new, faster catamaran service was due to start in 2024 but has not yet materialised.

on the other hand, we've also breezed across in dazzling sunlight as pods of dolphins leapt through rainbow spray, their gleaming bodies twisting and twirling in impossible aerial acrobatics to the delight of children and adults alike. It's up to Fate, really, what sort of crossing you get, but either way, when your feet touch firm land again on St Mary's, it's as if you've passed into another world.

Archipelago – the word recalls ancient Greece, with its sun-baked islands of stone temples and sacred groves, where seafarers set sail to adventure, the gods ride dolphin-back and the green waters conceal sea serpents and merfolk and even a lost city, Atlantis. And there is something of all of this in Scilly.

It was Stephen who first told me about the Scilly Isles and their enchantments. He'd visited before, once with his friends Lou and Nicky, and then, because he loved it so much, he'd come back alone. He'd wanted for a long time to take the kids and me, but it turned out to be almost impossible to get a summer-holiday booking in any of the off-island campsites because of (annoying) 'returners' – people who come back year after year. Then at last we managed it and we turned into returners too.

There is magic in these parts. It's heaven for a birdwatcher like Stephen, who excitedly devoted page after page in his notebook to avian encounters:

Shag – off all coasts in great numbers, sometimes in groups under water . . . swallows tumbling everywhere, also sand martins . . . the odd cormorant . . . oystercatchers! . . . gannets on rocks north of Eastern Islands . . . terns, I think both sandwich and common but hard to tell (for me) . . . rock

We Cannot Hold Back the Turning Wheel

pipits and stonechat near Hell Bay Hotel . . . northern wheatear on heather near Rushy Bay . . . a flock of sanderling at Green Bay . . . herons on the rocks . . . little egret at Popplestone Bay, and a good sighting of ringed plover at dusk . . . fulmar off St Martin's, flying into nests on cliff . . . great shearwater skimming surface (10cm!) . . . turnstone in St Mary's harbour . . .

It's paradise for the megalith hunter too, for on the handful of square miles that make up the Scilly Isles is one of the densest concentrations of megalithic remains in western Europe, with a bounty of entrance graves and cairns and a few interesting solitary standing stones. An enchanted land today as surely it was 4,000 years ago, still the last inhabited isles before the great watery nothingness begins. A domain where reality and the imagination co-exist, where the legends might just have some truth to them. Beyond the five inhabited islands of St Mary's, St Martin's, St Agnes, Tresco and Bryher, there are some 140 others, too many to visit or name. This plethora of islands implies the existence of another, shadowy Scilly that is now lost, the original unified land mass of which these islands were only the high ground. You can't see it if you look straight, but maybe you can glimpse it out of the corner of your eye.

Since at least the 15th century, there's been a Cornish legend that a whole kingdom, with its woods, meadows, farmland and churches, was drowned between Mount's Bay in Cornwall and Scilly. This legend became conflated with French Arthurian tales of a submerged land called Lyonesse, so that by 1586 William Camden was writing (in Latin) of the waters beyond

STONE LANDS

Land's End: 'People assert that there was a land, Lyonesse, so-called from some fable or other, covered over by an inrush of the sea.' In 1602, Richard Carew described the evidence for a lost city under the water between Land's End and Scilly: 'Fishermen also casting their hooks thereabouts have drawn up pieces of doors and windows.' This idea of a lost sunken kingdom called Lyonesse was widely popularised in the 19th century by Tennyson's *Idylls of the King*, in which Arthur's last battle, death and the isle of Avalon are all set in Lyonesse, 'A land of old upheaven from the abyss'.[66]

The reality underlying Scilly's Lyonesse legend is this. Around 7000 BCE, Scilly was a single island. By 4000 BCE, the sea had separated St Agnes, Annet and the Western Rocks from the main land mass to the north. The waters continued to rise and by around 2500 BCE, tidal flooding was encroaching on the northern island, increasing in severity until, by around 1500 BCE, Tresco, Bryher and Samson were the distinct entities they are today, separated by a huge intertidal area of saltmarsh. After *c.*1500 BCE the rate of change slowed, and it was not until the late 10th century CE that a permanent channel existed north of St Mary's and the saltmarsh was replaced by open water.[67]

Crossing between these shimmering islands and the sandbars that glitter like heaps of treasure, I would lean over the side of the Bryher ferry, the *Firethorn*, and peer down through the crystal water to try (without success) to spot submerged stone walls, road-like sandbars or seaweedy rings that might mark the sites of roundhouses.[68] Approaching St Agnes one day during the holiday we took after Stephen became ill, Ava clung to me with delighted shrieks as the swell made the little

We Cannot Hold Back the Turning Wheel

ferry dip and climb like a rollercoaster, and I had a sudden insight into how strange it was to be sailing over the drowned world with barely a thought for the people who'd once lived and worked there. Perhaps the loss of their land to the sea had been a cataclysm for those people, something initially unimaginable and horrific that slowly became a painful reality. They are long gone and now it's our time in the sun, but inevitably the wheel will turn for us too.

Nature has taken back this land but it's not entirely lost to us. Tantalising glimpses of the past remain. In 1756 the antiquarian William Borlase visited Scilly and was the first to record ancient walls – 'hedges of stone' – running down Samson Hill and into the water towards Tresco, and the ruins submerged on the Samson Flats.[69] At low tide, prehistoric walls are still visible today in Green Bay on Bryher, distinct lines of boulders running into what is now sea. It's long been speculated that paved roads – walkable at the lowest tides – still link the islands under the water. Old maps show sandbars connecting St Mary's with Tresco and St Martin's. 'A man may sometimes walk dry shod from St Mary Island to St Martin's and from thence to Tresco,' wrote John Troutbeck, Chaplain of St Mary's in 1796, and he was informed that a 'fine regular pavement of large flat stones is seen about eight feet under the water at spring tides, which are plain evidence of a former union subsisting between these now distinct islands'.[70]

Every year, a number of low 'walking' tides make it possible to wade between Bryher and Tresco. Sometimes, they are so low that an expanse of dry sand is revealed and the people of the two islands meet on the seabed for a party complete with

STONE LANDS

seafood stalls, 'sand bars' selling drinks, and live music. The convenient breaking down of the *Scillonian* in 2019 meant that, instead of having to go home, we got to go to the pop-up festival in the middle of the Tresco Channel too, crossing on foot along with hundreds of others.

On Par Beach, St Martin's, a prehistoric stone row[71] is supposed to be set into the seabed, hidden at high tide but otherwise visible, but despite searching the length of the beach and then splashing fully dressed into the sea, getting soaked to the waist while trying not to drop my phone in the water, I failed to find any trace of it. Certainly, it doesn't seem to be where The Megalithic Portal app says it should be. Perhaps it has been engulfed by the sands.

Trying to Hold Back the Wheel

Scilly reminds us of our puniness in the face of nature. When it blows here, it really *blows*. This archipelago of small, low-lying islands is exposed to the full wrath of the Atlantic, the winds and waves building up for thousands of miles until they dash themselves on the western shores of Bryher, St Agnes and St Mary's. When big seas are forecast, the *Scillonian* is cancelled. One August, there was not one but two hurricane-strength storms that tore down lesser tents than ours and many campers had to take refuge in the Bryher community centre. Though we couldn't do much beyond tighten guy-ropes, Stephen and I stayed awake most of the night, hoping that a combination of good engineering and the force of our consciousness would

We Cannot Hold Back the Turning Wheel

keep the tent upright, while monsters prowled around us, shaking the tent furiously, and rainbursts splattered against the fabric like the cries of hungry ghosts. It blew all night and then when daylight came it continued to blow.

The story of rising sea levels, which have been reshaping these isles for 6,000 years, is not yet over. Recorded surges in modern history demonstrate what the sea can do when it puts its mind to it: the storm on 26 September 1744, for example, that washed a house away in Hugh Town and flooded low-lying land on St Mary's, or the one on 7 March 1962 that ripped Higher Town quay on St Martin's to shreds and buried Old Town Road on St Mary's in 2 feet of sand and seaweed.[72] Scary future sea-level scenarios run by the Lyonesse Project predict 'a major change in the character of Scilly with the loss of very large intertidal areas'.[73]

When William Borlase came to Scilly in 1752, he was interrupted in the opening of a burial chamber on St Mary's by a rainstorm that by midnight became 'the most violent storm while it lasted, I ever knew'. His landlady told him that this 'outrageous' storm had destroyed the crops, and with it the people's means of paying their rent and feeding and clothing their families, and she asked if he had not been digging up the Giants' graves the day before, and said that 'many good people of the islands were of the opinion, that the Giants were offended and had really raised that storm'. On Bryher, Borlase was confronted by islanders demanding to know how much money he'd found and pointing out that everything they had in the ground was ruined.[74]

A connection between the ancient megalithic sites of Scilly and the destructive power of nature was also noted by Katharine

Sawyer in her *Isles of the Dead?*, the first comprehensive survey of Scilly's entrance graves and cists. According to her count, which includes sites she terms 'probable' and 'possible', an incredible 90 entrance graves and 61 cist graves plus 41 indeterminate sites are crammed into these 6 or 7 square miles of land.[75] Drawing on the work of the Lyonesse Project, which has dated the most significant period of land loss to the millennium between 2500 BCE and 1500 BCE,[76] Sawyer suggests that the large-scale construction of megalithic monuments on Scilly could have been a response to the inundation of land, an attempt to hold back the ever-rising waters[77] – to stop the unstoppable and prevent the wheel from turning further. She highlights the number of entrance graves surrounding the drowned land between St Mary's, St Martin's, Tresco and Bryher, and suggests that sightlines between these sites could possibly reflect a desire to protect this area, the megalith builders positioning clusters of monuments in attempts to hold back the sea.[78] From Bant's Carn on St Mary's, for example, there are sightlines to at least nine other prehistoric sites across the inundated area, including entrance graves on Samson's North Hill which are visible as mounds on the ridgeline.[79]

In Search of Stones

Sawyer's *Isles of the Dead?* includes an incredibly useful and endlessly entertaining (to the megalith geek anyway) catalogue of Scillonian entrance graves and cists, complete with description of what's visible on the ground, notes on archaeological finds and – handiest of all – grid references that can be plugged into the OS map app. Despite multiple sessions wandering phone-in-hand over Shipman Head Down, Porth Hellick Down, Castle Down, Chapel Down and other such places across the islands where megaliths are to be found, I've still only ticked off a fraction of the sites in Sawyer's gazetteer. True, many of them are highly ruinous and of the 'is that even a thing?' variety, but others, though camouflaged among heather-covered natural boulders, are unmistakably ancient constructions and a delight to track down. 'Tregarthen Hill D', for example, is a fantastic site looking down over the sea from the north of Tresco, with two capstones and a chamber with coursed walling and a gravelly floor, neat and dry like a hobbit hole, the kerbed mound covered with purple heather and bees humming all around. On Gugh, across the low-tide sandbar from St Agnes, there are entrance graves all over Kittern Hill, many so buried in gorse that they cannot be discerned, but I have ticked off 'Kittern Hill A', with its four capstones still in place, along with 'Kittern Hill B', two slabs set at right-angles that are classified as 'cist – probable'. Not far away from these Kittern Hill sites, leaning as if directing our attention over the water to St Mary's, is the Old Man of Gugh, the UK's southernmost standing stone, a pattern of runnels whipped into his back by millennia of rainstorms.

On the twin hills of the uninhabited island of Samson, which emerge from the sea like the breasts of the submerged Goddess, there are many cists and entrance graves to be discovered with the aid of Sawyer's gazetteer. There is no finer day out, I would say, than to kayak across from Green Bay on Bryher to Samson's dazzling white-shell sands and climb up to the prehistoric burial grounds. We clambered into the ruins of cottages abandoned when the last inhabitants left in 1855, and crawled into the hilltop entrance graves which survive, after several thousand years, still roofed with their capstones. From South Hill, the whole archipelago spread itself out beneath our feet and I felt as if we might soar into the sky alongside the terns and shearwaters.

Across the water from Samson, close to the top of Samson Hill at the south end of Bryher, is Bonfire Carn, a ring of huge white kerbstones that was hidden by gorse the first year we came but is now somewhat brutally (albeit helpfully) shorn of undergrowth. It's intriguing but quite ugly. Works Carn, on the other hand, lower down Samson Hill on its southernmost side, is a very beautiful place, a long entrance grave with a few capstones still lying across the exposed chamber, set in a wide ring of kerbstones on a shoulder of the hillside. Seen from above, as you descend Samson Hill, it looks as if the chamber is pointing across the water at the ancient burial ground on Samson's North Hill, and as if the whole landscape – the hillside, the scattered natural boulders, the rippling silk of the sea – has arranged itself to display this one site and give meaning to it.

There are three ancient sites listed by Sawyer on lovely Gweal Hill in the west of Bryher, set above the roaring ocean and a fantasy seascape of uninhabited isles that spread into the hazy distance. The most obvious is a cist inside a ring of stones; then, close by, there's the vague ruins of a chamber with two distinct parallelish lines of edging stones. The third site I confess I'm still not 100 per cent sure about, but I found something plausible and awarded myself the tick. A little above this plateau, at the very top of Gweal Hill, where the wind whistles strange music through the stone stacks, there's an outcrop naturally weathered into what could be taken for the head of an animal god, with flared nostrils and a stern, sloping jaw.

Once I went alone for a walk in a luminous silvery dusk that made every leaf look precious. The tide was very high and the sea in Hell's Bay was dashing itself on the rocks as if trying to exhaust all emotion and find some calm at the end of it. I climbed up to Shipman Head Down, which that evening was scented with honey and seemed more enchanted than ever, the jumbles of boulders around me transforming themselves with every step I took, revealing possible cairns and rows of stones set on end. I felt I was in a sacred place, treading on the bones of the ancestors.

And that evening I did find calm, lying on a slab at the top of the down, with granite under my palms and the surf in my ears and my breath floating out through my mouth and in through my nostrils. All anxieties fell away, and what was left was an overflowing love for the land, for this place, for the children, for Stephen . . . It was wonderful and deeply calming.

I was happy in that moment, and even better – and rarer – I knew it.

The Wheel Turns

In August, seven months after his cancer diagnosis, Stephen was swimming in the sea off Bryher and jumping off Church Quay along with the rest of us. He couldn't stay in the water for long, but he did it. One day we all cycled around the perimeter

STONE LANDS

of St Mary's, stopping off, as was our wont, at a number of prehistoric sites. Among the whispering pine trees above the Innisidgen Upper burial chamber, Stephen let a rope swing take him high into the blue sky, leaning back to increase his velocity – he always did love a rope swing – the muscles in his forearms taut as they took his weight, his arms thinner than before but strong still. In the tent each night, he turned and twitched, getting up from his sleeping bag and back down again, a quiet, desperate struggle to get comfortable. This holiday was not like other holidays: our friend Bob accompanied us on the outward journey, to help with the haulage and setting up the tent; my brother Duncan and his wife Lisa (with their little daughter Juno) joined us midway through, to help us get home again. It was not the same but it did us good. Dread and sadness were never absent but we came home feeling positive.

Less than a month later, back in London, Stephen discovered he no longer had the energy to ride his beloved bike. I was with him that afternoon. The Queen had just died and we were cycling over to Bermondsey to take a look at the Queue, but we abandoned the idea at Peckham Rye. We got off our bikes and lay on the grass under an old oak tree, not far from where we'd lived when Alex was born, the sun-rimmed leaves set against a sky that was an inappropriate joyful blue. Shadows trembled on the oak's trunk, cross-hatching it with bars like a ladder into the otherworld. On this common, William Blake once saw an oak tree filled with angels, their bright wings spangling every bough like stars.

There was a meeting at Guy's to review progress. Glum faces: the cancer 'is on the move', the main tumour increased in size since the previous scan and suspicious dots, tiny but sinister, showing up on the lungs. The GemCis chemo had reached the limits of its efficacy and there wasn't any point in trying any more of it. And what's more, no one had ever suggested that chemo could cure this incurable disease. So, time to try something different.

The idea of trials seemed to energise everyone. This was what we'd been waiting for – the promised miracles of modern science. There was not one but two possible trials Stephen could join. His oncologist also agreed to send a blood sample to the US for next-generation genome marker testing. Hope was in the air. Hope shot through with a fear that I mostly kept under control, sedated and locked up, but that sometimes broke free and overpowered me ... What if none of the trials worked? What if no genome markers were found? What if the second-line chemo was ineffective? Was this, in fact, the beginning of the end?

We kept going. At the end of September, hope became more tangible. Stephen was to move to the care of University College Hospital in order to start a Redx Pharma-run trial of RXC004, an inhibitor of Porcupine, whatever Porcupine was – it sounded spiky but not entirely unfriendly. What it turned out to be was 'a key activator of Wnt ligands'[80] and 'Wnt ligands' are, we discovered, a driver of biliary cancer. Bob sent me a link to an article about a woman from Cumbria who, against all the odds, was surviving bile duct cancer thanks to RXC004. The doctors said the trial was perfect for Stephen. We knew we shouldn't hope too much, but hope crept in. And hope felt good. Chemo couldn't cure him, we knew, but maybe RXC004 could.

In early October, just a couple of days before the trial was about to start, a phone call brought bad news. Stephen had been rejected from the RXC004 trial because of a bone density reading of -2.6 instead of -2.5. That night I couldn't sleep. The apparent arbitrariness of the decision drove me into a frenzy of frustration, arguments and counter-arguments looping round and round in my head. Stephen was being denied potentially life-saving treatment on the basis of a measurement of 0.1. How could this be possible? At 3 a.m. I got out of bed, turned on my laptop and started noting down the questions I wanted Stephen to put to the consultant at UCH.

I wanted to force Redx Pharma and UCH into letting him on the trial, but Stephen was project managing his own illness and didn't want me to cause trouble. Yet causing trouble is what everyone else was urging me to do, and anger was an easier emotion to bear than despair. We argued and I accused him of not fighting hard enough, of not letting me help. Then I hated myself for arguing with him when he was so sick.

He had to go back into hospital. He tried to smile when I came into his room, terribly thin and yellow in his NHS gown, hooked up to multiple tubes, barely able to raise himself from the pillow. I couldn't get at him to give him a proper cuddle, surrounded as he was by drips and drains. He tried to cheer me up about the RXC004; this was no wonder drug, he said, holding my hand, the first trial had been suspended because of the severity of the side-effects. RXC004 wasn't the answer, he said, let it go.

Stephen came home but things were bad now. A district nurse had to come most days to drain his stomach. Our bedroom was full of plastic bags containing tubes and bottles, gloves and dress-

We Cannot Hold Back the Turning Wheel

ing pads. At night, instead of sleeping, he was up for hours stretching and massaging his legs to try to calm the incessant twitching and jerking. And yet he was still going, on the steroid-fuelled days at least. He walked to the supermarket to buy fish pie so I could have a stress-free evening after work. He bought furnishings for our new bathroom, which he'd been project managing alongside his cancer. It turns out it's possible to think of soap dishes and toothbrush holders even when you're staring death in the face.

We had a meeting with the UCH consultant, a world-class expert in biliary cancer, who told us that we were 'on a hiding to nothing' trying to get onto the RXC004 trial (this trial that had been described to us as perfect for Stephen). The peripheral neuropathy was getting worse, he said, the numbness in Stephen's hands and his restless legs caused by a build-up of toxicity from the GemCis. It was probably the GemCis that had given him the osteoporosis that resulted in the fateful -2.6 not -2.5.

'I just don't understand why he can't go on the trial,' I said, breaking down in tears at last, and this was met with silence. I said: 'What we don't want is for him to go back on chemo and then be so weak that he can't get on a trial.' That, too, was met with silence. No, the consultant said, there was no point in taking the bone density test again.

The consultant talked about the serious peripheral neuropathy caused by the platins in the GemCis, so any chemo containing platins was now off the table. I knew about the neuropathy, but not that it was 'serious', just some tingling in the hands and feet, right, not something, surely, that could result in Stephen becoming bed-bound. But apparently it was that level of serious. The nurse asked a question and Stephen did not respond. 'He can't hear!' bellowed the consultant. Yes he'd been a bit deaf before and, yes, it had got a little worse recently, but was it necessary to shout at him and talk about him as if he wasn't there? There was something going on with the acoustics in the room because it did seem like Stephen was struggling to hear, and then I remembered the look of focus that often crossed his face as he watched my lips and the way he paused before replying, and I realised only then that the chemo he'd stopped in August was now, in October, making him deaf.

Later I thought of how much he would miss music, one of the few pleasures left to him, and how painful this process of slow – or worse, quick – decline was going to be, and I cried for him and for me and for our kids.

All through those terrible dark weeks, Stephen was trying to shield me from the true horror of what he must surely have known, and we were both trying to shield our children. It seemed to both of us that as long as there was a plan, as long as there was another step to take, it would be wrong to tell them that their dad was going to die. Those words would be irrevocable; they would destroy in one stroke, we thought, our children's happiness and innocence and lightness of heart. They would snatch their childhood away from them. And perhaps we were mistaken, but it seemed to us then that keeping that flame of hope alive was the most important and the only thing we could do. So we carried on through the maelstrom of hope and despair, living our everyday lives. The children went to school. I worked on new book proposals and reviewed people's manuscripts. Stephen made notes on his treatment options. He planned a trip we'd take, just the two of us, to a nice hotel in Somerset, to watch the starling murmurations over the Levels. He did not give up hope.

The levels of bilirubin in Stephen's blood began to rise. The stent was blocked and would have to be replaced before any second-line chemo option could commence. He had a scan and met the UCH consultant to discuss the stent operation – and was told that the stent was not blocked. The liver was simply full of cancer and no longer able to function. The devastating news was that he'd run out of treatment options. There would be no more chemo, no trials. He had at most three months left to live.

I wasn't there to hear this with him. I was at work – we'd thought it was just another routine appointment.

November now and darkness closing in. We had a surreal meeting at the hospice, talking about how Stephen would die. As his liver function decreased, he would get sleepier and sleepier, and perhaps become confused, but there would almost certainly, the hospice doctor told us kindly, be little pain. We set up a meeting with social workers to discuss how to tell the children that their dad was going to die. This, of all the sadnesses, was the hardest to bear. Stephen and I still could not bring ourselves to do it.

And then – miraculously – a stay of execution. Guy's offered us a second opinion and their second opinion was that a stent replacement could significantly improve the biliary drainage.

STONE LANDS

We seized on this hope: the stent replacement would bring down the bilirubin levels, chemo would become possible again and Stephen's health would stabilise. And, as he was now taking calcium supplements, surely the next bone density reading would be -2.5 instead of -2.6. He *would* get on a trial.

In late November, Guy's performed the endoscopy, removing the old temporary plastic stent and successfully inserting a large metal stent that was unlikely to block. He came out of hospital and we were quietly confident that there were more steps to be taken. Maybe the wheel could be held back after all, at least for a while.

Two days later Stephen's condition deteriorated unexpectedly and dramatically. He spent most of the day asleep and when he was awake he seemed confused. He'd try to focus on what I was saying, but his attention kept drifting off. He ate very little. All these were symptoms that had been described by the hospice doctor as signalling end of life.

I called the acute oncology line and Guy's arranged for one of the district nurses to take bloods. Stephen seemed a little better: more with it and able to get downstairs for some of the day. 'The endoscopy's taken it out of me, that's all,' he said. 'I'll get better when the new stent starts to do its work. Give it a week or two. You know what, I think I'm feeling a bit better already.' And he smiled to reassure me that he really was feeling better.

We waited and he did not improve. There was still time for the stent to start working, but he was so very thin now. It was shocking to see him without clothes, hollow chested, his body shrunk around his bones, a grim caricature of himself.

We Cannot Hold Back the Turning Wheel

On Friday the oncologist from Guy's called; she had the blood results, his calcium levels were too high, but the cure for that was drinking water so he might as well do that at home and come in for a check on the Monday. I focused – somewhat to Stephen's irritation – on getting him to drink more and more water and that did help reduce his blood pressure. He managed to get downstairs and watched a little *Breaking Bad* with me, but he was still sleepy and now he was feeling pain whenever he moved and that pain was getting worse.

First thing on Monday, as soon as the children had gone to school, I took Stephen into Guy's. He was so wobbly that he could barely stand unaided. I wasn't sure if I could get him down the stairs and wanted to call an ambulance but he said no – even in extremis, Stephen did not want to burden the public services (admirable albeit not entirely helpful in the circumstances). I gathered his things, called a taxi and we made it downstairs. He leaned on the doorjamb while I put his shoes on, unable to manage them himself, and it came into my mind that this might be his last time of walking down our stairs, his last time of crossing the threshold of our home.

The taxi driver, kind but detached, just a bit player in our drama, took us through Peckham, where we'd lived so happily for the first nine years of our life together. Past the common, across which two-year-old Alex had charged on his little legs shouting 'Running!'; past the Rye Hotel, scene of many fun, drunken nights together. I squeezed his hand and looked out of the window so he couldn't see the tears running down my face.

After a day receiving intravenous fluids in acute oncology, in

STONE LANDS

a chair next to two feisty old ladies chatting merrily about their Christmas plans (I thought I'd like to be like them when I am old and sick), he was moved to a high-dependency ward. There was still some hope and a plan: he had an abscess in his stomach that would be drained as soon as the infection responded to the antibiotics, and his liver function tests were showing some improvement. And yet a doctor asked us to confirm that he shouldn't be kept on a ventilator if anything went wrong during the abscess treatment. Another doctor asked us if we wanted to sign a 'do not resuscitate' order.

I went home that night and told the children, sitting between them on the sofa, my arms around them, that their dad wasn't going to get better. I said I hoped he'd have a last Christmas with us, that we'd have one more chance to look after him, to show him how much we loved him.

When I returned to Guy's early the next morning, I knew straightaway that Stephen was much worse. The nurse said he'd had a fall in the night, trying to get out of bed. No one could give me an answer about when the stomach abscess would be drained. A doctor told me that Stephen was going to get very, very sick – today or tomorrow. Over the course of that morning it became clear that he was going to die. A social worker came to talk to me about the children and urged that I get them in to say goodbye to him.

Worried messages were coming through from Stephen's mum and brother, and from my mum, and from our friends. I did not know what to say to them. It was all moving too fast and none of it seemed real. My brother Duncan brought in

We Cannot Hold Back the Turning Wheel

Alex and Ava. They looked pale and scared and tearful. I'd been concerned that their presence would upset Stephen, that he wouldn't have wanted to alarm them, but when he saw them he smiled the most beautiful loving smile, his entire face lit up as if nothing in the world was wrong, as if their presence made everything all right. They hugged their dad and told him they loved him, and he told them he loved them so much. Then Duncan took them away again.

They gave Stephen fluids and antibiotics and two blood transfusions, and none of it helped. The machines were beeping endlessly and distressing him, and I begged for a room to ourselves and for some peace and quiet. 'I'm so sick,' he said to me. 'I'm just so sick and so fed up with it. What's the point of being this sick?'

And then we found ourselves in a room alone together, the lights dimmed. No more needles, no more beeping. I held him, I lay next to him, I rested my head next to his, I told him I loved him over and over again. I stayed with him on his journey out of this life.

I found out afterwards that there had been a full moon that night. I hadn't noticed it; the outside world had ceased to matter. A London hospital is a city within a city, set apart from the rest of life. The occasional siren or shriek makes it through from outside, but has no meaning for us who are inside. It was the same when our children were born a couple of miles away at King's: in the maternity ward, lying next to a new-born baby, the Camberwell I knew so well seemed a world away, unreachable, irrelevant. And so it was in Guy's that night.

'Where are we going, Fi?' you said. 'I just want to go to sleep now.'

And then, later, you lifted your eyes to mine, with a look of such tenderness, gratitude and love. I bent my face to yours, rested my forehead on yours, and you said, 'I love you so much, Fi . . . We had a great time together, didn't we? You're a great mum. I'm just sorry it was so short.'

It was the most precious gift imaginable, this acknowledgement of our love, articulated amidst all the confusion at the end, when you didn't know where you were. And you were right: we'd had a great time. We'd had almost 20 brilliant years together and we'd created our extraordinary children and nothing will take that away from us.

The darkest hour. Stephen had been agitated, breathing hard. The nurse had given him a sedative but even so, he was restless. And then he became calmer and I thought that maybe he would be able to understand what I said, so I started to read out the text that his friend and climbing partner Luke had sent, thanking him for the amazing times they'd spent hanging off mountain walls together, thanking him for being a wonderful friend. I read out all the other messages from other friends, who loved him so much, from his mum, who'd wanted to come to see him to hold his hand one last time.

He was still now and his breath was slowing and then I realised he wasn't breathing at all.

I waited with him a long time, holding him, talking to him, telling him I loved him. As a new day dawned, gradually his face became cold. I asked a nurse to bring me scissors so I might cut a lock of his hair to keep. His eyes were open, his lips slightly ajar, as if he might stir and stay something at any moment. As if his spirit was lingering to comfort me during those last hours we had together.

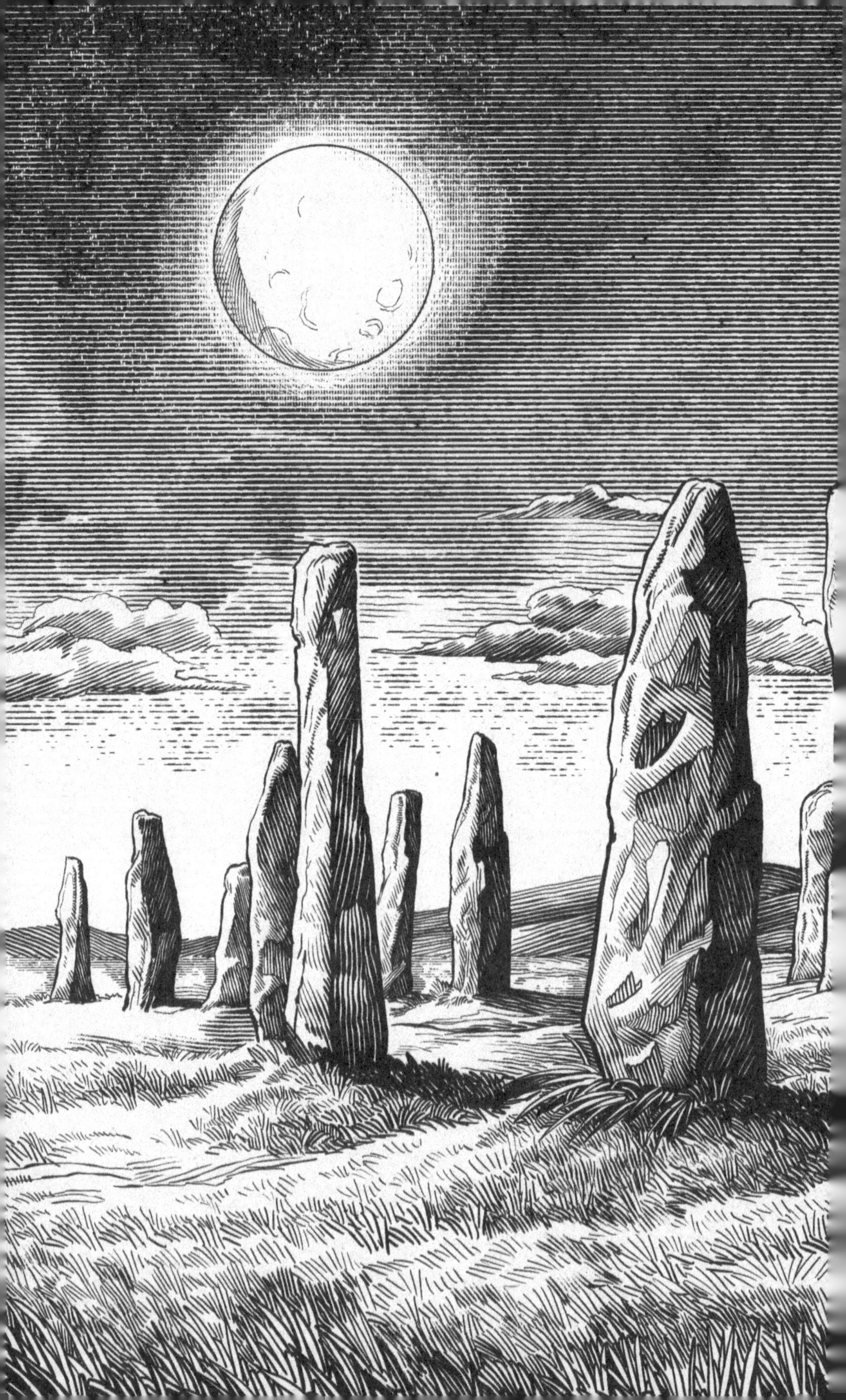

Chapter 7
THE STONES ENDURE, AND SO CAN WE

Calanais, ISLE OF LEWIS

SOMETIMES WHEN I CAN'T SLEEP, when the horror of losing Stephen clamps around my heart and jolts me awake, when I realise with a nauseous middle-of-the-night clarity that he is no longer here and I don't really know who I am any more, that I can't tell the difference between the real and the delusional, that I am leading the children through a mire in which we might all sink . . . sometimes, then, I imagine I'm that old stone standing on the moor, and that helps me to let go of the whirring dread and fall back into sleep.

The essential quality of a standing stone is its hardness. Think of a stone on the moor, still standing after thousands of years though the wind has done its best to blow it down, though it's been knocked countless times by sheep or cows, though it's been cracked by the ice and holed by millennia of falling raindrops. These hollows and runnels are the crow's feet of a stone, written on its surface by the passing of time and the shit that happens, just as our own lines are etched into our faces by sadness and worry, by love and laughter.

Stones are hard; they endure. And we can do that too. When I think of what Stephen must have endured from the moment he first heard the word 'incurable' and saw those grim survival statistics, of the dread that must have crept into the children's lives when cancer was first mentioned, of how I trudged on through everyday life as hope came and went, editing books, filling in forms, taking out the bins as if any of it mattered, of how we carried on putting one foot in front of the other and always with this unbearable but must-be-borne burden of sadness, I'm blown away by how strong and brave we all were.

One day, not long after he died, I was putting away the mountain of clean laundry that had accumulated on the basket in the hall and included many things that belonged to Stephen – holey socks, washed-out pants, frayed T-shirts (if he liked an item of clothing, he really did get the full wear from it) – and was assaulted by the horrific thought that he did not exist, though these mundane possessions of his insisted he must do. *There was nowhere in the world where he could be found.* I could not bear to tidy away the Fair Isle jumper he used to wear hiking and so I took it into bed to cling to when I woke at night.

I started sending him messages on WhatsApp. The ticks refused to go blue but I felt he was listening. I wanted to report back on what his work colleagues, academic collaborators and friends were saying: 'a marvellous Kittlerian', 'a man who could seamlessly weave Kant into a discussion of fixed-mobile convergence', 'extremely knowledgeable, yet humble and profoundly

The Stones Endure and So Can We

open-minded', 'a superb teacher', 'funny, loyal, curious, kind, a wonderful friend', 'deep deep-thinking, well read, worldly, critical, uncynical, quietly furious, consciously joyful, musically omnivorous, sympathetic, astute, confider and friend' . . . Oh God, I could go on and on with this, but I'll leave it there as it's making me cry. Stephen himself would have been so moved to hear it all, he never thought other people rated him that much and it just seemed illogical and impossible that he should not see this irrefutable evidence that they did. But that's the way of things.

There was nowhere in the world that he could be found and yet he was everywhere. I met him as I hunted through his notebooks for passwords and was confronted by ambitious lists of things-to-do that would never now be done. I met him in the park where we used to take the children each weekend, cheering them on as they wobbled on their bikes. I glimpsed him through our windows, picking up leaves in the garden and firing up the barbecue. When the doorbell rang, it was him, waiting impatiently with his bike because I'd forgotten to take off the door chain yet again . . . This, I realised, is what it means to be haunted. He was nowhere and everywhere.

I went through all our photographs to choose pictures for the funeral order-of-service and saw, for the first time ever, the whole pattern of our life together. It was only then that I understood that Stephen and I had grown older, and that when his world had narrowed during Covid he had become visibly sadder, even before the cancer diagnosis. I understood that our life together had seen a series of little deaths, of losses of our previous selves. Looking through the photos, I grieved every one of those losses, and I also saw how lucky we had been, our life filled with adventure and love.

When I think about how it must have felt to lose their dad and the life we had with him, and about how they will miss him for the rest of their lives, I want to tell Alex and Ava this: you have endured a lot and it has marked you but it has made you strong, too. Strong like a standing stone on the moor.

For a while I saw a bereavement therapist who specialises in embodiment, in the connection between mind and body and the way emotions are held in the body and can become trapped there. I contacted her to help me understand what support the children needed, as I couldn't really tell how they were doing and I was overwhelmed by the dread of what they might be thinking and feeling. The therapist said that she needed to spend some time working with me first. Without knowing that I have any special interest in stones, she asked me to hold a stone when I talked with her. I'd hold the Druid's egg I picked up on a beach in Pembrokeshire, the quartz pebble with the arc of small holes in it like the stone-holes of Waun Mawn. It fitted perfectly in the palm of my hand with my fingers curled around it. It felt cold against my forehead. It felt as if there were a matching stone inside my chest. Somehow it was helpful to hold this stone that had endured on this planet for thousands of years longer than any human, which the action of the waves over millennia and the clinking against its fellow pebbles had smoothed into a perfect oval.

I found it helpful, too, to remember. A memory is more intangible than a stone; you cannot weigh it in your hand, or feel its smoothness against your face. You cannot throw it to relieve your feelings, or shut it away in a wardrobe with someone's no-longer-needed clothes. And yet, despite its amorphous nature, memory is stronger than death. It is stronger than the fires of a cremation chamber that burn at 1,000 degrees Celsius and turn a body that once climbed and cycled and laughed and loved into a heap of grey ash. In memory, our past lives on.

The Oldest Rock

It is the Easter holidays and lockdown is still a year away and cancer just a sad thing that happens to other people. We're on the Isle of Lewis in the Outer Hebrides and we're flying high, up on a ridge with sweeping views over peaty moorland and shimmering water, surrounded by standing stones. The wind is pulling my hair vertically up into the air, tugging as if it's trying to lift me off the ground. 'You've got horns!' shouts Ava. The wind snatches the reply from my mouth and I laugh because the wind and rising emotion are conspiring to stop me articulating what I feel, even though what I feel basically amounts to just a single word: WOW!

All around us silver pillars stand like chess pieces frozen mid play, their arrangement resonating with an ancient meaning that we mere humans wandering the chessboard cannot comprehend. These are the *fir bhrèige* of Calanais (Callanish), the 'false men' turned to stone by an enchanter. I've never seen standing stones like these before: unbelievably beautiful slabs, very tall, elegant, and grainy and gnarled like wood but shimmering, even under grey skies, as if they'd been crafted from silver. World trees

STONE LANDS

of stone, connecting heaven and earth, quivering with life. As we enter the circle, by some miracle the clouds hiding the sun dissolve and sunlight blazes from the megaliths, streaked with silver, white and pink, every detail of the whorls and swirls and delicately frilled flakes standing out vividly as if the stones are deliberately revealing themselves to us in all their glory.

Needless to say, the children are oblivious to all this crazy magnificence and instead dart shrieking from stone to stone in a hybrid game of 'it' and hide-and-seek. Or not entirely oblivious: their excitement is surely fuelled by a sense that this place really is something out of the ordinary. As it turns out, Calanais is perfect for hide-and-seek; there's a small crowd of people here already, although it's quite early in the morning, and yet the 40 or so stones of the monument are able to absorb them, one moment revealing a multitude of colourful nylon anoraks, the next hiding them all so it's possible to imagine we're completely alone. While the children play, Stephen and I follow separate routes along the rows, avenue and circle that together make up the rough shape of a Celtic cross, from time to time intersecting to exchange observations. He stops to peer through his binoculars – a pair of pied wagtails! A duck with a white back and rump that's possibly a goosander! – while I consult the site guidebook and try to work out the cardinal directions and make out the Sleeping Beauty, the profile of a prone woman naturally sculpted by the hills across the loch.

Each of these stones is different, the fibrous rock sometimes resembling draped cloth, at other times the joints and limbs of a body. The animate quality of the stones becomes even more apparent from a distance, as we walk down the road away from

The Stones Endure and So Can We

the main site and see in profile the whole chessboard up on the ridge, the lesser pieces clustering around their queen, the land running steeply up to that amazing stone-filled horizon as if paying homage to the megaliths. And as we walk it becomes obvious that the sites are working together across the landscape: up on our right is the chessboard of Calanais I, to the left the slope is crowned with the stone circle of Cnoc Fhillibhir Bheag (Calanais III) and on the hill ahead is Cnoc Ceann a' Ghàrraidh (Calanais II): three marvellous stone circles within sight of one another – and there are many more ancient sites here. If ever there was a ritual landscape, this is it. We pass a roofless ruin, its glassless windows filled with sky like sorrowful grey eyes observing us among the stones. It must have been hard eking out a living from the land here, on this island that's now scarred in every corner with the shells of abandoned homes. I wonder if having the stones so close offered any compensation for the hardships.

The standing stones at Calanais are made of Lewisian gneiss, a beautiful, ancient rock that is named for the Isle of Lewis but is also found on other Hebridean islands including Skye and Iona and on the north-west Scottish mainland. Some of these Lewisian gneisses are as much as 2,900 million years old, Britain's oldest rocks, metamorphosed at a time before oxygen, before life existed, when the continents were still being shaped.[81] These slender, silvery, exceptionally long-lasting stones, very old and very hard, offer us humans a deep-time perspective and a sense of our own unimportance that I have always found mind-blowing – and comforting, too. This rock has been in the making for such a long time that a human life is nothing in

CALANAIS

CHAMBERED CAIRN

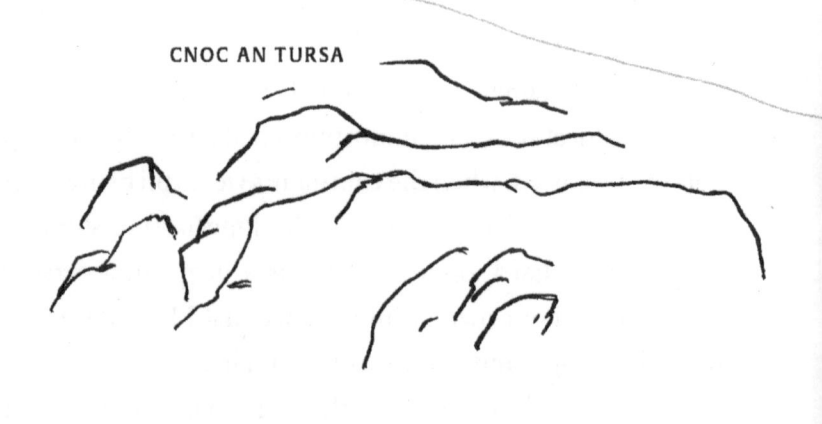

CNOC AN TURSA

↑N

50m

The Stones Endure and So Can We

comparison, any human life – however long we survive, it's all the same from the viewpoint of Lewisian gneiss: an infinitesimally tiny flash of wakefulness.

Stone mattered to the people who built Calanais. The landscape of Lewis is today smothered in peat, but 5,000–6,000 years ago it would have looked very different: the sea level as much as 5 metres lower and the uplands an otherworldly terrain of naked, jagged rock carved out by the glaciers.[82] Prehistoric people built 12 stone circles in the Calanais area, and there may be even more still hidden under the peat. Perhaps it was the distinctive qualities of this rock that inspired them to set up such an unusually high number of circles. As a result of the aeons-long tectonic process of repeated squashing and heating, which separated out the rock's constituent dark and light minerals,[83] Lewisian gneiss has a very striking appearance, patterned with swirls and stripes set in a quartz and feldspar matrix that sparkles in sunlight, especially when the stones are wet. Sometimes the gneiss contains distinctive black eye-shaped crystals; these hornblende inclusions appear in such large quantities on the stones of the main Calanais site that it seems probable that slabs featuring the crystals were deliberately chosen by the circle's builders.[84]

The stones of Calanais have endured for a long time, so long that the landscape around them has changed out of all recognition. What is now sea was once woods, grassland and marshes where people hunted and grazed animals. Where the land is now blanketed in peat, barley was once grown in long rigs. Radiocarbon dating has shown that the stone circle and the chambered cairn underneath the central pillar were built between 2900 and 2600 BCE; the central pillar and the surrounding stone circle were

STONE LANDS

put up first and the cairn some generations afterwards. It's often assumed the stone rows were constructed later than the circle, though not all archaeologists believe this is the case. What we do know is that the chambered cairn was ruined, perhaps deliberately, at some point during the second millennium BCE, and that the climate became colder and wetter, and that by around 800 BCE peat was drowning the stones and the site was abandoned. Then, for the next 2,600 years or so, what was here was a mini-Calanais, the stones submerged in peat up to 1.5 metres deep, only their tops sticking out. When the peat was cut back to the main circle's original base level in 1857, the five-millennia-old monument was fully revealed in a fantastically good state of preservation, the bottom halves of the megaliths bleached white by the acidic peat, looking strangely as if they were wearing trousers.

Thanks to having spent most of the historic era submerged in peat, only a few stones seem to be missing from the Neolithic layout of Calanais I, and one of these was found by Margaret Curtis, the woman dubbed a 'living legend' by the singer, megalith enthusiast and arch-drude Julian Cope, who admires the combination of vision, intuition and scientific rigour with which Curtis decoded the astronomical meaning of the stones. Cope describes in *The Modern Antiquarian* how Curtis was strolling down the northern avenue of the main circle one spring afternoon in the mid-'70s when she happened to spot the broken top of one of the standing stones embedded in a nearby wall. It was retrieved and duly stuck back on the following year. In 1977, probing the ground with a metal rod, Curtis located the lost stone from the end of the eastern row. She petitioned for several

The Stones Endure and So Can We

years for its re-erection[85] and the stone was finally restored to its rightful place in 1982, after excavators located the original stone-hole, complete with packing stones, which exactly fitted the profile of the base of the stone.[86]

Curtis (who died in 2022) was, like Aubrey Burl, the ultimate megalith enthusiasts' megalith enthusiast. Though she had no formal archaeological training, and developed an all-consuming passion for archaeology only after moving to Lewis with her young family in 1974, she was a hugely respected and delightfully idiosyncratic guide who took thousands of people around the stones. She was also the author, with her first husband Gerald Ponting and second husband Ron Curtis, of multiple guidebooks about Calanais. She really did have a powerful, almost dowser-like instinct for locating lost ancient stones. In addition to re-discovering the broken top and the buried stone at the main Calanais site, she spotted a hitherto-unknown stone circle – Druim Dubh – a few miles south-west of Stornoway while sitting on the top deck of a bus on the way to do her shopping.[87] She also identified a Bronze Age kerb-cairn at Olcote when road widening close to her home unearthed a heap of quartz chips.*

---

* Another site showing evidence of a prehistoric preoccupation with quartz (see Chapter 3).

STONE LANDS

The Moon Always Comes Back (Eventually)

At Calanais something much less tangible and yet no less striking than the magnificent monoliths has endured over thousands of years: the relationship that these stones have with the moon.

Margaret and her two husbands, Gerald and Ron, are most famous for their work in revealing lunar alignments at Calanais, especially in connection with the moon's major standstill that takes place every 18.6 years. Seen from the Calanais area, the Pairc hills of south-east Lewis appear to form the profile of a sleeping woman, her face, breasts, belly and knees delineated by the undulating horizon. This is the Sleeping Beauty, also known as the Cailleach na Mòinteach (Old Woman of the Moors). Curtis demonstrated how the moon, when viewed from most of the Calanais stone circles, will appear when in its extreme southernmost position at lunar standstill to rise directly from the Sleeping Beauty and skim low along her body. It is the end of the northern avenue at the main Calanais circle that gives the more impressive view of the phenomenon: seen from here, the moon appears to trace the outline of the Sleeping Beauty, then vanish into the rocky knoll known as Cnoc an Tursa ('hill of sorrow') and then, in a moment of great theatre, reappear from behind the knoll to set inside the stones of the circle itself.[88] Someone standing on Cnoc an Tursa would appear to any observers within the stones to be silhouetted against the moon, and the effect would be all the more spectacular if the moon was full. A photograph exists of either Margaret or her husband Ron recreating this effect, the

The Stones Endure and So Can We

figure on the knoll dramatically silhouetted against a huge glowing orb.[89] At lunar standstill, Cnoc an Tursa was, it seems, the perfect stage for ritual, and maybe prehistoric people knew it.

It's taken me a long time to get my head around the moon's 18.6-year cycle, but I think I have it now, thanks to Emma Rennie of the Callanish Blackhouse Tearoom sending me a link to a simple description of lunar standstill put together by Victor Reijs, her collaborator in the Callanish3D modelling project.[90] So here goes.

Imagine standing at a certain point (within a stone circle, say), plotting the rising and setting points of the sun along the eastern and western horizons through the year. If you are in the northern hemisphere, these rising and setting points will appear to move northward until the sun's northernmost point is reached at summer solstice, and then move southward until its southernmost point is reached at winter solstice. Every six months there will be a solstice (from the Latin *solstitium*, 'sun stands still') when the sun reaches either its extreme northerly (summer solstice) or its extreme southerly (winter solstice) position, and seems to pause there for a few days before heading back in the opposite direction.

So far, so easy to understand. The lunar standstill is equivalent to the solstice, only the moon, thanks to the tilt in its orbit, behaves in a much more erratic fashion than the sun, each month reaching new northerly and southerly positions in a complicated cycle that takes 18.6 years to complete.

Every 18.6 years, there is a major lunar standstill when the moon rises and sets in the most southerly position it will ever reach and is very low in the sky (this is the southern major lunar standstill), and then two weeks later rises and sets in the most northerly position it will ever reach and travels very high in the sky (this is the northern major lunar standstill). This effect doesn't occur during just one month; the moon will appear to the naked eye to reach its most southerly and northerly positions once a month for around nine months either side of the actual southernmost and northernmost lunar extremes.[91] So there is a lunar standstill period rather than a single southern or northern lunar standstill episode.

To confuse matters further, the lunar effect at Calanais would be most impressive at full moon and invisible at new moon, and of course entirely hidden if it was cloudy. The sheer complicatedness and long timescale of all of this might make you doubt that prehistoric people could really have observed the phenomenon and enshrined it in stone monuments, but it is possible. They would not have had to predict the various monthly positions of the moon, but simply to observe that every 20 years or so the moon hung especially low and huge on the horizon, sailing along the outline of the Sleeping Beauty. This phenomenon would have been observable once a month over 18 months, so one of these events would surely have coincided with a moon of reasonable size and with clear weather (especially as the climate was drier in Neolithic times).

I think the glimpses into ancient science and ritual offered by the Calanais stones, combined with the exceptional grandeur and beauty of the megalithic architecture here, is what makes this place so magical, mysterious and alluring for so many people. Since I first learned about the lunar standstill when editing Ken Taylor's *Celestial Geometry* in 2011, I've been fascinated by the idea of watching the low moon skim over the Sleeping Beauty and shine down the avenue into the circle of Calanais I. As I write this book in early 2024 we are heading into a lunar standstill period, so if I want to see it, I need to get up there again this year or next. Otherwise, there's another 18.6 years to wait.

Dowser, author and megalith researcher Grahame Gardner was at Calanais at the time of the last major lunar standstill in 2006. He'd waited patiently for the phenomenon to come around again, having found out about Margaret Curtis's theories just too late for the 1987 standstill. In the run-up to the June lunar standstill night in 2006, when the southernmost moon was going to be a full one, he spent his evenings at the stones, dowsing for ley lines and for water; he told me that he often finds water lines crossing underneath stone circles, and here at Calanais his dowsing indicated crossing points under the tall central pillar and under Cnoc an Tursa. 'The rock here is very energetic,' he says. 'You feel as if the ancestors are very present.'

On the night itself, crowds were gathering at the main circle, but Grahame waited for moonrise at Cnoc Fhillibhir Bheag (Calanais III). It was not until midnight that the clouds brightened over the Sleeping Beauty's thighs and the moon herself appeared to the accompaniment of an audible cheer from everyone assembled at Calanais I. Grahame continued to watch for an hour or so from Cnoc Fhillibhir Bheag, the circle now seeming to him different, charged by lunar energy, the stones come to life. Then he headed down to the crowds at Calanais I.

'There were lots of people there,' he said. 'A film crew, people with camera tripods, tents just outside the stones, people dancing . . . so many people, we thought we were going to miss the effect. But despite the clouds and all the people, we did see the moon setting into the circle, a brief coppery flash just at the end. I was standing just behind Margaret Curtis who'd come out with some chums and brought a sofa and a table for drinks. She was sitting there right at the end of the avenue and, I thought, *If she's there, I'll stand behind her; it must be the perfect spot!* And it was.'

'Once you've been to Calanais,' Grahame says, 'you can't deny that they were measuring this sort of stuff, because the alignment of the stones with the position of the moon is so precise.' He adds: 'The lunar standstill felt like an important moment. It was like when I saw the total eclipse of the sun down in Cornwall in 1999 and all the birds stopped singing. It felt like the clocks had been reset, the old cycle had ended and things were different now.'

Life is Tough so We Need to be Tough, Too

'If you'd told me years ago I'd end up living in the Outer Hebrides obsessed by standing stones, I never would have believed you,' says Emma Rennie, photographer of the stones, co-creator of the Callanish3D modelling project and owner of the Callanish Blackhouse Tearoom.[92] She hadn't even heard of Calanais before she came to the island with her family for a music festival in 2002, and though they had a blast at the festival, they left Lewis thinking they could never live on this remote island. But something came into alignment when they got back to their home in

Ireland, a ruin they'd been trying and failing to do up, and a man was standing there with an offer to take it off their hands. Four months later Emma and her husband had bought a house and the Blackhouse Tearoom on Lewis and moved there with their two small children.

Since then, she has become fascinated by standing stones and the potential of modern technology such as computer modelling to understand the technology of the past. In 2005 she commissioned laser scans of the main Calanais monument, expecting the project, in which over 50 million measurements were taken of the stones, to generate widespread enthusiasm and interest. It did not. 'I offered the data to all sorts of people and they just weren't interested,' she says. 'It took a year to get permission to do it and then afterwards all we had was: "But what are you going to do with that?"' It was only in 2022 that her collaborators, Victor Reijs and Alistair Carty of Archaeoptics and George Zotti of Stellarium, converted the 50 million measurements into something usable: a 3D model that was integrated into Stellarium, the online Open Source planetarium. The resulting model allows users to wander among the Calanais stones in three dimensions on their chosen date and time, and investigate potential astronomical alignments.[93] If you also download the ArchaeoLines plug-in, you'll be able to see the path of the sun and moon and check how these appear in relation to the stones during key celestial happenings such as the solstices, equinoxes and lunar standstills. 'Navigation takes a little bit of practice,' Emma says, 'but once you get the hang of it, it's fun.'

Emma loves the stones, but she's not a stone hugger. 'I interact with them respectfully and with my camera. Slightly detached, I suppose. I'm always aware that you bring yourself to these places, so whatever you see is going to be different from what the person next to you is seeing.' She does feel that she has an instinctive understanding of stones. 'I was brought up in South Africa with huge vistas and wild places and I suppose I just get them.'

In 2005 a hurricane blew the thatched roof off the tearoom and caused so much damage that it had to close. It has still not reopened. Life became very hard for Emma. 'I had no money so I got a job as a postie in Stornoway. I was a nervous wreck and I needed an outlet, so I started taking photos. I'd never really thought about doing photography properly before that.'

There were more hard times to come and 2013 was a particularly awful year. She split up with her husband, her kids left home, someone close to her was given a cancer diagnosis. Her brother was killed in a plane crash. Emma was struggling to make ends meet as a cleaner at a fish oil factory. One night she went up to the Calanais stones with her camera to try to photograph them with the aurora borealis overhead. She had no idea what settings to use for night photography, but she managed to get some decent pictures. 'And the next day, scrubbing underneath a vat of fish oil, my whole world still upside down, I found myself quite happily singing away. And that was it, I suppose. I was hooked on astro-photography.'

From then things gradually got better: she took more and more pictures of the stones set against the night sky, and started making a living through her art. Slowly, she regained her confidence and she's in a much better place now. 'Though,' she says, 'endlessly broke.'

For Emma, interacting with standing stones is about taking

the time to understand them. 'It has taken me years to figure out Calanais. You can't know something until you've experienced it, and with a moon working on an 18.6 year cycle that's going to take a long time. In 2006 I didn't really know anything about the lunar standstill, though we tried to livestream it. It's taken from then until now for me to really understand it. We all need a purpose and I feel that mine is trying to build a bridge back to a time when all we had was the sun, the moon and the stars. These stones have stood for so long and they still have mysteries that we're trying to figure out today. We think we know everything but we actually know very little.'

She's following in the tradition of Margaret Curtis, looking out for pieces of the puzzle as she walks with her dogs in the vicinity of Calanais. 'Margaret knew there was so much more to the complex,' she says. Out with her dogs one day, Emma found a place that she's fairly sure is an ancient site. 'There's this odd mound with a circular stone structure of some sort. It's two valleys over from Calanais, looking down over the mountains of the Cailleach.' Her tearoom next to the standing stones has not yet reopened, thanks to lack of money and a host of other difficulties. But she has architects and builders lined up and hopes that her dream of a tearoom and gallery filled with astrophotography – a place to exchange ideas about megaliths, alignments and astronomy – will soon be realised. 'I've stuck my ground and I'm still here,' she says. 'Life is tough, for everybody, and you just have to be tough to get through it. Life is also full of surprises and some of them are wonderful.'

STONE LANDS

Journeys of Transformation

Calanais, with its stone setting arranged in what we perceive today as a Celtic cross, and its 11 other stone circles and nine standing stones crammed into a few square miles, seems more than any other ancient place to inspire us to see patterns and alignments and try to make meaning of it all. And even if the meaning we make today is not the same as the meaning the original builders made, there's a lot of fun to be had in attempting to decode what they intended.

Although the moon is the star here (so to speak), there may be other alignments at play. The layout of the main Calanais monument with its radial arms seems to imply that these arms are pointing at something specific: sunset at the equinoxes has been suggested, as well as the first rising of the Pleiades, or Capella or Altair.[94] Although only a few stones in the southern row remain, excavation has discovered that the line of stones once continued southward along the ridge as far as the Cnoc an Tursa outcrop. Recent research suggests that this prominent rocky knoll may even be one of the reasons why standing stones were raised here in the first place. Among the massive boulders, there is a hollow with a dark opening, like the entrance to a cave. Excavation here has discovered prehistoric holes which could once have held posts marking out a kind of forecourt in front of the dark hollow, as well as another hole that could have been the socket of a huge standing stone right in front of the opening. In fact, this vanished stone could even have been the very slab that now forms the centrepiece of the Calanais I circle. People built fires in the

The Stones Endure and So Can We

forecourt, and left flints and pottery here. Was this, in fact, once sacred space?[95]

At midday one day in February 2013, local archaeoastronomer and stones guide Ian McHardy noticed a strange thing: a shaft of sunlight was coming through a slit in the back of the hollow and extending out through the entrance and onto the ground in front (where the forecourt would have been), which at that moment was in deep shade that made the sunbeam all the more striking. Over the next months, Margaret Curtis monitored the behaviour of the shaft of light and discovered that the phenomenon only occurred around the middle of the day, and that closest to midday the beam also lights up a seat-like stone within the tiny cave, and that in winter the beam is much longer than in summer. The result, Curtis and McHardy theorised, was a natural sundial, which, with the help of posts, could have enabled the monitoring of midday, midsummer and midwinter.[96] The beam of light extending from Cnoc an Tursa is in line with the circle's huge central standing stone in its current position, and perhaps implies that the circle of Calanais I, before the rows were added to focus the monument on the moon, was initially used for observing the *sun*. At midwinter the beam passing through the slit in Cnoc an Tursa would have been at its longest and most impressive, so perhaps this was a place of winter solstice ceremony, where people celebrated the ending of the sun's decline and the moment when the light began to grow again.[97]

It could even be, archaeologist Colin Richards suggests, that all the stone circles around Calanais were built to structure a transformational pilgrimage from the material world to the spiritual realm, with Cnoc an Tursa offering the ultimate

STONE LANDS

gateway to the sacred. Richards points out that this opening among rocks looks like nothing so much as the entrance to a cairn-covered chambered tomb such as Barpa Langass on North Uist (further down the island chain), and that chambered tombs were where the physical body decayed and the spiritual world was accessed.[98] Travelling across Lewis to Calanais, perhaps even following paths that still exist today, prehistoric people may have believed themselves to be crossing an increasingly sacred terrain, each stone circle on the horizon announcing a new stage in the journey.[99] Richards and his team believe that while the circles close to the main Calanais site were built to last, with proper sockets for the megaliths, the upland circles could have been designed to be seen from afar during the pilgrimage to the most important monument – the one focused on Cnoc an Tursa – rather than being visited themselves. This would explain why less effort was put into setting up the stones on higher ground and why they have all since fallen.

Like a shamanic pilgrimage, life is a journey that takes courage and persistence, and offers moments of joy and revelation too. Perhaps it is helpful to look at the sorrowful stretches of life, and even the plain boring ones too (the everyday drudgery of work and housework) in this light, as if it is all part of an on-going pilgrimage of transformation stretching from birth to death. An alchemical process of self-discovery. A journey in which we are scarred and battered by our experiences like a weather-beaten stone on the moor, and turn into harder and stronger versions of ourselves as a result.

For me, holidays have always been more than just a holiday. They're periods of intense aliveness in which I can find out

The Stones Endure and So Can We

about the world and myself, and be changed by coming into contact with wild and ancient places that give me access to a realm that's not quite of this world. Our journeys today may be haphazard, defined by annual leave allowance and the timing of school holidays rather than by the cycles of sun or moon, but perhaps in undertaking them we are tapping into some of the ancient experiences of pilgrimage and transformation. And the memories of these things don't leave you. They are an everlasting treasure, a source of comfort, nourishment and strength when life seems unendurable.

Whenever I want I can close my eyes and be back with Stephen, Alex and Ava on the coast north-east of Calanais, climbing the grassy lane to Clach an Truishal. This giant of a megalith, the very tallest standing stone in Scotland, rises close to 6 metres high and is wider at its base than most standing stones are high. It grows taller the closer we come, as if it is reaching out over our heads to the waves frothing on the shore below, to signal to the sailors whose boats no longer pass by. There is something deeply incongruous in its setting, this magnificent stone hemmed in by a puny fence and wall, with the power to crush anything in its path should it choose to fall. Downhill is a modern house, perhaps the farmer's, with one upstairs and one downstairs window overlooking the stone. We wonder what it's like to live there and be continually glimpsing Clach an Truishal at odd moments: drawing the curtains, setting the table, watching TV.

I can close my eyes and summon up the wind that blows furiously as we all lean against Clach Mhic Leoid, 'Macleod's Stone', above a white shell-sand beach on Harris, the southern part of the island shared with Lewis, while gannets dive into

STONE LANDS

milky-white waters luminous as glacier melt, and the shags on the rocks gracefully arch their long necks. This lovely quartz-veined, green-furred slab is as slender as a pencil side-on; from other angles it widens and the profile of its top edge appears to echo the fall and rise of the hills on the off-shore isle of Taransay. I rest my cheek against its gritty surface and listen to the squeaking of the oystercatchers and the rhythmic swell of the sea as it builds and crashes in harmony with the wind. We go down to the beach and Stephen strips off and dashes into the ocean, while I chase the children across the sand, a seaweed monster. Round and round in circles through the drizzle we go, the proof of our presence tracked into the virgin sands. Later, the tide will wash our footprints away.

I can close my eyes and see us entering, through a pair of portal stones, a circle with a setting so dazzlingly airy that if the passage graves were built to access the realm of darkness and the dead, then this monument, surely, was built to embrace the light and life. It is called Pobull Fhinn ('Fionn's people' or 'Fionn's tent'), also Sornach Coir' Fhinn ('the fireplace of Fionn's cauldron'), both names invoking the legendary Gaelic hero and seer Fionn mac Cumhaill. This is the kind of landscape of which legends are told. We have just walked over the hill from Barpa Langass, where the mouth to the ancient tomb yawns darkly within a mound of stones like the opening in Cnoc an Tursa at Calanais, and the grey-white rocks of the cairn are the lightest things in the North Uist moonscape, sooty rain-swollen clouds sagging over the endless brown peatland. Now we're on the other side of the hill, the perspective is brighter. We're encircled by standing stones on a platform that was cut into the hillside in prehistoric times and seems to be actively tilting us over the edge; below us, the long glittering arm of Loch Langass stretches up towards the volcano-like cone of Eaval, North Uist's highest mountain, fragmenting into sparkling fingers of water to embrace a mass of enticing but never-to-be-visited islets. Faint smudges on the horizon indicate the far-off mountains of Skye. The stones are furred with lichen and lean at angles as if they were the wings of a bird, as if they, like us, are on the point of rising into the air and joining in the lapwings' acrobatics.

We lie within the circle of welcoming stones on thick, rough grass that is, incredibly, dry; we eat our sandwiches and soak up the view. There isn't one word of moaning. We are transformed, again. We take a selfie to capture the moment: four smiling faces, wind-whipped hair, the old stones standing all around us.

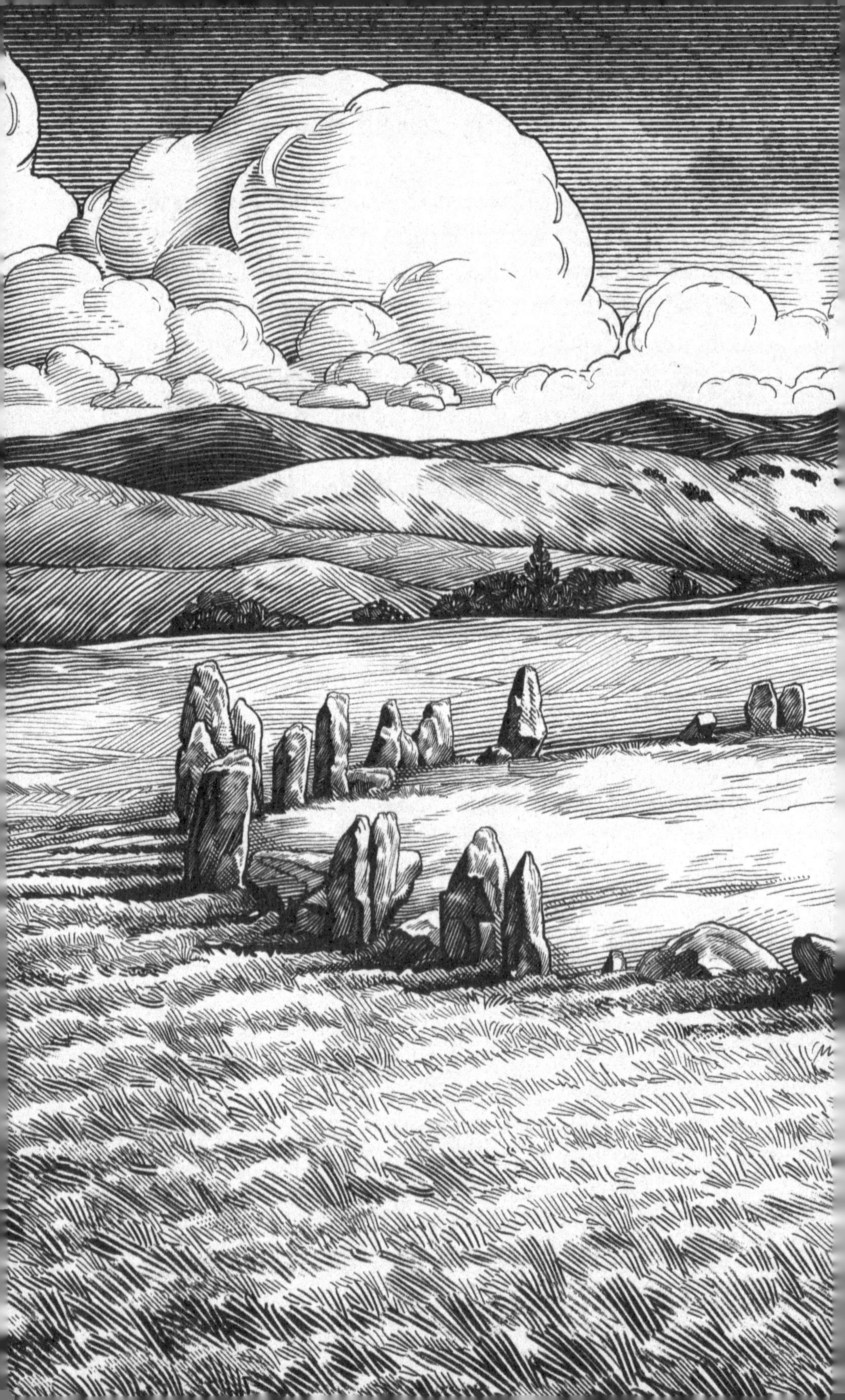

Chapter 8

THE LAND IS STILL ENCHANTED

Stones of the Lake District, CUMBRIA

EVERY MORNING I WAKE into dread and when I get into bed at night the dread is waiting for me. The light has grown as the year turns from winter to spring, but the darkness is still there, shadowing everything. 'No one ever told me that grief felt so like fear,' wrote C. S. Lewis in *A Grief Observed* after the death of his wife, Joy, from cancer, and he is right. It does feel like fear. Sometimes there's a silence in the house that's like death. The children are alone in their bedrooms and the thought of what must be going on inside their heads makes me even more afraid. I put on music to cover up the silence, never anything I used to listen to with Stephen, but the good thing about music is that there is an inexhaustible supply of new tunes. It brings some life into the house but underneath the music the silence is still there.

 We are on the train to Penrith. I've been having driving

STONE LANDS

lessons since Stephen was diagnosed but I'm not yet up to the journey from London to the Lake District. This is the same train we took a year ago, up to Glasgow on our way to Iona to get married. On that trip, Stephen had also not been up to the long drive, already worn out by the chemo and the cancer. The hills come close to the train and I remember the moment, last April, when the land rose either side of the track and my heart lifted: we were among mountains again, heading north on our pilgrimage to Iona, and everything was surely going to be all right. Now the land rises about us once more and I feel nothing.

Without Stephen I'm a stranger in my own life and the things we used to do feel empty and meaningless. There doesn't seem to be much point in dragging the children to the other side of the country but I'm doing it anyway, because we have to do something and I know Stephen would approve of me getting the kids into the mountains (and strongly disapprove of me allowing them to spend the entire Easter holidays on their screens). Alex has made a throwaway remark about loving the smell of the hills, which I've seized on as evidence that we need to go to Cumbria. And, also, there are stones.

When we get to Keswick, I find it is haunted. There is the sandwich shop that sold Stephen a tuna baguette that gave him food poisoning when we first came here almost 20 years ago. The row of gaunt, grey guest houses where the two of us stayed. The mountain-gear shops, the racks of discounted waterproofs, the pub with photos of climbers and walking routes on its walls. And beside me, ahead of me, waiting on every corner, is Stephen, map in hand, a rope slung around his shoulders, quickdraws jangling from his climbing harness. I try to tell the

The Land is Still Enchanted

children some of this but I think it's too painful for them to hear me. On a bridge we pause to look at the dusk river and the mountains black against the sun's afterglow, and we see bats flitting over the silver waters that curve into the distance with the promise of adventure, and there is Stephen again, bat-watching with us on the little green by the river at Buckfastleigh, where we stayed when we went to Dartmoor not yet one year ago. The children rest their elbows on the stone wall, silent for a moment, and I have a strong and comforting sense that his spirit is near and he's looking after us. And he's still with me, later, when the kids go crazy as they always do on the first night of a holiday; only before there had been two of us to cope with them, and now there's only me and it's overwhelming, but he's there, encouraging me to be patient.

He's with me as I run out of Keswick and up the hill to Castlerigg circle, past the bench inscribed with the words 'Rest your bones on the way to the stones', past gnarly old trees that guard the way, stretching out their branches to touch twig-tips and form a natural roof over the road. I'm short of breath from the running and the brimming-over emotion, and when I reach the parking lay-by and the gap in the hedge into the field of the stones, I have a powerful sensation of existing simultaneously in the past and the present: I'm here now, alone, on this sun-dappled April afternoon, and I'm here with Stephen on a foggy November morning almost two decades ago when we came to Castlerigg for the first time, entering the field to get our first sight of the stones: small grey triangles like little devil horns capping the grassy slope. Now, as then, I walk higher up the

STONE LANDS

field and the stone circle reveals itself.

And then: wow, what insane magnificence and crazy beauty! This expansive circle of stones is set within a ring of mountains – Blencathra and Skiddaw, High Seat and Helvellyn and more – and raised up on a plateau so that it floats between valley and sky, like a megalithic offering to the hills and their gods. Beyond the stones, the plateau appears to stop short, a sharp line of demarcation beyond which rise the mountains, as if this were a kind of runway offering a direct flight to the home of the gods. When I came here the first time, the mountains drifted in and out of a sea of cloud and mist, and it was hard to make out where land ended and sky began. Today there is an intense clarity to everything and an inner luminosity, as if it has all been crafted out of stained glass. Even the cloud shadows are sharply defined, moving across the fells like giant grazing sheep. The standing stones are the most precisely delineated of all, every bump and crevice standing out clearly, each one of the stones expressing its singular inner nature.

Even the constant stream of other people can't spoil it. I notice how everyone, adults and children alike, seems to head instinctively for the Sanctuary, the mysterious rectangle of ten or so stones set inside the eastern part of the circle. Kids climb on the stones of this structure and jump in the puddles, while the grown-ups seem particularly drawn to lean against the throne-like megalith that stands just outside the Sanctuary, a huge, chunky stone with a tall back and a kind of seat worn smooth and shiny by thousands of years of human contact.

A woman with berry-red hair takes off her shoes and walks

around the stones, touching each one. I do the same, but with my shoes on. We pass each other and I feel a connection and a solidarity with her, though I don't want to interrupt her ritual by making eye contact, or more to the point risk her interrupting mine. There's something profound going on for me now: I'm feeling a deep sense of gratitude to this place for being just as enchanting and awe-inspiring as when we first encountered it all those years ago; and for encoding Stephen into its past and holding him there, for making me understand that his being is now part of the fabric of the universe and so a part of these mountains, a part of the birds that are scattering over the stones, an aspect of the stones themselves and of anything that stirs my soul. Nothing is born or dies, but there is a mixture and separation of things that are.

Quests to the Home of the Gods

For ancient people, day-to-day reality must have been interwoven with the mythic realm in a way that modern secular rationalists cannot comprehend, except maybe occasionally, when confronted with some numinous place, a cathedral or a stone circle perhaps, that wakes us up and reminds us that, really, life and death and the existence of the universe are still great mysteries, even if most of the time we choose to ignore them, and that we know very little, if anything, about the meaning of it all.

It's been suggested that the large stone circles of Cumbria, which were among the earliest megalithic rings to be built

STONE LANDS

(around 3,000 BCE in the case of Castlerigg*[100]), seem to have been connected with the prehistoric axe industry. This is more interesting than it sounds. The tuff outcrops of the Langdale Pikes were ancient factories, the source of many thousands of stone axes, and in-progress and finished axes have been found close to Castlerigg, Swinside and Long Meg stone circles, with several axes actually unearthed inside Castlerigg itself. Words such as 'industry' and 'factory' can give a misleading impression. These axes did have practical uses as weapons and tools, but some of them were clearly valued as purely symbolic objects, ground, polished and never used. It takes at least 40 hours to polish a large axe, hours that are lost from the crucial business of survival without increasing the tool's cutting performance. Those 40 hours were spent on making the axe more beautiful, perhaps increasing its spiritual potency, perhaps enhancing the characteristics of the stone so that people could more easily identify where it came from.[101]

And where the stone came from was the tops of mountains. The Preseli Hills were the source of axes found at Bournemouth as well as the bluestones erected at Stonehenge.[102] Jadeite used to make gorgeous glassy green axes like the one discovered in the Thames at Mortlake came from high in the Italian Alps. The Mortlake axe was so thin that it would have broken if it had been used to cut down trees, but it would have sparkled entrancingly in sun and firelight and a magical nimbus would have

---

* Or even earlier. It's been suggested by archaeologist Steve Dickinson that the Sanctuary replicates in stone the structure of rectangular wooden buildings used *c.*3700–3600 BCE.

The Land is Still Enchanted

appeared to surround its delicate edges if it had been held up to the flames. It would, perhaps, have appeared magical. Tuff used to make the Cumbrian axes came from high, steep outcrops such as those at the Langdale Pikes and Scafell Pike; extracting it would have been difficult and dangerous, and perhaps the difficulty and danger was the point. The peaks of the Langdale Pikes dominate the surrounding landscape with a lordliness and ominous beauty that must surely have been as impressive to Neolithic people as to us now; they are like great beasts reclining on the horizon, at rest for the moment but with the potential to rise up and wreak havoc on the valleys below. Perhaps this is where the gods lived, or perhaps these august peaks were even gods themselves, and the perilous journeys to source the axes a sacred quest for those who undertook them.

It's possible, even likely, that prehistoric people did not distinguish between the source of special ritual items (such as Preseli bluestone or Langdale Pikes tuff) and the realm of the ancestors or gods. When they climbed up Pike o' Stickle – a 'steep ladder to heaven' as Alfred Wainwright put it – to hack out tuff, or descended into the Neolithic mine shafts at Grimes Graves in Norfolk and crawled into the blackness of the galleries to extract flint, did they feel that they were travelling through a mythic terrain? Was their sense of geography bound up with the sacred?[103] We can't ever know, but prehistoric people didn't have a mindset that separates the rational from the spiritual, that puts total credence in the former while dismissing the latter entirely.

STONE LANDS

Re-entering the Mythic Realm

Even today, after thousands of years and inconceivable changes in our way of life, we can still trace some of the features of the prehistoric world and by doing so perhaps get hints of how ancient people might have understood their surroundings, and even re-enchant the landscape for ourselves. It sends a shiver down my spine to consider that the roads we use today may have been those trodden 4,000 years ago; people once walked along the valley beside the River Greta from the henges of Penrith to Castlerigg, and now the busy A66 takes the same route.[104]

I also love the idea that we may, by looking at the landscape surrounding a stone circle, see what the ancient monument builders saw and understand why they put the stones in those exact positions. It was the engineer and archaeoastronomer Alexander Thom who from the 1930s to the 1970s researched and popularised the idea that standing stones were placed to line up with each other and with notable points on the horizon in order to mark key astronomical events, such as the rising or setting of the sun at the solstices. Margaret Curtis, who famously interpreted the Calanais circles in terms of their sightlines to the moon at lunar standstill, was just one megalith enthusiast influenced by Thom's ideas. Although archaeologists may sometimes pour cold water on the whole alignment thing, commenting that in many cases the purported sightlines could have been generated by chance as much as by design, there is something profoundly moving about the thought that, several thousand years after the stone monuments were built, the earth and

The Land is Still Enchanted

the sun are continuing their age-old dance of light and darkness, and that by waiting within a stone circle at equinox or solstice-time, we are marking a turning point in the year as ancient people also did, in their own way.

Castlerigg, with its incredible setting within a complete circle of mountains, is well supplied with potential alignments. According to Alexander Thom, this stone circle was an observatory for a number of astronomical events including the lunar standstills. From the centre of the circle, for example, watchers can observe the sun rise over Helvellyn at the Celtic crossquarter festival of Samhain, midway between the autumn equinox and winter solstice. The big event at Castlerigg these days is summer solstice, when a crowd gathers to watch the sun setting over Skiddaw and waits through the night to see it rise again behind Blencathra.[105] Who knows whether midsummer was actually observed at Castlerigg by the prehistoric builders, but it is meaningful to people now and that's what matters.

Some archaeologists point out that the widespread focus on (obsession with) discovering alignments of standing stones to the sun and moon means that other views, which perhaps were more important to the prehistoric builders, may be overlooked.[106] For Richard Bradley, stone circles are a microcosm of the whole surrounding landscape; in the case of Castlerigg, the ring of standing stones works as a metaphor for the encircling mountains. He describes large, bank-free and open stone circles such as Castlerigg as 'theatre in the round', contrasting them with henges such as Mayburgh, at Penrith, where there is also a continuous hilly horizon around the site but the view of it would have been hidden from those inside the monument by

STONE LANDS

its high bank. Castlerigg invites people inside the circle to relate to the surrounding mountains (and any monuments located there); it reproduces the mountains in its stones, encapsulating their very nature.[107]

Included in the mountainscape visible from Castlerigg are the distant Langdale hills, the source of the stone axes. At Copt Howe, in the Great Langdale valley, there's a huge boulder carved with a marvellous panel of prehistoric art including concentric circles, half-moon shapes, cup-and-rings, chevrons and triple grooves – symbols that seem laden with meaning and almost comprehensible, like an overheard conversation that you can't quite make out. And behind the boulder, there is a tremendous view up to the horns of the Langdale Pikes, site of the ancient axe factories. Could it be that the art relates to the mythic realm that lies in the hills beyond – a map, perhaps, with instructions on how to enter the domain of the gods?

The concentric circles and rainbow arcs of prehistoric rock carvings often seem to have a blurred, trippy look that could possibly represent the visual hallucinations of altered states of consciousness. Experiments have found that these distinctive motifs of Neolithic art have a remarkable similarity to the doodles drawn by those hallucinating in laboratory conditions.[108] A clue may have been discovered at Balfarg in Fife, where a pot unearthed among the remains of a Neolithic henge and stone circle contained pollen from deadly nightshade and henbane: evidence, perhaps, of consciousness-altering rituals taking place in what was once an important ceremonial centre (only two stones remain standing today, encircled by a 1970s housing estate named The Henge).[109] The structure of the human brain that created entopic phenomena thousands of years ago is the same brain structure we have today. Does that mean that, perhaps with the help of hallucinogens, it is possible for us to enter the mythic realm, too?

Even if the path to the otherworld is hard to find in our modern era, we can still access enchantment in places such as Castlerigg, through being touched by what we interpret today as 'beauty'. That feeling of joy and uplift that strikes the heart at the sight of a stone circle set within a ring of mountains was, perhaps, how ancient people connected to their gods. It can do something similar for us still.

A Valley that Belongs to the Stones

The breathtaking beauty of Castlerigg brings its own problems: this is one of the most visited of stone circles and unless it's the middle of the night or tipping down with rain, you're unlikely to have it to yourself. On a sunny afternoon there are liable to be coaches parked down the lane and the site overrun with tourists sitting or (worse!) standing on the stones, and cluttering up the interior of the circle as they take endless pictures of each other. Swinside is another Lake District circle possessed of heart-stopping beauty, but it's tucked away in the less-visited south-western fells, two or three miles west of Broughton-in-Furness, and is accessed by a walk of a mile or so from the tiny parking spot at Crag Hall, so there's a real possibility of encountering no one at all when you get there.

The Swinside stones are lovely: 55 glistening slate megaliths,

STONE LANDS

known locally as 'grey cobbles', many with multiple sharp-edged planes, some horizontally banded like a knitted jumper, some sprinkled with iridescent gold lichen. One is completely split from top to bottom. Another, the tallest pillar which marks due north, glistens red at its crown, as if splattered with fresh blood. And the whole wide valley and encircling hills belong to them; as you approach, it's impossible not to have your eye immediately drawn to this ring of stones huddling side by side on an artificially flattened platform, a sort of Round Table around which the stones stand, slump or lie, as if you've caught them at the end of a long, drunken feast. Absorbed in each other, they ignore us but command our attention.

This place is also known as Sunkenkirk, for the legend that these stones are all that remains of a church that the people tried to build each day but the Devil dragged below the earth each night. Between the Devil and the pillar that appears to be daubed with blood, you'd think there would be a sense of foreboding here, but there isn't, or at least not when we arrive on Easter Saturday in glorious spring sunshine. It is dry underfoot, the day is warm and there is no one else around, so I am drawn to lie on the ground inside the circle. I would probably feel too self-conscious to do this somewhere busy such as Castlerigg or Avebury, but here it seems like exactly the right thing to do. I don't have any definite beliefs about standing stones having spiritual power, and yet I do feel there is something special and 'other' about the interior of a circle described by ancient stones. To me, it feels like sacred space. As I lie with the sun on my face, the warm earth supporting me, I have a sense that the ring of stones is acting upon me in some beneficial,

The Land is Still Enchanted

healing way. My breathing relaxes into an easy rhythm, as if it has fallen in with the beating of the earth's own heart.

Alex, Ava and I have come here with my friend and colleague Uzma, who thanks to the joys of remote working has managed to escape London for a more nature-oriented life in the Lake District, and her old friend Daniel, who has kindly driven us here from the bus stop at Ambleside. Uzma is a kind of hippy-ish person like me and first she comes to lie down next to me, then comes Ava (who is always game for something new) and then Daniel (also of a mind-body-spirit mindset). Alex, understandably, is resistant to the suggestion that he might join us and remains by the stone wall looking at his phone. The rest of us lie there in a row surrounded by a wheel of stones, which are themselves surrounded by the encircling fells and mountains, which are in turn surrounded by the ever-spinning heavens. Wheel inside wheel inside wheel; this stone circle is an omphalos, the navel of the earth, and we are at its very heart. I lift my head and see that some sheep have entered the circle and are eyeing these peculiar humans curiously.

All around is a spectacular circular panorama: Black Combe, Raven Crag, Lath Rigg, Knott Hill, the distant Old Man of Coniston and more; this is as much of a natural amphitheatre as Castlerigg. It is Knott Hill, the breast-shaped mound swelling from the earth to the south-east, which is the closest and most obvious land form; and Alexander Thom pointed out that this hill, viewed from inside the circle, marks sunrise at winter solstice.

Daniel has brought his dowsing rods – coat hangers bent into an L-shape – and he holds them loosely in his hands as he walks through the stones. They twist and cross as he enters and leaves the circle and when he passes over its centre. Ava and I, as well as Uzma, who has tried dowsing before and been impressed by its efficacy, all give it a go. As I pass through the stones into the circle, I send a thought to Stephen, asking if he is there, and at that very moment the rods twist right round. It's the wind, I am sure, and just a coincidence, but I find it serendipitous and comforting.

When Ava tries dowsing, the rods twist for her too. In the interests of full disclosure, she said afterwards, 'One time there was a lot of wind and the rods twisted, and the other time there wasn't any wind and the rods still twisted but not so much. So I'm not sure...'

Fear is Part of the Journey

These days, without Stephen, I am often afraid. Before, when I was kept awake by spiralling thoughts of doom, I had only to reach out to touch the warm body lying next to me to feel grounded again. Often (not always of course, but often), that was enough for the worry cloud to dissipate and allow sleep to come. He was my anchor. Without him, I am adrift and when the fear comes, late at night when all my defences are down, there is nowhere to hide. I used to enjoy dropping off to sleep, mulling over this and that, but there is no pleasant night-time ambling through my mind now. I am sick and tired of turning on my pillow trying to evade the dark thoughts and finding comfort nowhere.

The Land is Still Enchanted

However bright the day has been, every night the fear comes. The fear that the happiest years of my life are behind me and that I spoiled them with stupid arguments over who did what around the house, who valued who most, who got more evenings out, such pointless petty wrangling (when we were waiting for the scan results, I promised myself that if we got through this, I'd never give him a hard time over anything again, but by then it was too late). The fear that Stephen had lost his joy even before he'd got sick, that I did not try hard enough to protect him from the things that made him anxious, that this anxiety had caused the cancer. The fear that work will overwhelm me, that I'll drop all the balls and lose my job and our income. The fear of what will happen to the children growing up without the steadying and motivating influence of their dad, that I will be too taken up with work to notice when things start going wrong for them. That they will slip out of my life and I will be left completely alone. That I will drive into a lorry and kill us all. Or worse: kill the children but not me.

The thought of driving was really frightening. I did actually manage to pass my driving text while I was at university and then I didn't drive for another 30 years. I just didn't see myself as someone who would be capable of driving. My spatial awareness was poor (I thought) and I was mesmerised by the oncoming traffic and sure I would end up giving in to the urge to drive into it. Because I lived in London with its plentiful public transport options, I could get away with this ridiculousness. If we were going anywhere that required driving, Stephen drove. Over the years, he must have driven me thousands of miles, from the north coast of Scotland to the western tip of Cornwall to the far west of Wales to Brittany and to the Pyrenees. After the babies were born, at least I could contribute something: I became the distractor-in-chief: the (dreadful) singer, tiny-foot-stroker, storyteller, dispenser of snacks, player of car games (such as the fruit game, which involves going through types of fruit one by one to guess what fruit the other person is thinking of – strangely satisfying), in short supplying anything that was needed to keep them quiet while Stephen concentrated on the fast-moving crazies on the road. I also worked the CD player and read out the over-by-over cricket report. But despite all this, the balance of effort was very much on Stephen's side; we visited hundreds of standing stone sites together and he was always the driver.

One of the first things I did after Stephen was diagnosed with cancer was book some driving lessons. I wanted to be able to drive him to his hospital appointments. I wanted him to enjoy being chauffeured about, just as I had been all these years. But relearning was a slow and painful process. I'd drive forwards a few metres, then my lovely and incredibly patient instructor Gemma would reverse the car so I could do it again. Eventually I felt brave enough to drive round the block, moving more slowly than the pedestrians. After a few lessons, we made it onto the main road, where Gemma had to keep grabbing the wheel to counter my tendency to veer left in order to evade the oncoming traffic. ('Watch your left!' was a constant refrain.) And so it went on for several months. I still believed I wasn't a driver, could never be a driver.

And then Stephen died, so in the end, despite having so many lessons while he was still alive and proudly reporting my progress ('I drove at 30mph today!', 'I got into fourth gear!'), I didn't drive him anywhere.

I should probably have given up on the car-hire idea; it was too soon, I wasn't ready, but I was determined to try to drive to at least one standing stone site while we were in the Lake District. If Stephen wasn't around to drive us to stones, then I needed to be able to do it myself. The night before the planned trip to Long Meg and Her Daughters, I had terrible insomnia. The wind was going crazy outside, apparently determined to rip the tiles off the roof, and my mind was full of dread potentials: serial killers creeping about downstairs; twinges in my stomach signalling an illness that would leave Alex and Ava orphaned; the prospect, increasingly certain as the clock passed 3 a.m., of killing the children when I fell asleep at the wheel.

In the event, tiredness was not a problem: the terror kept me alert. The day was in equal parts awesome and awful. When we arrived at the Penrith car-rental, the small automatic I'd ordered had (so they said) been crashed the day before by another customer and was now unavailable. As a replacement, I was offered a tank-like automatic estate or any manual. I didn't fancy attempting to manoeuvre the enormous estate so I chose a small manual as the lesser of two evils. I'd done most of my relearning on a manual and though I'd been switched to a (much, much easier) automatic a month earlier, I was more-or-less competent on the manual. How hard could it be . . . ?

Shortly after exiting the forecourt, I stalled at a junction and couldn't work out how to restart. The traffic quickly built up behind us and a deluge of honking commenced. I was in a tearful panic ('I can't do this!'), the kids were trying to phone the

STONE LANDS

car-hire people to come and rescue us, the honking was intensifying. The driver of the lorry stuck behind us exited his cab and came over to my window to find out what was going on. I said I couldn't start the car and he pointed out that the electronic parking brake was on.

This humiliating incident behind us, we were on our way. This was the good bit: quiet, sunlit country roads, whizzing through the tree shadows, and the joy of pulling up in one piece at the Long Meg and Her Daughters car park. My first drive to a standing stone site, what joy and pride! The children didn't seem unduly shaken by the stalling debacle.

And what a fantastic site this is. As you approach the circle, the outlier stone, Long Meg, grows higher and the mountains rise too, until you can see all the way to the Pennines, and to Helvellyn in the Lake District, and you get the full measure of Long Meg. She stands somewhat apart from the stone circle, outside its south-west entrance, a very tall, leaning pillar of red sandstone, one of her faces inscribed with art: spirals, concentric circles, arcs. I trace these markings gently with my fingers, feeling wonder at their mystery and the direct connection they give me with their long-ago carver, and the fact that they are still here after thousands of years of exposure to sun and frost. I also giggle a bit at the possibility that, while we treat these carvings with reverence now, they might mean something prosaic: 'Special offer: hazelnuts 1 flint a bag' or 'Swiftfoot was here'.

Long Meg is special, the only quarried stone here (the stones in the circle are all natural erratics, boulders transported to the local landscape by glacial action). She was taken from the cliffs above the River Eden and put up before the circle was built;

and it may be that she was even the reason for the circle's construction. When you face the spirals on Long Meg, you also face the Lake District mountains; perhaps, as with the panel at Copt Howe, the carvings describe the sacred realm that they overlook.[110] There is a winter solstice sightline from the centre of the stone circle through Long Meg to Helvellyn and the setting of the midwinter sun. From a certain angle, she looks like the head of a giant, with a long nose, strong, frowning mouth and a high forehead, but perhaps it is not a forehead but a pointy hat that we see: Long Meg is a witch, some legends say, possibly named after an early 17th-century witch called Meg of Meldon.

It's not clear whether the stones of the circle are Meg's daughters, fellow coven members or multiple lovers. 'These soliciting her to an Unlawfull Love by an Enchantment are turned with her to stone,' wrote the traveller Celia Fiennes at the start of the 18th century.[111] The 70-odd granite boulders stand or lie in a wide circle that's one of Britain's very largest and also, judging by the hazel charcoal found in a stone-hole and dated to 3340–3100 BCE, one of its very earliest.[112] There were 77 stones here when the topographer William Camden came in 1599; by Stukeley's visit in 1725 some of those stones had been broken up. Others slipped into the ditch of an earlier and now-vanished Neolithic enclosure that adjoined the circle on its northern side. But even if somewhat depleted, and scarred by a farm track running right through it, this circle remains a marvellous one. The massive block in the south-west would, it is estimated, have taken 120 people to set upright. Two enormous boulders mark due east and west, perhaps deliberately placed to honour the equinoxes.

STONE LANDS

I would like to spend the whole day at Long Meg but I have committed to the stone avenue and circle at Shap, a mere 30 minutes' drive away. The thought of this drive is bothering me. Better to get it over and done with. The one thing I really don't want to do is go on the M6; I have never been on a motorway and I need a few more lessons with Gemma before attempting that.

At Penrith I get in the wrong lane at the roundabout and we are headed for the M6. 'Mum, no no no, not that way,' shout the kids, but it's too late to change lanes . . . I'm curving round the slip road with a sick sense of dread – how did this happen? – argh, we're on the motorway! It's like the 'we're on the freeway' scene in *Clueless*.

There's a lorry behind and a lorry in front, my heart is pounding out of my ears, my hands are sweaty on the wheel and there's no way I'm getting out of the slow lane. I get into fourth gear because I've never been in fifth and I'm terrified that if I try to do that we'll stall and a lorry will plough into us.

The kids are amazing, calmly monitoring our progress on Google Maps and encouraging me – 'Only 10 miles to the exit, Mum, you're doing great, keep going . . .' – despite being deeply unnerved themselves. I have a strong sense that Stephen is looking down on us with a mix of exasperation and encouragement.

And after all the drama, when we get there and pull up at an untidy angle in the car park, Shap is disappointing, which is a shame because it's a stones enthusiast's paradise, not so much for what is there now, but for what there was once and for the possibility of rediscovering some of it. Once, an avenue of at least 500 granite megaliths stretched northward for 1.5 miles from

The Land is Still Enchanted

Kemp Howe stone circle all the way to a barrow on Skellaw Hill, the 'hill of skulls'. Lady Lowther painted the avenue as it stood in 1775, with the stones of the Kemp Howe circle (then called Shapsey) recognisable in the foreground and the vanished double row heading northwards (the A6 then a quiet country lane). A plan drawn by Dr Simpson, Vicar of Shap from 1857 to 1863, shows the double row leading from Kemp Howe circle to another, much larger stone circle surrounding a huge monolith, and from this second circle a single stone row extending on, but the avenue had been destroyed many years before Simpson recorded the site so who knows.[113]

Officially, just 14 stones remain in Shap Avenue today, dotted around the fields west of the village and along the A6, which marks the route of the southern stretch of the ancient double row. However, it is likely that many of the standing stones were reused as building material and if you look at the site entry on The Megalithic Portal, you'll see stones enthusiasts in their element, posting pictures of possible avenue stones now embedded in the field and village walls.

The weather has turned and we tramp in drizzle on muddy tracks between fields, and up and down the A6 looking for stones. The children are over it and who can blame them, and I'm not feeling great, disturbed by the unintentional foray onto the motorway and dreading the drive home. There is too much missing from this experience: we are not only lacking Stephen, but the stones themselves are barely present. It is too much to expect us to revel in the ghosts of stones when we are haunted by a ghost of our own. If Stephen were here, there would not have been any stressful driving dramas. If he were here,

STONE LANDS

tracking down missing stones would have been fun, and I would have had the heart to try to visualise the lost avenue and draw the others into my imaginings. In this moment, it all feels hollow and pointless.

I want to treat the kids to a pub lunch to try to make up for the weirdness, but the pub isn't open. We eat Co-op meal deals by the Goggleby stone, a chunky glacial erratic surrounded by sheep poo, and we clamber over a dry-stone wall to view the slumped Aspers Field stone. The rain comes down harder and the traffic rumbles by as we trudge down the A6 to Kemp Howe, at the south end of the village. The circle is uninspiring, half of it missing, mown down by the railway in the 19th century, and the remaining stones all fallen like a semicircle of bloated dead seals. The kids refuse to climb over the gate with me and instead yell warnings from the roadside: 'The sheep are going for you, Mum, get out nooooow!' At one point the shouting turns into screaming and I discover why when I get back to the gate: they have spotted six dead rats strung up on the barbed-wire fence like a ritual sacrifice or a warning to trespassing stones enthusiasts. (Later we discover that these were moles, not rats, left there by the mole-catcher who is paid by the farmer on a per-mole basis.)

We retreat back to Penrith, though not before a further stalling incident in which an impatient lorry squeezes past us and scratches the hire car, and then a re-encounter with the bewildering and scary Penrith interchange. I burst into a laughing-crying fit when we finally get back to the rental place.

When the hysteria and the shame at my general flakiness and inability to use a satnav subside, what I'm left with is a sense that, despite the horrible driving and the disappointment at Shap, the

The Land is Still Enchanted

three of us have come through an adventure together, a sort of modern-day pilgrimage to the stones. Maybe it didn't work out as I'd hoped, but we completed the quest. During that night of sleeplessness worrying about driving to Long Meg, a thought had come to me that was so comforting that I got out of bed to write it down: *We're on uncertain ground, finding our way through a bog like the one at Lochbuie, but I know our stones trips make us happy and I can hold on to that.* I think on this now and somehow it is very reassuring. However sad or scary or dreary things get, this land of ours is still enchanted and there are adventures to be had. Also, I intend to go back to Shap one day and give it another go.

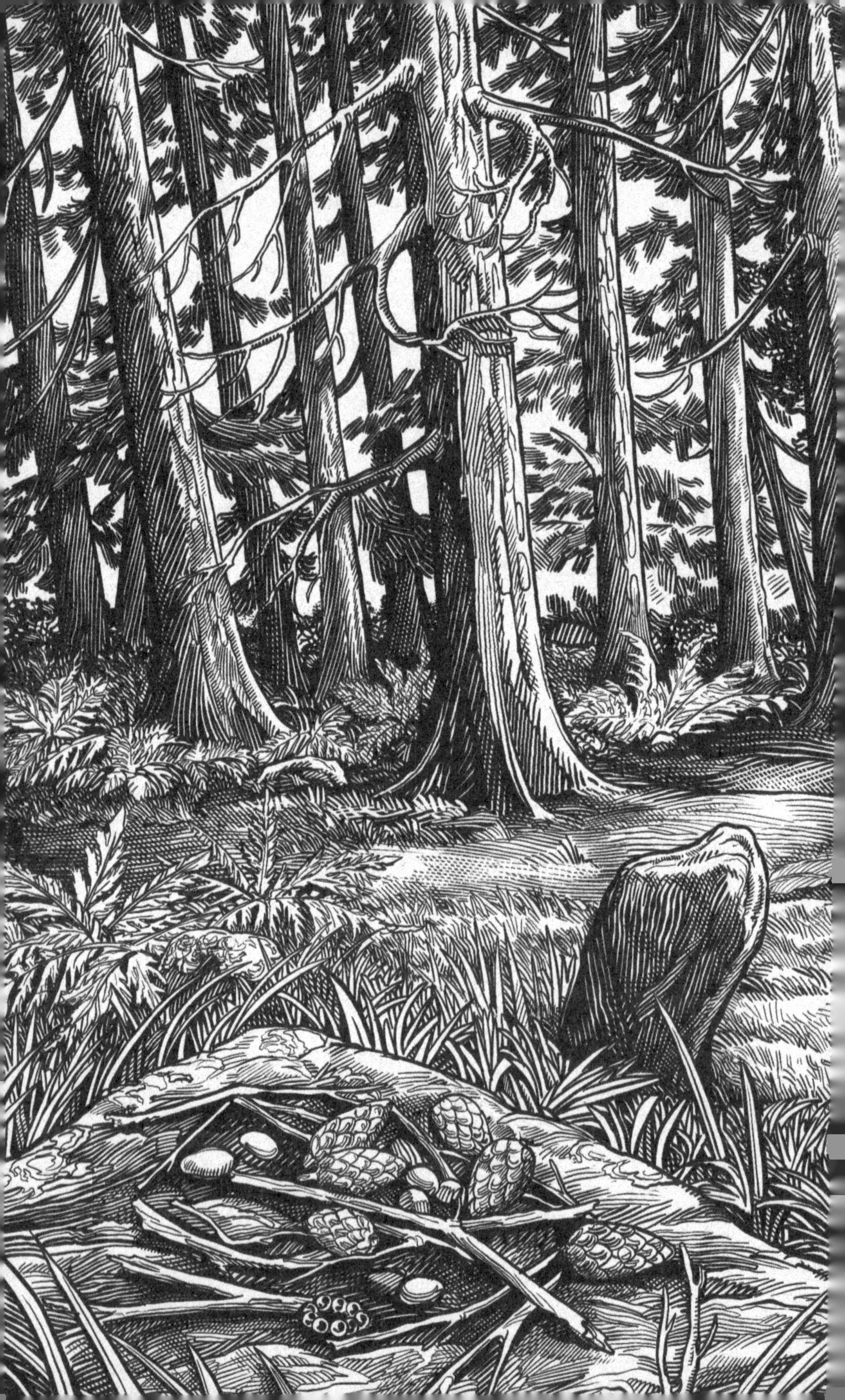

Chapter 9

THE STONES BRING US TOGETHER

Stones of the Medway, KENT
Stones of the Peak District, DERBYSHIRE

Megalithic Adventures in Kent

IT'S JUNE NOW, GETTING on for summer solstice. Already more than six months since Stephen died: time flows relentlessly onward, taking us away from him. Ava and I are crossing a furrowed field spiky with flints alongside my old friend Sarah and her daughter Robin (who is also my goddaughter – or rather my 'godlessdaughter', as Sarah puts it). Sarah is wearing a large, floppy straw hat against the sun and marching along in her usual determined way in Doc Marten sandals while simultaneously tapping notes into her phone and smoking a roll-up. I have known her since we worked together in the early 1990s, and our daughters are good friends. The girls both have an intricate garland of silvery green flowers painted from forehead to cheekbone, the art of a talented face-painter at Trosley Country Park. Below us is the church of St Peter and St Paul at Trottiscliffe, where the artist Graham Sutherland is buried and from where a secret

STONE LANDS

tunnel is rumoured to extend as far as the Coldrum long barrow. I am keeping an eye out for ancient arrowheads and as usual failing to find any. We pass a road sign that reads 'Dead Slow Please', apparently requesting the spirits not to rush on their way to the stones.

And Coldrum has been a place of the dead for a very long time. Human bones found in the burial chamber here have been dated to an incredibly ancient early fourth millennium BCE,[114] yet even today people are still being laid to rest by the long barrow: a crematorium notice of dispersal of ashes dangles from a branch, alongside all the ribbons, letters, petitions, strings of crystals and Kentish hagstones. Robin, the man had been called. It's the same name that belongs to the girl who now leans on a lichen-splodged sandstone megalith next to her friend Ava, looking down over the waves of barley flowing across the Medway chalklands, telling each other stories, dreaming their adult selves into being.

Stephen was waiting for me here, as I knew he would be. The Medway megaliths are the nearest old stones to London and we often drove out here with the children for a Sunday day-trip, either to Coldrum or a few miles further east to Blue Bell Hill for Kit's Coty House and Little Kit's Coty. Further east still, near Chilham and the River Stour, is Julliberrie's Grave, a Neolithic mound that lacks any stones at all. We had a picnic on top of it on 22 March 2020, the last day of freedom before lockdown began.

The last time we visited Coldrum together was in the November before Stephen's diagnosis. He was already feeling not totally himself and lay on the grass among a scattering of coppery beech leaves by the edge where the ground falls steeply away and many of the long barrow's stones have tumbled down. The kids scrambled up and down the slope, in and out of the burial chamber, and over and around the stones. Their tiny cousin Juno insisted on being lifted up to see the view from the top of the megaliths too.

I was scared that it would be overwhelmingly painful to come back to Coldrum without Stephen, the memories of us all here together an unbearable reminder of loss. But there is comfort in knowing he's still here. He's striding to the stones through a bitter winter's afternoon after a Sunday roast at The George in Trottiscliffe, encouraging us all to keep moving to stay warm. He's instructing the kids on a blustery spring day, when primroses are growing in the shadow of the burial chamber, to stop moaning because *yes we are doing the full circular walk* and *no it really isn't that far*. He's gathering twigs and bits of dry grass from around the long barrow to get the Kelly kettle going during a mildly illicit mid-lockdown outing. There is comfort, too, in being here with Sarah, who misses Stephen in the form in which she knew him before, but describes him as 'transmuted, not gone'. She tells me that she still often asks for his advice on things.

Today there's pride mixed in with all the other feelings. I've driven us all here on the motorway from London, and without any significant trouble. The Penrith roundabout debacle had knocked my confidence and freaked out the kids, who were not keen on the idea of getting into a car with me ever again. But I got back on the horse, had numerous motorway lessons with Gemma, pestered my friend Jim to accompany me round and round the Sidcup roundabouts, watched the Conquer Driving YouTube videos, rehearsed motorway slip-road procedure until the sequence was embedded in my brain, repeated my mantra: 'I *love* driving – calm, confident and in control!' over and over again... And I was helped and encouraged in all of this by Ava, who despite being only ten had taken to the whole driving thing and was good at intuiting when other drivers were about to cut in front of us (as we live in London, this happened often).

A couple of weeks later came another red-letter day when for the first time I drove on the motorway *on my own*, on my way to Blue Bell Hill in Kent to meet Elena, a fellow megalith enthusiast who I'd connected with via Instagram. I was late thanks to following the satnav's directions into the woods and down a very steep, bumpy track to a dead end, and then having to reverse with great difficulty back up again, but Elena didn't seem to mind. As we walked, we chatted about stones and the joy of walking along an ancient path – part of our walk followed the Pilgrims' Way, which runs from Winchester to the shrine of Thomas Becket at Canterbury. She told me how, Stonehenge aside, Kit's Coty 'was the first monument I ever visited and the start of all my folkloring adventures'. She was so struck by these stones that she began her Instagram page, @elena_of_the_ways, as a place to record her experiences.

At Kit's Coty House the grass is threaded with poppies and alive with butterflies, a heat haze shimmering over the Medway valley and the chalk-scarred North Downs. The clean lines of the dolmen are strong against the burning midsummer sky, its chunky, pitted capstone raised high on the three uprights, the interior of the chamber in inky black shade, the sandstone walls

The Stones Bring Us Together

reflecting the sun's blinding glare back at us. The stones are scratched with 19th-century graffiti and still hemmed around by the railings put up at the behest of Victorian archaeologist Lt General Augustus Pitt Rivers, who wanted to protect ancient places from vandals and souvenir hunters, and succeeded in doing so but at the cost of penning in the stones. It's still not possible to touch them. There was a long barrow here once, but that has been entirely ploughed away, its kerb of stones long removed. It's not a perfect standing stone site, then, but I've been here many times with Stephen, Alex and Ava, and I'm very fond of it.

It's so bitter-sweet being here and I don't want to alarm Elena by starting to cry, so I'm secretly relieved when we leave Kit's Coty and continue down Blue Bell Hill to a site I've never seen before: the White Horse Stone. In a clearing in woodland, we find a group of neo-Pagans celebrating summer solstice, four men and one woman in a circle by the altar-like block of sandstone. A statue of a goat deity has been placed on the flat top of the stone, and one of the men is carrying a staff capped by the figure of a raven, another a hunting horn. The sycamores murmur and splashes of sunlight dance with the leaf shadows on the earth and over the stone itself, flecking it with gold. In turn, the group greet Odin, Herne the Hunter and Sunna. The man with the hunting horn whispers a reassuring aside for our benefit: 'We're not fascists, you know.'

The woman gives the others a slip of paper each and asks them to write down something they want to achieve – not for healing or for prosperity or for the benefit of anyone else, but simply for themselves – then collects the slips in a jar for a

STONE LANDS

further ritual to take place at full moon. After a whispered consultation, Elena and I leave to give them some privacy. An hour or so later, after a picnic above the cutting through which the Eurostar rumbles, we return to the now-deserted clearing to see the White Horse Stone at close quarters. There is indeed something equine about it, a sense of muscles moving under moulded flesh that draws me to stroke it, as if I am running my hands along a real horse's flank. The stone's name is linked to the legend of Hengist and Horsa, Saxon brothers who are supposed to have invaded Kent in the 5th century under the flag of a white horse. In one version of the story, Horsa was buried here after the Battle of Aylesford, and the white horse flag was draped across this stone. It's actually not certain if it's a prehistoric standing stone at all; this stone may have taken on the identity and legends of another megalith – the Lower White Horse Stone – which was destroyed around 1823 and stood about 300 metres away, under what is now the A229 dual carriageway. But whatever its true provenance, the White Horse Stone is clearly special to some people now.

We tear strips of paper out of my notebook and make our own wishes. With some difficulty, as the paper doesn't seem to want to take, we set the strips alight, hoping that the smoke will carry the wishes to whoever or whatever it is that makes these things come out right. My wish is to be able, one day, to finish writing this book.

Elena also takes me to the Coffin Stone, in a vineyard accessed from the Pilgrims' Way, which at this point is no longer a pleasant footpath through the woods but a pavementless and fast country road. I follow her along the verge, nervous about the traffic and, once in the vineyard, about the possibility of trespasser-averse guard dogs, but I'm fired up with determination to find a new stone. It turns out to be a large slab of sandstone, fallen, sunken in weeds and partially covered by a field clearance rock – perhaps a site for the dedicated megalith enthusiast only – but there is nonetheless something thrilling about this ancient stone that survives between the regimented lines of vines. The prehistoric lives on in modern Kent.

On the way back for a final look at the main Kit's Coty site, we visit Little Kit's Coty, an extremely ruinous burial chamber that's also known as the Countless Stones, the name coming from the story that it's impossible to count them all accurately. This legend, according to folklorist Lesley Grinsell, also applies to ten other megalithic sites, from Swinside to Rollright and Stonehenge to the Hurlers.[115] It seems especially apt at Little Kit's Coty; it really is not possible to count up this muddled heap of stones and achieve the same total twice. We try several times and fail.

It is a good day out.

Places of Community

A few weeks later and Alex, Ava and I are in the Peak District. Knowing that this summer would be very hard for us, my brother Duncan and sister-in-law Lisa have invited us on holiday with them and their daughter Juno: we decide on a week in a rented cottage in Hathersage, conveniently close to a number of standing stone sites. My driving (though I say so myself) is not bad at all now, especially when I have Ava to work Spotify and tell me I'm in the wrong lane.

I have been to Hathersage before. There's a photograph of Stephen that I took on a trip here long ago, before the children were born. He is flanked by our climbing partners Luke and Lauren, the three of them lit up by a beam of early-evening sunshine that has slipped between the stone walls of the village houses. We are on our way back from cragging at Stanage Edge and they're all grinning, fired up by a successful day of climbing. I remember exactly how that moment felt – the joy of the hills and old stone walls gilded by the fading sun, the sense of comradeship, the anticipation of a well-earned session in the pub, and the compulsion to take a photo so I'd never forget it.

We lost touch with Lauren some time after that happy climbing trip, and then during lockdown we learned that she had died. A year later, it was Stephen's turn to go. Lauren and Stephen had no idea, that summer evening in Hathersage, how their lives would pan out. If they'd known, would they have done anything differently? Perhaps not. I remember thinking, back then, how similar the two of them were in their determination to squeeze every last drop of meaning and enjoyment out of life.

I remembered that moment so well and yet I could not work out where I'd taken the picture. Day after day I tried all the possible roads and footpaths in and around Hathersage, scouring the hillside up to the campsite and the bunkhouses above the village, but no joy. I had this idea that if I found the actual spot, I might be able to catch an echo of the four of us passing by all those years before. Returning in tears from one failed expedition, I was stopped by a neighbour, who asked me what

The Stones Bring Us Together

the matter was and instead of being flummoxed by my too-detailed response, got me to send him the photo to put on the local Facebook groups. This quiet act of kindness from a stranger touched me deeply.

I've been thinking a lot about community and all the things people did for us after Stephen was diagnosed. The help with researching treatments and finding doctors, with hauling our camping baggage to Scilly and back. The freezer full of nourishing home-made meals. The books and chocolates sent to Stephen in the hope of distracting him. The people always there at the other end of the phone, texting me solace and encouragement, always available to speak even when struggling with their own anxieties and depression. The colleagues who weren't fazed by my breaking down in tears during work meetings. Our house full of flowers and fruit baskets and boxes of Christmas gifts. All the people who helped with childcare, welcoming in my kids as if they were their own.

I've always been someone who is most at ease alone; even in the company of people I know well, there is usually a sliver of self-consciousness that makes me uneasy and clumsy in social interactions. It was different with Stephen. Right from when I first met him, Stephen was someone who I could just *be* with, two human animals existing side by side. And now he is gone, I am torn between wanting to be with other people and wanting to be away from them, and neither feels right. Drinking used to make things flow but it isn't as fun as it used to be, not when I know that a hangover will bring with it an inability to fend off the horror. But I do understand, now, that I can't do without other people.

STONE LANDS

Standing stones are often interpreted by archaeologists in terms of community: one example is the theory that the stone circles of Orkney were built with stones from different locations to bind together disparate groups.[116] Another is the idea that the Stonehenge bluestones (whether previously standing in a circle or not) were transported from the Preseli Hills to Salisbury Plain as the ancestral totems of a people moving eastwards to new lands.[117] And, in many ways, standing stones act as icons of community still and continue to bring people together, from those who share their photos of sites on social media to those who gather in their thousands at stone circles to celebrate the solstice. A stone circle remains a good metaphor for equality and community.

I meet up with other standing stones enthusiasts at the bimonthly Stone Club gathering in London, which by a strange and poignant coincidence takes place at The Social on Little Portland Street, the very place where I first met Stephen (the brown leatherette banquettes are still there). Stone Club, which organises events around the country as well as encouraging members to meet up for informal trips to ancient sites, was started by artists Lally MacBeth and Matthew Shaw in November 2021 as an online and real-world community 'for stone enthusiasts to congregate, to muse and most importantly to stomp to stones'. They'd initially envisaged it as being for their friends only, but word spread through Instagram and soon they were mailing out thousands of membership packs complete with Mên-an-Tol badge and membership card, everything with a deliberately home-made vibe.

The Stones Bring Us Together

When I asked why she felt Stone Club had landed so well, Lally said, 'Matthew and I wanted to create a space which was open and inclusive, where we could go for walks, make work about the ancient landscape and bring people together. I think Stone Club's success is partly down to a need to come together post Covid, partly to our emphasis on information sharing and on everybody having a voice within the community, and partly to the more general re-engagement with landscape and locality that happened during lockdown.'

Standing stones enthusiasts love nothing more than to talk about stones with each other, and I can attest that a room packed full of them is a fine and inspiring thing. My first encounter with the mighty power of a stones community came through my work in publishing, when I commissioned Andy Burnham, the founder of The Megalithic Portal, to write *The Old Stones*. We wanted this guide to the prehistoric sites of Britain and Ireland to include the full range of stones-enthusiast perspectives, from professional archaeologists and archaeoastronomers to fringe theorists and people who just like to go on a weekend walk to a stone – all of whom are represented within The Megalithic Portal community.

Andy explains how the book was created: 'Community involvement was key. I used our database to work out the most popular thousand or so sites in the UK and Ireland, then I invited a core team of Portal members to whittle down the site selection and check the information for their areas. I also approached our members for permission to use photos they'd submitted to the website. With that and all the editing queries, 10,000 emails must

STONE LANDS

have gone back and forth during the creation of the book, which was quite overwhelming.'*

Andy describes how The Megalithic Portal got started, in the days before Google: 'Back then there were no historic environment resources online; you had to go to the council offices to get the information and I'm sure very few people did. So, I decided to create my own web directory of prehistoric sites, following in the inspirational footsteps of the Stone Pages website set up by Paola Arosio and Diego Meozzi. I wrote to Aubrey Burl and he kindly sent me a floppy disc containing all the location data from his books on stone circles and rows.

'At that time, stones enthusiasts were in touch and chatting via the Stones Mailing List run by Chris Tweed. This was before social media as we now know it existed; you just sent an email and it was forwarded to everyone on the list. People ran these things themselves back then – unlike today, there were no big corporations controlling our interactions. The Stones Mailing List was a very mixed group, combining Pagans, eco-warriors, techies, academics and casual enthusiasts.

'I was contacted by Chris (Holy) McGrail, who told me he'd been tasked with creating an interactive website to accompany Julian Cope's book *The Modern Antiquarian*. He came to my house and I helped out with suggestions for categorising and arranging things. After he left, I realised this was going to be a game-changer: an interactive site with the clout of the arch-drude Cope would soon outshine what our little community had been doing. I immediately set to work to automate our site

---

* Indeed. But all worth it in the end!

database, and within a few weeks I had something up and running.

'This was in early 2001, which coincided with the worst-ever outbreak of foot-and-mouth disease in the UK. That spring and summer the countryside was completely closed off to visitors, which wasn't exactly the best way to launch a web resource based on visiting ancient sites. But after that initial delay, contributions went from strength to strength. I have to admit to being driven by competition from The Modern Antiquarian website (and similar) to innovate as best I could. Some of their inner sanctum didn't like me very much in those days but I think we've made up after all these years.'

These days, Andy says, the real competition to The Megalithic Portal comes from social media and the instant gratification it offers via 'likes', etc., but as he points out, 'contributions to The Megalithic Portal endure long after the few days it takes for things to drop down a social media timeline, never to be seen again. We are backed by a society of supporters and we're here for the long term.'

Forging Community at Nine Ladies

It's a fine August day and there are six of us tramping over Stanton Moor: Duncan, Lisa and Juno, plus Alex, Ava and me. We are all (or at least the adults) in a state of high excitement because this moor is a prehistoric wonderland that includes the Nine Ladies circle, famous for UFO sightings and a long-lasting environmental protest, as well as three other embanked stone

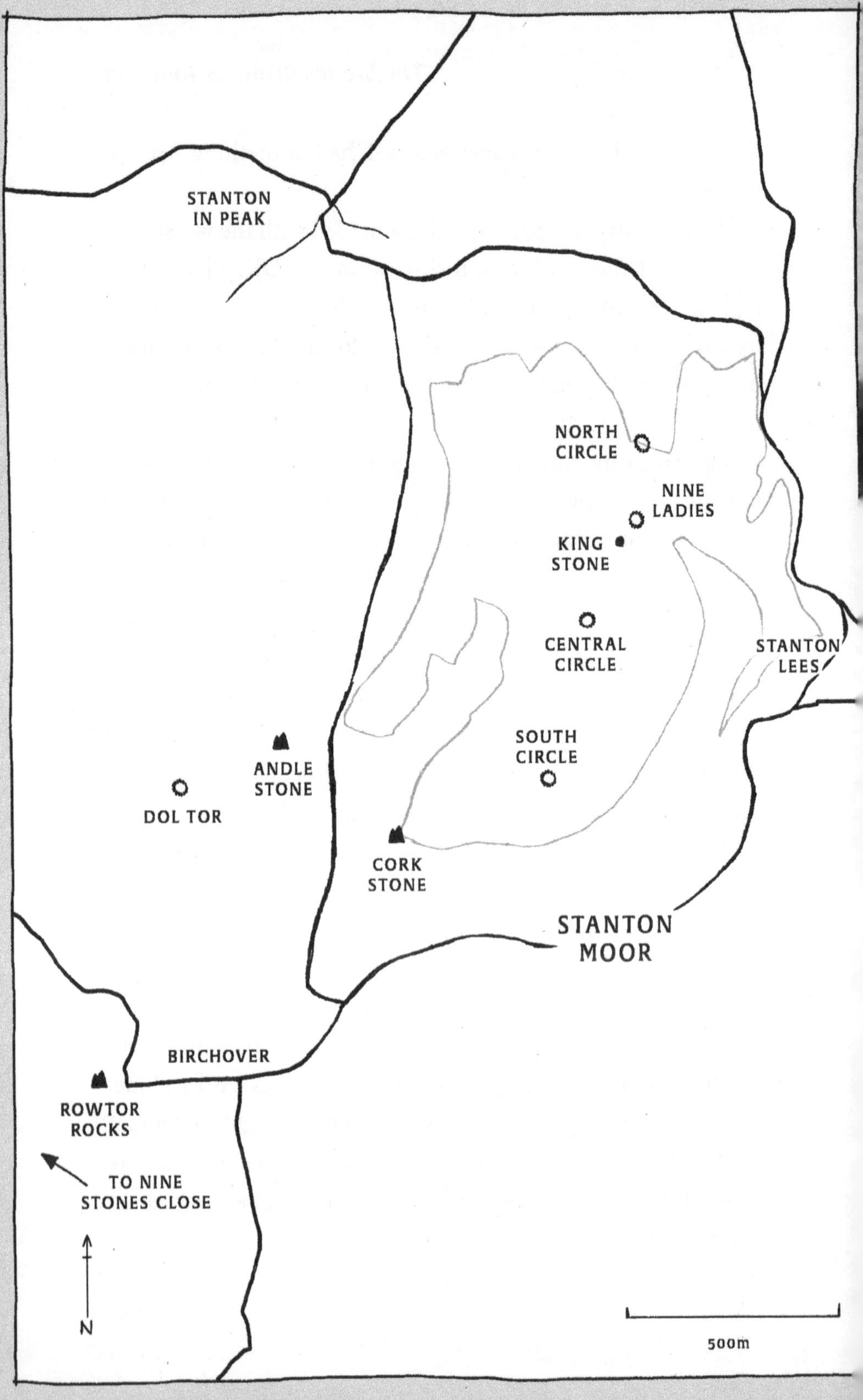
STANTON IN PEAK
NORTH CIRCLE
NINE LADIES
KING STONE
CENTRAL CIRCLE
STANTON LEES
SOUTH CIRCLE
ANDLE STONE
DOL TOR
CORK STONE
STANTON MOOR
BIRCHOVER
ROWTOR ROCKS
TO NINE STONES CLOSE
N
500m

circles, over 70 ancient cairns hidden among the heather and gorse, and in addition to all this, two further stone circles – Doll Tor and Nine Stones Close – very close by.

I call the first site – 'stones over there!' – but Alex insists those whitish blobs are only sheep, and he's proved right when one of them moves. It's not that easy to make out the cairns among all the other heather and bilberry-covered mounds. We leave the sandy path and make our way through a ghostly birch wood in search of the South Circle. There's little undergrowth here and the sunlight slashes through the tree trunks to create a chequerboard of light and shadow. It's evocative but there are still no stones to be seen.

Two walkers in anoraks are wandering through the birches, stopping every few steps to consult their map. Stones enthusiasts, for sure. I accost them and ask if they're looking for South Circle, which it turns out they are. Baffled, we scratch our heads together.

And then . . . in a clearing I see what appears to be a slight embankment, nothing more than an indistinct bump in the ground, and then a stone, small and leaning next to a few even smaller stones . . . possibly the cairn which, according to The Megalithic Portal, is supposed to be inside the circle. There's a set of tiny stones that could be the entrance stones, and across the embanked oval is another set. These stones are so small that I can't believe they are actually bona fide prehistoric 'entrance stones'. But maybe they are! People were smaller in prehistoric times, right?

At this point Duncan reminds me that three-year-old Juno's patience won't last for ever, and looking at the mutinous faces of Alex and Ava it seems like theirs is running out fast too, so I decide to leave off hunting for overgrown cairns and miniature stones.

We have no trouble locating the Nine Ladies circle – its stones may be small for megaliths, but they are undeniably there. Like their unfortunate Cornish peers, the Nine Maidens and Merry Maidens, they are women turned to stone for the sin of dancing on the Sabbath; the grassy bank in which they are set is the hem of their dresses, brushing the ground as they twirl. These nine gritstone uprights have a companion: a fallen tenth, which was exposed by the drought of 1976. And along a path through ferns and within sight of the circle is an outlier stone, another small megalith that does not really live up to the imposing name of King Stone.

All around are silver birch, ash and beech, and a wishing oak bedecked with ribbons and tokens; sylvan onlookers who have drawn back to allow the humans access to the stones. My first memory of the Nine Ladies, from a very wet and not entirely successful camping trip to the Peak District I took as a student (it ended when our tent collapsed during a midnight storm and we decided to cut our losses and go home), is of the stones set in front of these trees, somehow echoing and channelling their energy. When people talk about the Nine Ladies, they often seem to bring up the trees. Gareth Wilson, for example, who is a landscape consultant with a professional eye for the aesthetic qualities of Derbyshire stone, and also a committed megalith geek who has visited every standing stone in the county, said to me of the Nine Ladies: 'The trees around that stone circle are

The Stones Bring Us Together

very spiritual. The silver birch especially; that's the lady of the woods. Being a horticulturalist, I often go foraging there and it's lovely, but I never quite feel like I'm on my own. It's a strange feeling: there's always a sense that the tree spirits are watching.'

The hot August Sunday we visit, Nine Ladies is like Piccadilly Circus, what with all the dog-walkers and picnickers, neo-Pagans and stones enthusiasts. Like other Peak District sites, Nine Ladies may not have the most impressive megaliths in the world but it is within easy day-trip distance of Sheffield, Manchester, Nottingham, Birmingham and more, and so is much visited and very well loved. Too much visited and loved, some might say. The damage caused to the Nine Ladies by people camping near by and building fires inside the circle, carving graffiti and daubing paint onto the stones, setting the moor alight with their fag butts and simply wearing away the ground by endlessly walking round and round, has been a cause for concern for a long time.[118] As far back as the 19th century, in fact: the 'BILL STUMPS' graffiti carved into the King Stone (probably inspired by *The Pickwick Papers*) was noted with dismay by Augustus Pitt Rivers, who included Stanton Moor in the first list of megalithic sites to receive government protection.

Of all stone circles, Nine Ladies is perhaps the one most closely linked to the idea of community, which was forged there in the furnace of a passionate protest against quarrying that burned for a decade between 1999 and 2009. In resistance to Stancliffe Stone's plan to reopen the Lees Cross and Endcliffe sandstone quarries, the protestors of the Nine Ladies Anti-Quarry Campaign set up camp to defend what they held to be the sacred landscape of Stanton Moor, eventually building an elaborate settlement of tunnels, benders, tree houses, walkways and sky rafts not far from the stone circle.

A student when the protest started, Aimee Blease-Bourne became caught up in the campaign and eventually wrote a book about it.[119] 'My ex-partner took me up to Nine Ladies and I heard there were some people down the hill who'd made a load of tree houses and that there was a threat, and I desperately needed to know more about it all. This multi-layered landscape – the stone circles, the moorland, the trees, the quarry – just blew my brain open. It changed my consciousness. We spent a couple of nights at the camp and had a fantastic time, met different people, played drums, watched the fire poi and I was just hooked.'

She started an MA in cultural theory looking at what was happening at Nine Ladies, which then turned into a PhD. Aimee was now up at Nine Ladies pretty much every weekend. 'Most of the people I knew back then came from Nine Ladies. We were all there for similar reasons: to celebrate nature, to kind of connect with our ancestors up there, and to protect the site. I'd visit the protestors and I'd often take equipment, batteries or towels or whatever. I feel like I became an unofficial guardian of the stones.

'The stone circle has an interesting power – and other people have said this too: if you try to manifest something there, things do seem to find their way and come true. I felt I could just go to the Nine Ladies and resolve all my problems. It's also a very healing place. There's a legend that Robin Hood brought Maid Marian to the Nine Ladies to heal her after a battle. I love that this landscape has so many different layers, which makes it a kind of queer landscape, because it's undefinable. It means many

The Stones Bring Us Together

different things to many different people. That really sparked with me because I'm queer myself. I saw myself reflected in the landscape.'

Like Aimee, I too find it fascinating that people connect with standing stones emotionally in all sorts of different ways. That the people who go to a site such as Nine Ladies come to feel that it belongs to them, and in turn may be shaped into a community by it.

The Nine Ladies Anti-Quarry Campaign had many allies, from archaeologists and walkers to the local Stanton Lees Action Group (SLAG), but not all the locals looked on the protestors kindly. Worries about drug-dealing, littering, out-of-control dogs, threatening behaviour and, most of all, the fear that the camp might become a permanent Traveller site, led to hostilities. The locals themselves were bitterly divided, with the two nearby villages, Stanton Lees and Stanton in the Peak, feuding over the location of the quarry. Eggs were thrown at parked cars and tyres let down.[120]

In 2009, permission to quarry at Lees Cross and Endcliffe was revoked. So the protestors got what they wanted? 'Yes and no,' said Aimee when I asked her. 'There's just been an extension of the quarry across the road. There was always going to be a new quarry; the battle was between Stanton Lees and Stanton in the Peak over where it was going to be, and it ended up pretty much equidistant between the two villages. It's not in the most sensitive area close to the stones. It's still massive and polluting and not ideal, but it gives jobs to local people and we need stone. The quarrying debate is difficult.'

In 2009, the camp was carefully dismantled and the site

tidied up and left to nature, as the protestors had promised it would be all along. 'We were there for a reason, and when that reason was gone, everyone moved on. As hard as it was.' Aimee took part in the dismantling. 'It was beautiful, a very cathartic, amazing process, but also heart-wrenching to do everything for the last time. I kept thinking, *This is the last fire*, and, *This is the last time I'm going to walk up to Nine Ladies from the site*. It was really sad. Some people had lived there ten years and they'd built their whole life around it.'

It must have been heartbreaking for the protestors when they had to strike camp and leave behind that intense period of their lives. I understand that. The wheel turned and they had to move on. And yet it sounds like they are still connected by these standing stones, which they had come together to protect.

'The stone circle is still a hub for the protestors. I try to get up there for the solstices,' Aimee says. 'Everyone's dispersed, but I still see some of the old faces there. And lots of new faces, too. I love going up there.'

Guardians of Stones

There's a seventh person out with us on Stanton Moor today and that's Stephen. I think we all feel it. For me, he's evoked by the young men at Rowtor Rocks with bouldering mats on their backs. When Alex and Ava climb up the staples to the top of the giant natural pillar known as the Cork Stone, I hear him cheering them on. I see him scrambling gracefully up after them.

The Stones Bring Us Together

The Andle Stone is another glacial erratic that Stephen would have scaled without a moment's hesitation, a massive sandstone outcrop set in a barley field on the way to Doll Tor stone circle. Like the Cork Stone, this huge, natural rock is so much more physically imposing than any of the standing stones around here, and so completely alien in the landscape, so strangely sculpted and weird, that it seems possible that it could have been an initial focus of reverence in the area, before the stone circles were built.

A track leads through golden barley that shimmers as the wind gently ruffles it this way and that, like it's stroking a cat. The sun is high and the colours are intense: against the glowing barley, which is almost too bright to look at, the clustering pines are dark and sinister. The track leads us downhill towards them, through a rickety gate and into a hay field, and then along the edge of the conifers, which whistle and creak ominously. The information board on Stanton Moor had said that Doll Tor is on private property and therefore inaccessible, and the consciousness that we are trespassing adds to the sense of edginess. This place has a reputation – 'There's something weird there,' someone said on Twitter/X. And yes, I get that.

When we reach the clearing where the six stones of Doll Tor stand, we find them huddled together, as if they're whispering secrets to each other, the clearing filled with an unearthly light. We are at the edge of the wood and beyond this fringe of trees the land falls away, so there's a great sense of air and space even among the tall trunks of the conifers. All around are signs of witchcraft – a pentagram made from sunflowers; a tripod altar constructed of branches lashed together with stems and ferns; a stone slab decorated with coins, crystals, cones and shells;

STONE LANDS

and berries and cones wedged into the crevices of the stones. It is a place of community and ritual. Real witches come here.

We sit on the ground beside the stones, and hand around the snacks and water bottles. In this lonely place, there is a definite *Blair Witch* edge, so I leave a chocolate on the altar as a placatory offering. A combine harvester starts up its earth-shaking rumble in the field outside as we leave, and there is some discussion about whether the farmer would mow down trespassers or not. It's the spookiest stone circle I've ever been to and utterly magical.

Doll Tor circle has been attacked on several occasions. During excavations in the 1930s, three of the standing stones were smashed into pieces and had to be stuck back together with concrete. It suffered an unauthorised 'restoration' in 1993, when a person or persons unknown, apparently intent on creating a better space for a spring equinox ceremony, set up eight extra stones in addition to the original Bronze Age six, and removed stones from the circle's kerb and a prehistoric cairn, piling them up in a heap. The site was painstakingly restored the following year, and the two megaliths that had been moved from the circle put back where they belonged, but the kerb and cairn were so disturbed that it was not possible to replace the individual stones precisely, only to try to create something approximating the historic drawings of the site.[121]

In 2020, the circle was damaged again. An anonymous poster wrote on The Megalithic Portal how they'd discovered that stones had been removed from the cairn to create fire pits and left in a heap, burned and cracked, and how they'd tried to clear

The Stones Bring Us Together

up the mess: 'I'm aware moving the stones isn't ideal but I wasn't just going to leave them piled up.' 'Good work,' wrote another Portal poster in reply, 'it means a lot to many people.' These ancient places that lie unprotected in our countryside will always be vulnerable to those who want to damage them, but luckily many more people are inclined to look after them than the reverse. There are many unofficial guardians of the stones out there.

Juno and Ava are over it, so Lisa drives them back to the cottage, but Duncan, Alex and I carry on to the circle known as Nine Stones Close. The sun is lower now, the colours deeper and everything touched with magic and strangeness. We pass through Rowtor Rocks, where seats, steps and alcoves have been carved out of the living stone, and shadows flee across the rock as if someone we are seeking has only just slipped around the corner. I catch myself wondering where Stephen is and for an out-of-time moment have a sense that he's been with us all day and has just nipped off to do some bouldering.

The twin-peaked outcrop Robin Hood's Stride watches moodily over Nine Stones Close, as if the horned head of the Devil has burst out of the earth. The outcrop's 'horns', seen from the stone circle, are said to frame the setting of the moon at the major lunar standstill.[122] There are four stones standing at Nine Stones Close (not nine*) though in the mid-19th century seven were recorded; a suspiciously large stone embedded in a

---

* The number nine crops up repeatedly in the names of standing stone sites – the Nine Maidens, the Nine Stones – although there very rarely seems to be actually nine of them.

field wall near by, as well as a megalith lying in the next field, could account for two of the missing stones.

These are the tallest stones in Derbyshire and beautiful ones at that, each stone different. One is shaped like a fishtail, another incised with a ridge of runnels. One is like a sculpted hand, the fingers closed and pointing upwards; another has indentations and nobbles as if it were a chunk of the moon. Near by stands an oak tree that reaches out its branches towards the stones and dwarfs them, reminding them that in this region stones are not supposed to be that big. It has become an integral part of the monument; the guardian of Nine Stones Close, perhaps.

Moments Like These

At times I am very low, thinking about how different this holiday is without Stephen and about what we as a family have lost. I know that we will never again experience that bliss of the four of us escaping reality on one of our adventures, leaving work and school behind for two weeks' camping and stone hunting and sea-swimming in Brittany or Scilly or Cornwall. How incredible were those fortnights away from mundane life: a true immersion in magic. Of course, the children are growing older and we would soon have lost their enthusiastic participation in these escapes from reality, had in fact been losing it already. But now my fellow adventurer is gone, I'm scared, sometimes, that my own story is coming to an end too.

And yet there are moments like this still to be had. I am eating a Bakewell tart inside the Seven Stones of Hordron Edge,

The Stones Bring Us Together

leaning up against the Fairy Stone, the biggest in this circle of modestly sized megaliths. Duncan and Alex are here too, sprawled on the damp, tufty moorland grass. To my great delight, Alex has chosen to join Duncan and me on a 12-mile hike instead of going shopping in Sheffield with Lisa and the girls. We have walked north from Hathersage onto Stanage Edge, then along the blustery Edge to Moscar Moor, and then south to find the Seven Stones.

This is a remote and marvellous place. To our east, the upsweep of moor is terminated by Stanage, the severe rock wall that guards the horizon. To our south is Bamford Moor, where the Old Woman Stone lies broken on the ground, felled by the landowner in the early 20th century so that walkers could not use it to help them find their way on private land. Not far from this fallen stone, somewhere in that ocean of purple heather, is Bamford Moor South stone circle. On the horizon to our west are the volcano-like mounds of Win Hill and Lose Hill, their profile said to be deliberately echoed by the top edge of my current backrest, the Fairy Stone. Kinder Scout, site of the famous 1932 mass trespass that was a landmark in the history of the land-access movement, is visible in the misty distance. All around us the views extend over rippling moorland to the blue hills on the horizon, and there is not another person in sight. Heaven.

Duncan, Alex and I are laughing about how the names of Win Hill and Lose Hill, which refer to a battle that is supposed to have taken place in the 7th century between Edwin of Northumbria (the winner) and Cynegils of Wessex (the loser), are a bit basic and on-the-nose. We discuss the potentially magical nature of a circle with an indefinite and shifting number of stones; some sources say ten, some 11, some 23 . . . All that can be said for sure about the number of stones at the Seven Stones of Hordron is that there definitely aren't seven of them.

And as we talk, I am thinking to myself how pleased and proud Stephen would have been at the sight of his son, grown so much taller already, his long hair flying in the wind like Medusa's snakes, voluntarily taking part in this day of moorland tramping – and even, dare I say it, enjoying it!

Here's another happy moment of togetherness and stone hunting, from the year before Covid turned the world upside-down. Stephen and I are at Arbor Low, the most magnificent of the Peak District's ancient sites thanks to its ridge-top setting, a high, lonely, ancient place, with views that sweep far and wide and seem to travel in time as well as space. To the lark song is added the chirruping of four children: our two and the two boys belonging to Stephen's climbing partner Toby and his wife Caroline. The eight of us have been camping and climbing in the Peak District, and we have stopped at Arbor Low on our way back to London. We've had a wonderful weekend full of laughter, as the only two competent climbers (Stephen and Toby) hauled the rest of us, giggling and flaking out, up the millstone grit.

When I saw Arbor Low for the very first time it was in an aerial photograph, and I was startled by the resemblance of the henge, with its grassy outer bank, and its ditch and raised inner platform fringed with a circle of fallen stones, to a great green eye complete with pupil and eyelashes staring unblinking out of the earth. The site has turned out to be as atmospheric in reality as the pictures promised, and we are excited to learn that it is said to be haunted by boggarts, who harass those who venture up here after dark.

We climb up Gib Hill, to the south-west of the henge, which was perhaps (gruesome thought) named for a gibbet that once stood here, displaying the bodies of executed criminals as a warning to those passing on the road below. Gib Hill is man-made, a Neolithic long barrow that might have been the very first monument built on the plateau. In the Bronze Age, long after Arbor Low henge was dug and a circle of stones raised (and shallow sockets imply that they *were* raised, although they've all fallen now), a further barrow was built on top of Gib Hill, and another large barrow set into the bank of the henge. Many more barrows were constructed in the landscape for miles around. This was a sacred place for a thousand years, a site that kept drawing the monument builders back.

From up here, the horizon spreads so wide it hints at the curvature of the Earth. We can see the mighty gritstone edges, distant waves of rock caught forever on the point of crashing down. The gnarly white limestone megaliths all lie peacefully on the ground, as if they gave in to the wind long ago and are now resigned to staying in their comfortable beds of dandelions, buttercups and soft grass. This weekend is going to be the last time I ever climb with Stephen, and yet there is none of the sadness of an ending about this trip, no inkling of dread. The eight of us huddle together to share a picnic in the ancient ditch, out of the wind, among the long grasses and wildflowers.

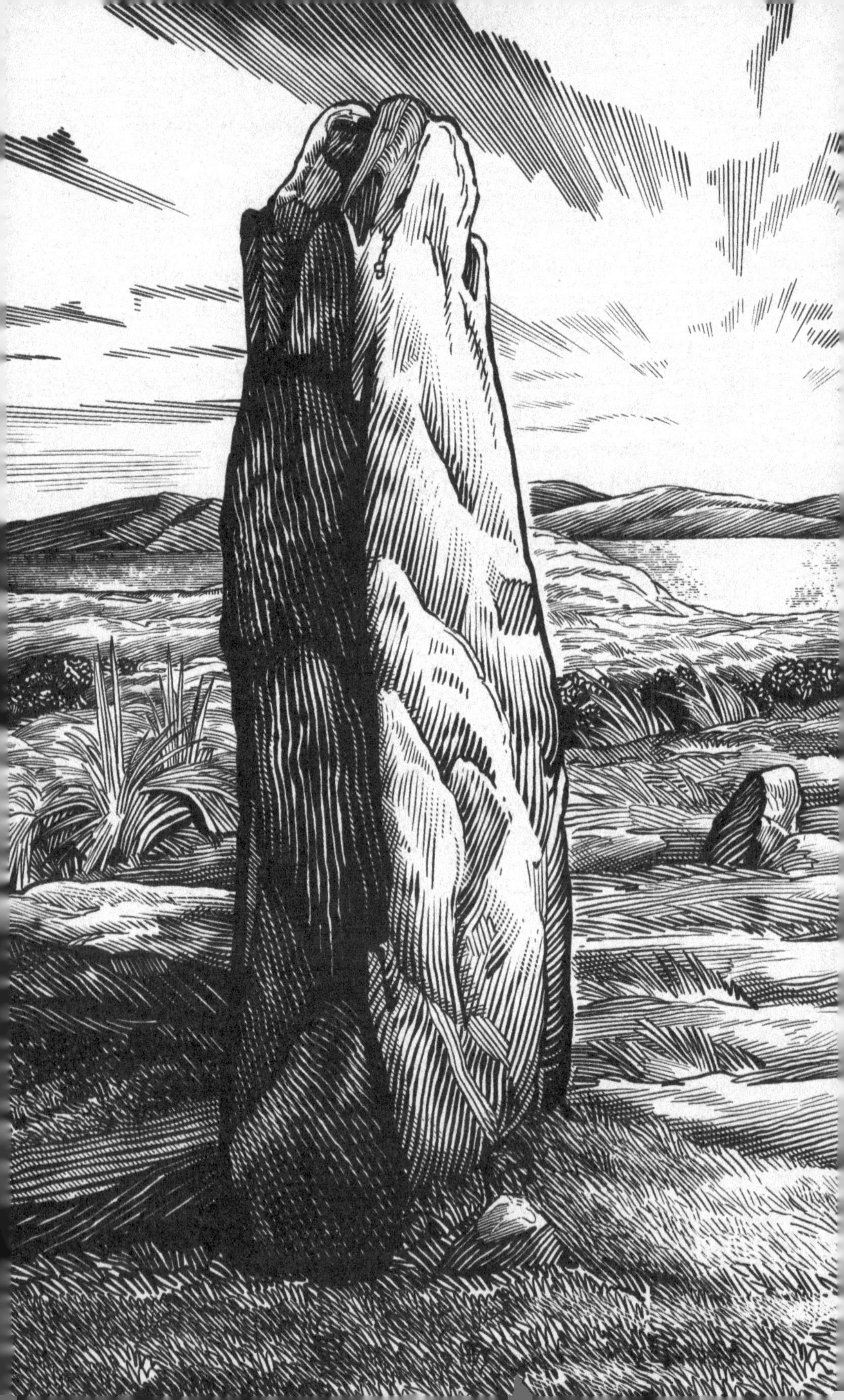

Chapter 10

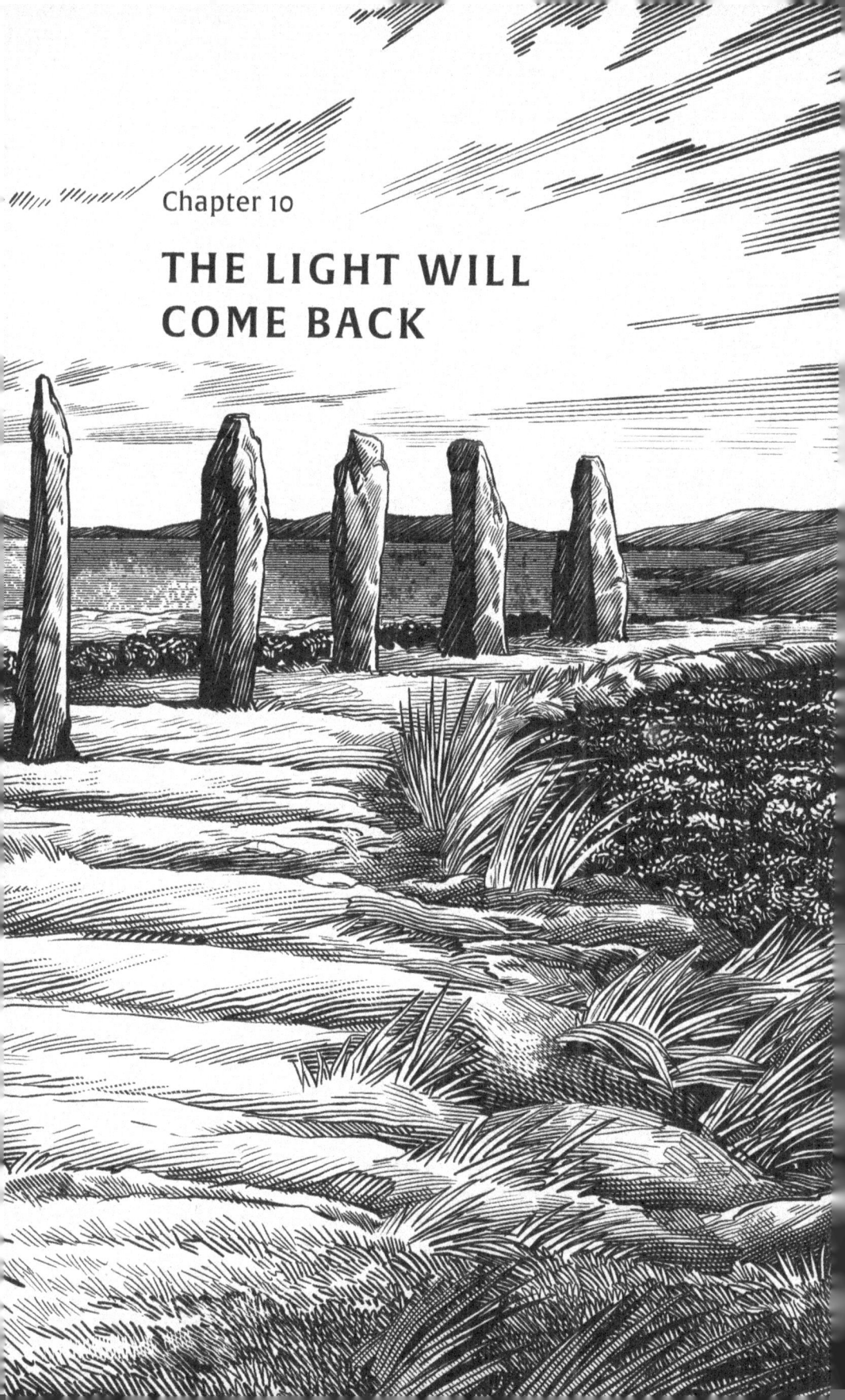

THE LIGHT WILL COME BACK

- c.3700 BCE: Earliest evidence of Neolithic activity in Orkney

- c.3500 BCE: Earliest evidence of activity at the Ness of Brodgar complex

- c.3400 BCE: Midhowe in use by now

- c.3300 BCE: First buildings at Skara Brae

- c.3300–3100 BCE: Unstan in use by now

- c.3200 BCE: First buildings at Barnhouse

- c.3100 BCE: Structures 1, 8, 12, 14 at Ness of Brodgar built on top of earlier buildings

- c.3000–2900 BCE: Stones of Stenness ditch dug

- c.2900 BCE: Structure 10 built at Ness of Brodgar

- c.2700 BCE: Maeshowe ditch dug

- c.2600–2400 BCE: Ring of Brodgar ditch dug

Stones of Orkney

AS THE DAYS SHORTEN and the light fades, my sense of dread is growing. The wheel slowly turns: we pass the autumn equinox and then we pass Samhain, at the midpoint between the equinox and the winter solstice, and then, before I know it, it's 8 December again. A year on from the day Stephen died. It's almost midwinter and things seem very dark.

I'm burying myself in work and in writing this book. I worry that I'm working too hard and it's not healthy to carry on like this but I'm finding the writing helpful. It's a controlled way of understanding what's happened and it stops me from thinking too much about what's going on right now. It lets me cry as if I were crying for someone else. Every night, at a certain point after I doze off, I'm suddenly wide awake again, as if two wires have touched in my brain to spark a terrifyingly clear insight into all the things that can – and will – go wrong. And then

STONE LANDS

I can't sleep for ruminating on the doom scenarios.

I consult child-bereavement specialists and they assure me that my kids are OK; in fact, they are both coping well. But the dread remains. How can they be OK, when they have lost their dad, who loved them so much? When his going has proved that death is real, that it won't turn out right in the end, not for me and not for them and not for anyone, that we are all hurtling towards the same destination and some of us will get there much sooner than we think?

In December, on the anniversary of Stephen's death, I take the day off work and the kids out of school, and we go to the crematorium to see his memorial stone installed. We eat mince pies and drink tea by the stone, pouring some of Stephen's favourite Earl Grey (sweetened with a third of a teaspoon of sugar) on the ground. We leave behind a chunk of quartz from Preseli, and sprigs of holly from the garden, and some shells and sea-smoothed pebbles, and a mince pie for the foxes. Then the three of us go to choose a Christmas tree, and carry it through the streets to the car together and work out how to cram it and us back in. We drive home, decorate the tree, look at old photos and watch *Hot Fuzz*. We get through it together.

On the morning of the 22nd, the shortest day of the year, I leave the house while the kids are still sleeping (it's the school holidays and they have both firmly declined this early start) and arrive at Hilly Fields in Brockley just as the night sky is starting to lighten. The stone circle here is by far our nearest megalithic site but it's not a very old one, having been put up to celebrate the Millennium. A lot of thought went into this circle's construction: the stones form a sundial in which the person using the sundial is themselves the gnomon, their shadow indicating time of day via one of the 12 granite boulders of the circle. A flat engraved stone in the centre of the circle marks the different positions in which the human gnomon must stand for this to work, varying according to the time of year.[123] This circle may not be ancient, but like Stonehenge it observes and celebrates the sun's yearly journey around the sky, and it has recently acquired a new resonance for me. A little way from the ring of stones, a young tree is growing in a mesh guard; this is the greengage that Stephen's workmate Martin planted in his memory.

In the dim light of dawn, I see that other people have come here to mark the winter solstice. They are all facing St Norbert's Gate, the two tall pillars of Caithness flagstone that stand just outside the circle. I take up a position at the back of the circle and look around me: solitary figures are hunched into their coats and scarves, silhouettes in the darkness. Seagulls spray out scattergun overhead, and then my friend and fellow editor and megalith enthusiast Adam arrives. Two years ago, Adam and I had marked the exact moment of the winter solstice by lighting a candle and sharing a minute of silence in an office emptied by working-from-home, and I had felt it to be a significant act, a recognition that I was about to turn 50 and a whole new decade of life lay ahead. That evening, when I was back from work, Stephen and I had built a solstice fire, written down three things that we wanted to attract into our lives and then burned those strips in the fire. I think Stephen thought the whole wish-burning thing a bit silly, but he liked having a midwinter fire and that we were thinking properly, for once, about what we wanted to do next. I don't

STONE LANDS

know what he asked for. What he got, less than a month later, was a cancer diagnosis.

A year on and I was sitting by another winter solstice fire in our back garden with Alex and Ava, Duncan and Lisa, Sarah and Robin. That day I'd seen Stephen's body in the funeral parlour and I'd known it was just a shell, no longer him, his spirit gone. Some of us had written messages to him to put in the fire. I had this feeling that the smoke might somehow take my words to him, wherever he was. I'd just wanted to update him on all the lovely things people had been saying about him; it had seemed impossible that he could not be told.

Time flowed on and now I'm another year downstream, waiting within the stones for sunrise on the shortest day of the year. Now more people are entering the circle: groups of parents with pushchairs, a dog-walking woman with reindeer horns on her head. I'm touched that we cynical Londoners have spontaneously turned up to celebrate the dawning of the light, that we've come together in this unrehearsed ritual to be connected with each other, with the people of the deep past and with the epic mechanics of our solar system. It feels moving and important, although the sun is hidden by thick cloud and the stone circle less than a quarter of a century old. Adam checks the time and advises that the moment of sunrise has passed. The shortest day has begun. The reindeer-horn woman wishes us a happy solstice and we return the greeting.

A few days later, my old school friend Debbie forwards me a link to a poem about winter solstice by Joseph Fasano, offered by him on Twitter/X 'to anyone in the dark'. It's short and powerfully uplifting and ends with these words: 'you have hated your one life long enough. Try something wondrous.'

And so I do. I book a trip to Orkney.

Light in the Darkness

Stephen and I had long planned to go to Orkney. In one of his notebooks there's a page titled 'Fi', with a heart drawn next to my name. It's hard to look at now, this list of things he wanted to do with me. He must have written it soon after we met because the items include 'Meet her mum' and 'Meet my parents' and we did that early on, when his dad Philip was still alive (he died in December the year we met; my own dad, Robert, had died the previous year so Stephen never got to meet him and that's a shame because they would have liked each other). Many of the places on his list we did end up visiting together, from Cornwall and Scilly to the Lake District and the Usk valley. We did move in together, we did (eventually) get married and we did have our children. But some things we never got around to doing and Orkney is one of them.

For many megalith enthusiasts, Orkney is the ultimate stone land, famous for its extraordinary Neolithic architecture – its spectacularly well-preserved stone villages and chambered tombs, its awesome stone circles and the huge ceremonial halls that have recently been unearthed and are unparalleled anywhere in Britain. Five thousand years ago, these islands 9 miles off the coast of northern Scotland were a centre of cultural innovation, from where the practice of building stone circles is thought to have spread down to southern England. People travelled by boat to Orkney from places such as Ireland and Cumbria and even continental Europe. Far from being a backwater, Neolithic Orkney was at the centre of its world.

Every year, these wind-pummelled islands in the very far north of Britain (only Shetland lies further north) experience extremes of both light and darkness. At midsummer, there are 18 hours of light each day, and even at night a lingering twilight signals that the sun is not far away. At midwinter, there are 18 hours of darkness, hemmed about with creeping dusk and, more than likely, black-bellied rain clouds that obscure the sun even in the day. Every year, the pendulum swings from darkness to light and back again, the growing or declining of light from day to day a constant reminder that nothing stays still, that everything changes and that every human life has its seasons too. Those long winter nights of the past, when there was nothing much to do but sit by a fire and listen to stories, must be one reason why Orkney is so rich in folk tales, in its legends of mermaids and selkies, of the sea-dwelling Fin Folk, and the trows who lived in the ancient mounds and whose power grew strong at midsummer and midwinter[124] – pivotal times of intense light or darkness.

If the winter solstice feels important to us now in our modern world of artificial light and central heating, how much more so must it have been for ancient people who relied directly on the sun for light, warmth and the growth of food. Many prehistoric monuments around the world seem to have been built in alignment with one or other (or both) of the solstices. There's Stonehenge, of course, with its well-known midwinter

The Light Will Come Back

sunset–midsummer sunrise axis, but many others too. Just south of Inverness, the Clava Cairns (aka Balnuaran of Clava) is a magical site with three large Bronze Age cairns each set in its own circle of standing stones, the whole prehistoric cemetery itself encircled by a ring of graceful, silvery beeches that offer children some good climbing. When we stopped there on the way to the Orkney ferry at Scrabster, I was thinking about our upcoming visit to Maeshowe and had winter solstice on my mind, so was excited when the information boards revealed that the three Clava Cairns were themselves all oriented on the winter solstice, either via a passage that would have let the light of the setting midwinter sun into the chamber or through the use of especially tall kerbstones to mark the south-west, the direction of sunset on the shortest day.

The most famous winter solstice alignment must be the one at Newgrange, the massive Neolithic passage tomb with its startling white reconstructed quartz façade which stands in a rich prehistoric landscape in the Boyne Valley in Ireland. At midwinter, the Newgrange 'roof-box' – an unusual slit in the stone above the entrance to the mound – channels a beam of the rising sun along the passage and into the chamber. As the sun rises (clouds permitting) on the mornings on and around the winter solstice, the beam widens, flooding the dark interior of the tomb with light.

And then there is Maeshowe, built on Orkney's Mainland c.3000–2700 BCE (at least a century after Newgrange) and also renowned for its winter solstice alignment and its outstanding Neolithic architecture. A bitter early April wind is blowing and the hills are shrouded in mist when Ava and I finally find

STONE LANDS

ourselves outside Maeshowe's smooth, rounded grassy mound, which in its current form (its top was once more pointy) resembles a fairy mound such as Sithean Mòr on Iona. The little gate to the passageway contributes to the impression that someone lives here and in fact someone does (or did): a mound dweller called Hogboy known for his great strength and bad temper – Maeshowe's Victorian excavator was warned about disturbing him. Alex has refused to join us, citing the bad weather and the pressures of being in the first year of his GCSEs ('I need to have a lie-in, I'm a busy man, you know'). Ava, sensing I'd be disappointed if neither child accompanied me, has bitten the bullet and come, probably lured mostly by the thought of the gift shop but nonetheless looking about her with mild interest.

This isn't like any chambered tomb I've seen before. The mound with its pinched stone mouth sits on a round platform and is encircled by a wide ditch (there's no causeway so it's not clear how the moat was crossed), and then further ringed by a bank where a stone wall and at least one standing stone (and perhaps a whole stone circle) once stood. It's as if the bones of the Old Ones left within Maeshowe were imbued with such power that they had to be kept contained within multiple rings of stone, earth and water.

Our 10 a.m. tour group shuffles into the mound down a long, austere passageway made of giant megaliths, crouching low to avoid banging our heads. There's a distinct feeling of travelling back into the past, that the monument itself is forcing us into the prayerful stance of pilgrims, just as it has forced anyone entering via this passage since it was first built. There are gasps as people unfold themselves within the sickly electric light of

The Light Will Come Back

the chamber and take in this place of ancient ritual: the four huge megaliths that stand in each corner, the impossibly neat stonework, the ancient corbelling that skilfully curves the walls inward until they stop abruptly in a modern concrete dome, the three side-cells floored and roofed with single great slabs of stone. The four massive standing stones in the main chamber have no structural function, the guide tells us, and are lightly weathered so perhaps once briefly stood outside. It may even be that they were used to mark the position of the setting midwinter sun, and that the walls of the chamber and the passage were then raised around them to ensure the monument was perfectly aligned to catch the light of sunset on the year's shortest day.

The chill air of this grand chamber is somehow not of this age, as if here the Neolithic lives on, preserved within this stone-walled, clay-skinned ancient space. I would like to come here alone, to stand still in the darkness and try to catch an echo of the people who built this place, who carefully placed stone on stone to create smooth walls and a perfectly judged corbelled roof that would still be intact today had the Vikings and the Victorians not broken in that way, who carved mysterious geometric patterns into the stonework of the passage and the side-cells. Even among a chattering tour group, it feels very weird to be inside this incredibly old building.

'Surely there could be no darker place in the bewintered world than the interior of Maeshowe,' wrote the Orcadian poet George Mackay Brown. He was describing what happens each year on the afternoon of the winter solstice (and for three weeks either side of that), when the sun drops between the two great

STONE LANDS

hills of the island of Hoy and its rays fall first on the Barnhouse Stone, 750 metres to the south-west of Maeshowe, and then reach the cairn itself, travel down the passageway and hit the back wall of the chamber, turning darkness into glorious, golden light. 'One of the light rays is caught in this stone web of death,' Mackay Brown wrote, the illumination of the dark interior 'a pledge of renewal, a cry of resurrection.'[125] Every year, on the darkest of days, the sun comes back to Maeshowe to promise the return of the light.

Set against the wall in Maeshowe's passageway is a massive slab that archaeologists believe would have been pivoted to block up the entrance, leaving a slit at the top which, like the Newgrange roof-box, could have channelled the sun's rays into a single focused beam, enhancing the midwinter solar effect for those inside. You can witness the phenomenon for yourself if you visit around winter solstice and take the 2 p.m. tour, says the guide, but due to the currently prevailing weather conditions in Orkney, there's only a 1 in 7 chance of seeing it. The weather was better in Neolithic times.

A Day of Light

It is Easter Saturday, the day after our arrival on Orkney, and I have woken to see this enchanted realm in daylight for the first time: the sky is a crazy, unfeasible, cloudless blue, crystalline sunlight bouncing off the sea loch and into our converted barn where it flickers and sparkles over the white-painted walls and ceiling as if this living room were a mermaid's grotto.

The Light Will Come Back

Oblivious, both kids are determined to have a lie-in, and that is fine by me. The stones are calling. Grabbing a banana for breakfast, I'm on my way.

Our holiday rental is only 10 minutes' drive (and this is not a coincidence) from the Mainland's 'Heart of Neolithic Orkney', where the strip of land known as the Ness of Brodgar divides the lochs of Stenness and Harray, and the two incredible stone circles of Stenness and Brodgar stand. As I drive over the hill and down towards the A965 to the yearning strains of 'Farewell to Stromness' on Spotify, with the waters of Stenness spreading out sapphire blue below me and the swans chopping up trails of diamonds as they take flight, I'm filled with such overwhelming emotion that I have to slow down while I blink away the tears.

I turn off the main road and there are the Stones of Stenness, its massive megaliths like the unfurled sails of a tall ship. And in the distance, what look like human figures up on the ridge: the Ring of Brodgar! Inconceivable to be here at last, and to be here without Stephen. I feel like my heart will burst with the beauty and sadness of it all.

Here is the colossal Watchstone, a slab standing 5.6 metres high, guarding the approach to the bridge to the Ness of Brodgar. Driving onto the narrow, stone-walled bridge, water on either side, reminds me of a dream I often had as a child of an endless pier stretching out into deep water, a committing path into the void. In the garden of the cottage by the road are two standing stones, probably not much noticed among all the archaeological treasures here. Beyond the fence is the Ness of Brodgar excavation site, where every summer for two decades archaeologists

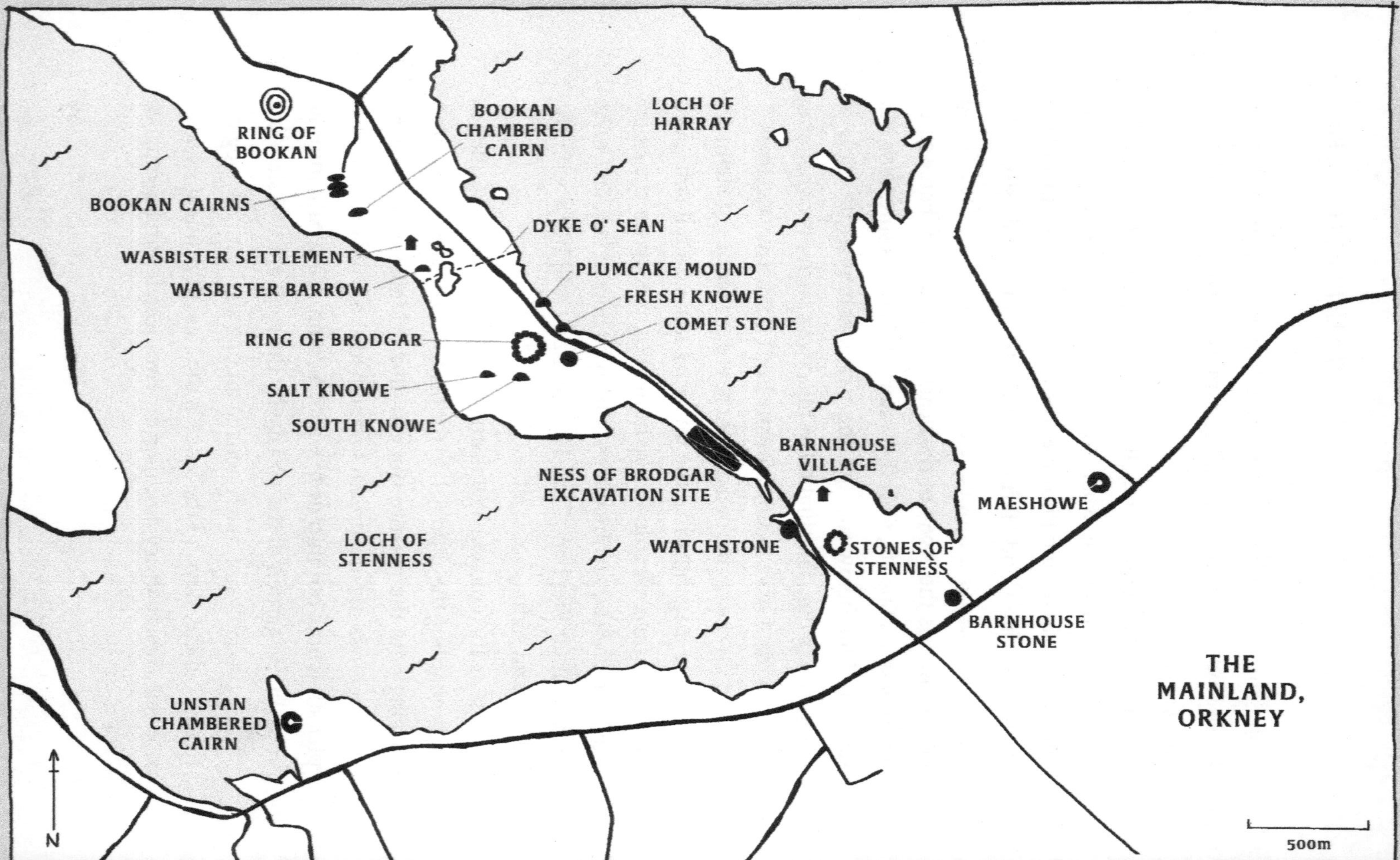
RING OF BOOKAN
BOOKAN CHAMBERED CAIRN
LOCH OF HARRAY
BOOKAN CAIRNS
DYKE O' SEAN
WASBISTER SETTLEMENT
PLUMCAKE MOUND
WASBISTER BARROW
FRESH KNOWE
COMET STONE
RING OF BRODGAR
SALT KNOWE
SOUTH KNOWE
BARNHOUSE VILLAGE
NESS OF BRODGAR EXCAVATION SITE
MAESHOWE
LOCH OF STENNESS
WATCHSTONE
STONES OF STENNESS
BARNHOUSE STONE
THE MAINLAND, ORKNEY
UNSTAN CHAMBERED CAIRN
N
500m

The Light Will Come Back

have been unearthing an astounding complex of huge Neolithic halls.

Duckboards lead from the Ring of Brodgar car park across marshy ground towards the circle. The puddles between the reeds glint in the morning sun as if a hoard of gold coins is lying there. I'm in a daze. There's a ditch all around the Brodgar stones, so I scramble down into the soggy mulch and then climb up to the circle, the stones hanging in the sky above me. As I enter the circle, a rabbit's tail flashes and the creature scampers into the ditch. It feels like a sign.

The 27 surviving upright stones of the Ring of Brodgar are set in little clusters, the gaps in the circle evoking the ghosts of the lost megaliths – perhaps 60 (or even more) of them in total once stood here. It's an expansive and airy circle, set on sloping ground and enclosing an arena of wild, heathery moorland from which comes a great twittering, whirring and chirruping of birds and insects. I walk around sunwise, touching every stone and every stump of a stone; there are many stumps protruding from the earth and sometimes the snapped-off pieces of megaliths are lying next to them.

There's something very human about this place, the stones like people (exceptionally tall ones, sure) with all their individual characteristics and imperfections, gathered for a ritual or a negotiation or a dance. In the upper part of the circle, where most stones survive, the shadows reach out from one stone almost to the next, as if they're trying to touch one another. Some of the stones are planed like a pack of cards, and in some cases the pack is well worn and falling open, the cards splayed apart.

The Ring of Brodgar (or at least its ditch – the stone circle could be earlier) was built *c.*2600–2400 BCE, maybe 500 years after the Stones of Stenness and perhaps a millennium after the earliest confirmed activity at the Ness of Brodgar complex. Looking out from the top of the circle, I get a feel for how the monuments on the peninsula, built over a span of hundreds of years, interact with, and draw power from, the landscape. The horizon, an unbroken circle of low hills, defines a vast natural stage for the sites now as it did five millennia ago, below the great sweeping dome of the sky. The sense of space is extraordinary and this cannot have changed since prehistoric times, even if some of what is now the Loch of Stenness was then marsh, and if what seems now an isolated, empty location was then busy with people, filled with their houses and temples, fires and livestock. Now as then, the raised ridge of the Ness of Brodgar has the appearance of a ceremonial path along which monuments are placed, today running between two lochs while in prehistoric times it marked a dry route through shifting wetlands. From the bottom of the Ring of Brodgar, the twin hills of Hoy are barely visible, but as I rise up the circle, they rise too, and from the top of the circle they dominate the horizon, as if the very point of the circle is to reveal them.

Another woman is walking around the circle, closely examining the uprights one by one, stopping every so often to place her forehead onto stone – she reminds me of me, being scruffy and middle aged and clearly taking a keen interest in megaliths. When we cross paths, she asks if I'd like my picture taken next to the slab that I'm leaning against, enjoying the feel of dry, gritty prehistoric stone against my palms. 'Yes but I'm the world's most

The Light Will Come Back

unphotogenic person,' I say, and she replies, 'But it's all about the stones', and she's not wrong there.

Archaeologists led by Jane Downes and Colin Richards have identified seven different types of sandstone at the Ring of Brodgar, indicating that the megaliths were brought here from at least seven different quarries. They also point out that the sockets of the Brodgar stones are much shallower than those of the Stenness circle, implying (as with the upland circles of Calanais) that they were put up relatively quickly, without concern for longevity – strange given the immense effort that would have gone into cutting Brodgar's enormous ditch from solid bedrock. The archaeologists' suggestion is that it was the *building* of the site that mattered (not the finished project), the different stones representing – and brought here by – different communities, the creation of the circle a way of binding these groups together.[126]

In the spirit of building community, I go to fetch Alex and Ava and they agree to a walk around the Ness of Brodgar with reasonable good humour. At the Ring of Brodgar, Ava finds a stone with a scattering of depressions that she says could be ancient people's fingerprints, fitting her own fingertips into them. We eat a Co-op meal deal on the top of Salt Knowe, an enigmatic Neolithic mound close by the Ring of Brodgar which is as big as Maeshowe but, like Silbury Hill, contains nothing inside. Ava runs down the mound to pick daisies and do cartwheels on the grass. Then we go down to skim pebbles on Stenness loch – Alex is the best of the three of us, well trained in skimming by his dad.

The Stenness stone circle has a different atmosphere: less human than the frail, crumbling stones of Brodgar, more

STONE LANDS

polished and perfect, as if the massive slabs had been laser cut for a modern art gallery. The stones jut from the earth like enormous scalpels, their blades glinting in the sun: an aesthetic of strength and power. Incredible how sharp-edged and pristine the stones look considering how very ancient this circle is. The ditch has recently been dated to around 3000–2900 BCE,[127] which gives the stone circle a date that roughly matches Castlerigg's. It may be that the ditch was dug to enclose stones that were already standing, in which case the stones would be much older. Either way, this could be the first stone circle ever built in Britain.

There could have originally been ten or 11 stones in the Stenness circle; three giants survive, the tallest close to 6 metres high, plus a fourth much smaller, crooked and possibly inauthentic stone. Inside the arc of megaliths are two smaller uprights next to a prone slab: the remains of a 'dolmen' that was constructed in 1906 out of the remains of an unknown prehistoric setting. There's also a stone-lined hearth, which is strange to see inside a stone circle and makes me imagine the dramatic fiery rituals that might have taken place here.

Somewhere close by stood the famous holed Stone of Odin, through which people used to clasp hands to seal marriages and business agreements. Babies would be passed through the hole to ensure lifelong good health, and crippled limbs were inserted in the hope of a cure. It was destroyed in 1814 by the locally despised tenant landowner Captain W. Mackay, and the last surviving piece of it, the holed section which had been used as an anchor for a mill-shaft, was broken up in the 1940s.

I'm awestruck by the sheer massiveness of the three supersized Stenness megaliths. It would have been incredibly challenging to quarry, transport and erect these stones using whatever limited equipment they had (perhaps wooden sleds and rollers, ropes, trestles made of stacked stones, etc.), requiring a huge investment of time, labour, resources and faith. I'm impressed by what Colin Richards has written about the grave risks involved: not just the danger of being physically crushed at any point during the process, but also the risk of public loss of face, political catastrophe, spiritual ruin. If anything had gone wrong, the consequences for the people who tried and failed to raise these stones could have been dire.[128] Nevertheless, they did try.

These standing stones tell us that ancient people were prepared to risk everything; and that sometimes they succeeded, while at other times – as is shown by fallen and broken megaliths found at prehistoric quarries and standing stone sites – they failed. I find this comforting. It makes me feel better about trying to write this book, which involves all sorts of risks. It also makes me think about the risks involved in love. There is always the danger that you will invest your heart only to have it broken. Love often does lead to loss and pain, but love remains a risk worth taking. We have to screw our courage to the sticking place, and take some risks. Otherwise what is the point of it all?

Alex and Ava's patience is taxed by the minimal remains of Barnhouse village, and by Stenness they're totally fed up, so I take them home. At dusk I return for the third time that day, alone. Brodgar is utterly enchanting. As I clamber into the ditch, the golden light on the back of the stones fades, and a soft purple glow settles over the circle. There are other people here but they are speaking in hushed voices, slipping in and out of the stones, barely present. Through the silhouettes of stones I watch the sky as the cloud trails thicken and disperse. The sun is hidden but then, in a moment of heart-clutching beauty, it drops below the veils and its beams pour like honey onto the Loch of Stenness. Another day is ending, another day is coming – there's always this flow of new days, of new beginnings, for so long as we have life. What a gift it is just to be alive! The moorland is a shimmering plain of gold and the stone people are in their circle, holding the power, keeping the faith.

The Ness at Midwinter

What was it about the Ness of Brodgar peninsula that drew people here in prehistory? Stone circles, standing stones, barrows, mounds... And then there's the Ness of Brodgar complex itself, which was approaching its 20th and final season of excavation when I came to Orkney. The site was only open to the public for a few weeks in summer so I couldn't visit it, but each time I crossed the peninsula on my way from the Stones of Stenness to the Ring of Brodgar and back, I passed the fenced-off area of raised ground that I knew concealed layer upon layer of buildings that in their size and complexity were unique in the Neolithic of western Europe. Archaeological exploration had only begun here in 2003, after ploughing exposed a worked and notched slab, and the subsequent excavation was to change our understanding of Neolithic Orkney. The archipelago was already famous for being home to numerous Neolithic stone-built dwellings, but the buildings within the Ness complex were much larger and more elaborate – more hall than house, with mighty walls and roofs of stone tiles. The largest collection of sherds of Grooved Ware pottery ever found has been unearthed here, as well as thousands of decorated stones featuring 'butterfly' and other incised motifs, and even traces of paint.[129] And the mind-blowing reality is that only a fraction of the 2.5 hectare site has been revealed: geophysical surveys indicate that below ground there are more structures extending in all directions, and older buildings underlie the ones that have been exposed.

It's thought that the ceremonial complex at the Ness of Brodgar was a place of feasting and gathering, drawing people from all over Orkney and far beyond. And maybe there was a special connection with midwinter. The Orkney folklorist and archaeologist Sigurd Towrie, who is closely involved with the dig, points out that the peninsula is roughly aligned with (in opposite directions) the midsummer sunset–midwinter sunrise axis, and offers an especially magnificent view of winter solstice sunrise (clouds permitting, of course), the spit of land marking out the point in the hilly south-eastern horizon where the midwinter sun will finally appear. Sigurd wonders if the ridge's natural solstice alignment was one of the reasons that drew people to the Ness of Brodgar in prehistory, just as it was the midsummer sunrise–midwinter sunset orientation of chalk stripes on the ground at Stonehenge that led to the construction of the Avenue and the solstice alignment of the stone circle.

When I contacted Sigurd to ask if the excavation had unearthed any more signs of a midwinter alignment, he said,

STONE LANDS

'None of the buildings excavated so far have anything that could be considered as alignments to winter solstice sunrise or sunset. However, we're looking at building on top of building on top of building, so that may not be the case for the earlier unexcavated structures.'

I asked him how people were feeling about the prospect of the excavations ending after so long. 'It will be a miss, the site having played such a major role in many people's lives since 2003. However, it is the time to stop. There's plenty of archaeology left, but that will be for future generations to look at. We've got the vital post-excavation work to concentrate on now.'

I was hoping for selfish reasons that the site might be kept open for visitors, but the structures, Sigurd said, would have to be reburied at the end of the 2024 season. 'The stone used to build them laminates when exposed to the elements. Left uncovered there would be nothing left in a few years.'

There's something very poignant about the thought that these incredible remains will be sealed once more within the earth, not lost but preserved for future generations of archaeologists to uncover and interrogate with even more sophisticated techniques than they have now, to conjure up through their modern magic the deep past once more.

Tales of Stones and the Turning Year

Born on a small farm by the sea at Tankerness in East Mainland, Tom Muir is a storyteller, author and folklorist intent on preserving Orkney's rich heritage of folk tales. He's also an

The Light Will Come Back

archaeologist who took part in Colin Richards's 2008 dig at the Ring of Brodgar: 'The first Orcadian to be at the bottom of the ditch for 5,000 years'. He described to me how they dug down below the level of a previous excavation to reach the blue clay at the base of the ditch, and how it became clear that the ditch had been originally created by digging a series of pits, presumably positioned in a circle via a rope extended from a central point, these pits then extended and joined 'like a string of sausages'. Tom was used to having to lug buckets of earth out of a trench, so the elevator that took the excavated soil up to the surface in 2008 felt like an indulgence. He speculates that Salt Knowe could have been built from the earth that came out of the ditch. 'The spoil would've had to go somewhere. If you're expending a lot of time and energy and expense into digging a ditch around a monument which has significance for you, then maybe the rock and earth you're digging out might be considered in some ways sacred or important. You wouldn't just dump it somewhere. Maybe that is why Salt Knowe was built, and maybe Silbury Hill was something along the same lines.'

This explanation of the 'empty' Neolithic mounds Salt Knowe and Silbury Hill makes sense to me! I ask Tom what he thinks about midwinter in Orkney and he tells me about the three standing stones in Orkney that have legends linking them to New Year's Eve. 'At midnight on Hogmanay, the Watch Stone by the Ness of Brodgar bridge will move from its position to take a drink from Stenness Loch. And nobody can see it; if you try, something will always happen to stop you. Then there's the Stone o' Quoybune, which goes down to the Loch of Boardhouse at Hogmanay, but it kills anybody that tries to see it. And the

STONE LANDS

Yetnasteen in Rousay is the Tigger of standing stones, because on New Year's Eve it bounces down to the shore for a drink and then bounces back in just three big bounds.'

The story associated with the Ring of Brodgar is about giants: 'They all got together and danced in a big circle. There was a fiddle playing and all the giants were dancing. And they were enjoying themselves so much, they lost track of time, the sun rose and they were all turned to stone.'

The circle of giants became the Ring of Brodgar, and the fiddler became the stone circle's outlier: the Comet Stone. In the 19th century, Tom says, people used to doff their caps when they passed the Comet Stone, though when they were asked why they did it, they could not say. 'It was just something that had always been done, and they were carrying on the tradition.' At that time, the stone was known as the Ulie Stane ('oily stone'), perhaps hinting at a long-forgotten practice of ritually anointing this stone with fish oil.

There's a wonderful folk tale Tom knows that encapsulates the idea of an eternal back-and-forth between summer and winter, the ever-tilting balance of darkness and light.

'We have this story about the Mother of the Sea. It was believed that she rules the sea in the summer, and she calms the storms and gives life to all the creatures in the sea. But during the course of the year she starts to weaken and her arch-enemy Teran, the evil male spirit who is held captive under the sea throughout the summer, breaks his bonds and the two of them fight. This is the time of the autumn equinox. We get storms about September, with gales and heavy seas, and that's the two of them fighting under the sea. Then Teran defeats the Mother of the Sea and drives her onto the land, where she has to live in exile throughout the winter while Teran rules the sea. He brings with him destruction and death. Teran's reign is when the boats are wrecked and the food is in short supply. He unleashes the Nuckelavee, a hideous creature, half-human, half-horse, with no skin on its body and a hatred for mankind, who will kill anyone that it comes across.

'But during the course of the winter, Teran starts to lose his power, and the Mother of the Sea grows in strength. At springtime, she goes back into the sea and the two of them fight again at spring equinox, with more gales and heavy seas. This time the Mother of the Sea defeats Teran and binds him at the bottom of the ocean. She locks up the Nuckelavee again, and brings calm to the waters and gives life to all the sea-creatures again. Life is good while the Mother of the Sea rules.'[130]

It's an old tale, Tom believes, and perhaps a very old one because it's definitely not Christian. 'You're not going to have the world and everything created by God in six days, and then he rules over everything except the sea which is ruled by a goddess. That's heresy. You'd have found yourself on the wrong side of a box of matches if you started saying that.' Nor is this folk tale preserved among the Viking legends, so where does it come from? Perhaps it dates back to very ancient times.

The idea that some of the beliefs of prehistory might be preserved in folk tales still told today sends a shiver down my spine. Whatever its age, the message of the Mother of the Sea's story seems a perennially relevant one: everything changes, all the time. Winter triumphs over summer, then summer over winter. And so it goes on, from darkness to light and back again.

STONE LANDS

The Tides of Time

We are finding our way forward, together. There are three of us now, not four, and in Orkney we knit ourselves together as a team. Alex is now keen to assist with the car navigation and the Spotify management, and when he does this Ava is on alert in the back seat, intervening when she feels he's too engrossed in his phone, which is often. We are on the lookout for seals, because seals make us think of Stephen, agile in his wetsuit, swimming and surfing. There was that time at Orford Ness, the former atomic test site on the Suffolk coast that's now a nature reserve, when he took off his trousers and shirt and jumped into the sea for an impromptu dip, while the rest of us stayed shivering on the shingle, and then we were all pointing and shouting because close to him a seal's head had popped up. It stayed there, bobbing and staring like a star-struck teenager while he swam. Stephen had been charmed and flattered by the seal's attention: 'wonderful experience', he wrote in his birding notebook, alongside mention of lapwing, egret and herons on the marsh and meadow pipit on the scrubby heath. 'Fi and lots on the beach saw' – he needed the evidence of our eyes as proof that it had really happened. I'd wondered at the time if a selkie had come to lure him away. And if ever there was a place haunted by selkies, it is Orkney.

We go cairn-hunting together. A Neolithic chambered cairn is definitely more fun for kids than standing stones and Orkney has around 90 of them, some in a mind-blowing state of preservation. At Unstan, Alex and Ava rush ahead onto the promontory that sticks out into the Loch of Stenness and burrow eagerly into the stone passage like rabbit-hunting terriers. You have to crouch and squeeze between the stone walls and then you find yourself in a light and spacious chamber that's lit by a window in the modern roof. Green algae-stained slabs scratched with Victorian graffiti subdivide the chamber into stalls, where bodies were left in a crouching position to decay and bones were heaped up in piles.

We visit the Dwarfie Stane on Hoy, in the desolate glacier-sculpted Rackwick Glen. Behind the monument the land sweeps up to meet the immense vertical sheet of rock that is known as Dwarfie Hamars; opposite is Ward Hill, the highest point on Hoy and in all Orkney. The earth is barren, treeless, shrivelled, unremittingly brown. Apart from the tarmacked road and the duckboards snaking across this boggy moonscape up to the stone chamber – and the pylons marching across the lower slopes of Ward Hill – there are no signs of the modern world. Perhaps this scene would have been perceived as just as weird, otherworldly and awe-inspiring 5,000 years ago.

The Dwarfie Stane is the only one of its kind in all Britain: a rock-cut chambered tomb (if it ever was a tomb), hollowed out from a single massive bunker-like block of sandstone. It must have been painstaking toil to chip an entrance passage and two chambers out of the rock, shaping what looks like a stone pillow in one of them, and then grind the interior surface beautifully smooth. It was pleasantly dry when we crawled inside, no trace of moss or mould though the surrounding peatland is sodden.

It may be that the Neolithic builders of the Dwarfie Stane were inspired sound engineers as well as skilled masons. Dr

STONE LANDS

Aaron Watson's experiments here in the 1990s showed that the stone chamber amplified humming or singing so intensely that listeners outside perceived the monument to be shaking, while the beating of drums outside the Stane echoed off the surrounding rock faces like a peal of thunder.[131] It must have been incredible to witness. My own acoustic experiments inside the tomb were cut short at Alex and Ava's embarrassed urging as another visitor was approaching up the duckboard path.

At Wideford Hill chambered cairn on the Mainland, you descend into the darkness of the tall corbelled chamber via a trapdoor in the roof and a ladder. It took us a long time to work out that the trapdoor opens by sliding and not by lifting. The entrances to the side-cells are low and you have to get right down on the muddy gravel to crawl into them. Even more fun is Taversöe Tuick on Rousay, a double-storey cairn with two burial chambers built one on top of the other, the interior luminous with green lichen and linked by a ladder through a hole in the flagstones. Alex was down the ladder first: 'I quite like this one,' he called up from the lower chamber, which is pretty enthusiastic from him.

Of all the chambered cairns on Orkney, perhaps the most awesome is Midhowe, on the south-western shore of Rousay. The seascape is especially dramatic here, a steep grassy hillside sloping down to shelves of jet-black rock, where knife-edged geos cut deeply into the land, and seals tumble through the waves. This lonely stretch of coast is littered with traces of past lives: an Iron Age broch, the square foundation of a medieval hall, a 16th-century church, and then what looks like a big modern barn concealing the biggest surprise of all: a Neolithic

The Light Will Come Back

Ship of Death. The vast chambered cairn is elongated and rounded like an upturned hull, its mound of stacked stones faced with herringbone-style walling and split down its middle by a long passageway, with pairs of upright slabs forming stalls. In these stalls, bodies were left on stone benches to decay, the bones then mixed up and arranged in heaps throughout the cairn. Overhead walkways take you right over the monument, to look straight down into this Neolithic ferry to the afterlife.

Across the valley from Wideford Hill on the Mainland is the Cuween Hill cairn, or the Tomb of the Dogs as it's often called, named in modern times for the 24 dogs whose skulls were found here. This site was recommended to us by Bernie Bell and her husband Mike, who we met on the white sands at Evie on the Mainland's north coast. We struck up a conversation and it turned out that Bernie and Mike had moved to Orkney about 20 years ago and ever since have been exploring the ancient sites here. Mike writes poetry about megaliths, and Bernie often writes about standing stones for the *Orkney News*. We must go to the Tomb of the Dogs, she said. 'I used to avoid it, thinking it was linked to dog-killers, but our little dog Ben didn't seem fazed, so I thought it must be OK.' Now it is one of her and Mike's best-loved places.

They also love the Tomb of the Eagles high on the cliffs of Isbister on South Ronaldsay, the site named for the bones and talons of sea eagles found here alongside the remains of at least 324 people, but it closed during Covid and has still not reopened. On their last visit, just after lockdown, Bernie and Mike found the entrance to the cairn blocked off. They poured a libation of whisky onto the stonework as they watched the sunset and said

STONE LANDS

goodbye to the place – they had a feeling they would not be able to go there again.

Bernie sent me links to some of her fascinating megalith-themed articles, including one with a photo of her leaning against one of the Brodgar stones.[132] 'Here's something if you're interested in whether folk see the stones as healing places,' she wrote. 'For years now, I've rested against this stone when my back has been hurting, and it is always eased. I'm not claiming to know why or how, but it eases my back, and that's what matters to me.'

At Cuween Hill, I crawled into the cairn and sat in the darkness, watching the light fall through the passageway onto the old stones. I peered into the side-cells using the torch of my phone, and in one of them I stood up and put my hand on a little shelf at about chin height and felt the moss and the damp, the chill of this very old place. The torchlight revealed an entire corbelled ceiling – probably the original prehistoric roof. So strange and moving to think of the people who lived close by, who built this tomb and whose work outlasted them by thousands of years, connecting them with us who live today.

When someone dies, at first it's like they've just left the room. You can't believe they've really gone and you keep thinking of things you need to tell them, keep trying to call them back. There's something that needs fixing – a lost wifi connection, a games platform upgrade, a child's anxiety – and instinctively you reach out for them, only to be reminded, with renewed despair, that they're not there. They are not anywhere: an impossible truth that must be relearned again and again. Day and night are

The Light Will Come Back

pierced by these torturous moments of realisation and there's no respite.

You are sailing along the shore and you're waving at them. They're running along the sand waving back and calling to you. Surely it must be possible to reach them. They're so close that you can almost touch them, but you can't reach them and it's excruciating. This is the culmination of your journey and theirs: you in the boat calling to them, and them unreachable on the shore.

Then one day you realise that the tide has taken your boat far away from the shore and you've reached a new land where the person you've lost has never lived. It turns out that your journey hasn't come to an end, and that those years you spent with them are just one stretch of the terrain you will cross from birth to death. Only, you haven't left them behind. They're in the boat with you and wherever you go now, they will go too.

Time flows on, taking us with it. There are tides in the lives of people and those tides cannot be held back, no more than the moon or the sun can be stopped in their journeying across the sky through the days, months and years, through the decades, centuries and millennia. The cycles of day and night, of summer and winter, of life and death, structure our lives now as they did the lives of people 5,000 years ago.

I am crawling towards the cliff edge above the Old Man of Hoy, the stone guardian of the flank of Orkney, as the wind does its best to push me into oblivion. Gripped between finger and thumb are a few tiny strands of a lock of Stephen's hair that I cut from his head in hospital after he died and have carried with me in my purse ever since. The last remnants of his body

STONE LANDS

as it was in life. Like many climbers, he'd had a dream of one day getting up this 137-metre sandstone stack rising sheer from the sea, an iconic and difficult climb. I think maybe this was why we never went to Orkney together; he'd wanted to be ready to climb the Old Man and he never was.

He would have loved it here, I tell the children, explaining that I want to leave behind a few of the precious strands of his hair. The words catch in my throat but I manage to get them out.

'Dear Stephen, you're here at last,' I whisper as I inch forward and let the wind take the strands from my fingers. 'I love you . . . Go on then . . . get to the top.'

On our last evening in Orkney, I take a moment in between stuffing the bags and loading up the car in preparation for an early start, to stand at the edge of the darkening bay. The sky and loch are swathed in purple and blue silk, and white seabirds (Arctic terns, I think) skim the water, threading lines of white ripples through the shimmering silk, then soaring high. And then I see them: two, three and more rounded heads in the water . . . ten of them, maybe more. The bay is full of seals. Speaking softly but urgently into my phone, I summon Alex and Ava, and they come and stand by me, marvelling and slightly impatient.

When we get back to London, it is at least 15°C warmer than in Scotland and a mass of greenery has sprung up beside the pavements and in front gardens. Spring is here at last. I turn the key in the front door and for a moment, after our week of absence, I smell the house as others must smell it. This smell of home is deeply familiar, though mostly I don't notice it, and it summons up a thousand memories from different eras of the past: Alex and Ava as babies, as toddlers, as growing children; the friends and family who have walked through this door; and, of course, Stephen and all the returns home we made together. The flood of memories, the sense of loss, is intense: painful and joyful at once. The strongest impression of all is that Stephen is *here*. He has not gone anywhere; he lives on in this house, an essential part of what makes it a home. He has been with me all through our trip to Orkney but I had not expected him to be so present when we returned, to find him waiting for us.

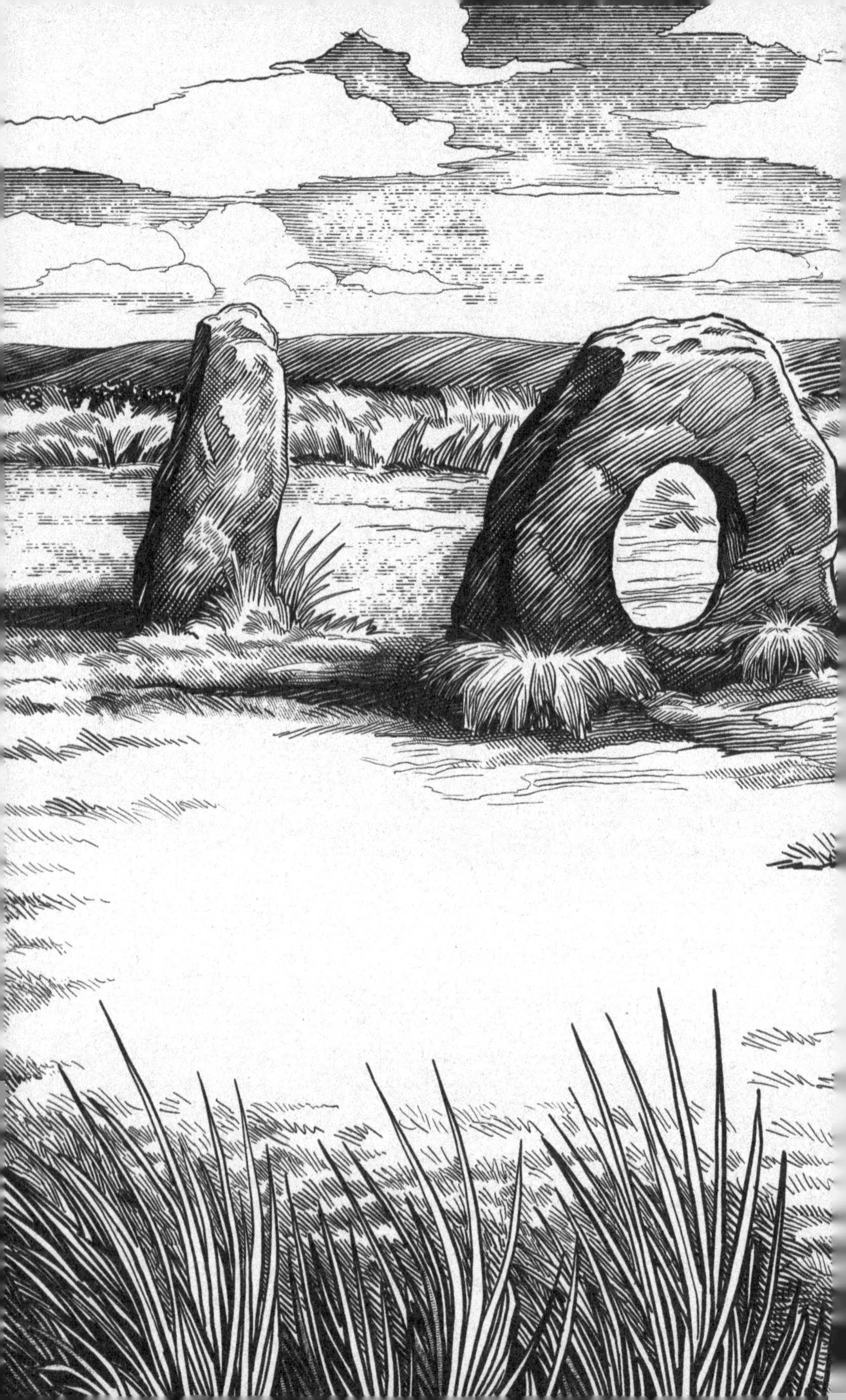

Chapter 11

THIS IS A WORLD OF WONDER

Stones of West Penwith, CORNWALL

THERE'S A VIDEO I SHOT, a few years ago now, of Stephen, Alex and Ava crawling through the Mên-an-Tol. First goes Stephen, long limbed and slender, placing his hands on stone and earth with the practised efficiency of a climber. He passes easily through the hole in the megalith and stands gracefully, shaking out his shoulders and lifting his bespectacled face to the wind and the sun. Then little Alex follows, and even littler Ava. There's a short delay during which I must have handed the camera to Stephen, and then I appear on screen, grinning from ear to ear, and I too crawl through the stone and stand tall, opening myself to the breeze and the feeling of rebirth. It is midday and the sunward faces of the holed stone and its two flanking pillars are bleached white, while the cloud shadows cut strangely black across the moor, like splashes of paint that expose what we take to be reality as an artist's illusion. Shadows

STONE LANDS

that remind us that the darkness is always present, even at high noon, and that make the colours of gorse and grass, of our bright summer clothes and the cornflower-blue dome of the sky all the more rich and intense. Open heathland runs up to the rim of the great bowl in which Mên-an-Tol is set, and on the horizon the engine house of Ding Dong mine sticks up its finger, a 19th-century manifestation of the age-old human impulse to mark our presence in the world with stone.

Like countless numbers have done before us, as the large patch of worn, bare earth around the holed stone attests, we have completed the Mên-an-Tol ritual – or at least our version of it. Sunlight glimmers in the hole through which we have all just passed, catching the threads of quartz in the granite, and projecting a second hole onto the red earth. A portal of sunlight into the otherworld, perhaps. We are all wearing sturdy hiking boots – even four-year-old Ava has a tiny pair of them – ready for a good day out tramping the moorland. It is our first visit to the enchanted realm of West Penwith, and there are to be many more.

The Land's End peninsula, or West Penwith as it's also known (the name persisting from one of the old administrative hundreds of Cornwall), is a stone land characterised by granite and by an incredible density of ancient sites, the highest concentration of them surviving here, it is said, in all Europe. Now that Lyonesse is under water, this is the furthest west you can travel on the English mainland before hitting the sea, and like other land's ends – Finisterre, Pembrokeshire – it is a place apart, a magical region of folklore and legend, witches and piskies, holy wells and standing stones. This land of granite can also, despite

This is a World of Wonder

all its magic, be hard and unrelenting for those who struggle to make a living here, a place of poverty, of unemployment, low wages and homelessness. Experiencing West Penwith only as a holiday-maker, I have been privileged to know it as a place where it's possible, perhaps more than anywhere else, to feel the wonder of the world and the joy of being alive.

The Mên-an-Tol ('holed stone') may be surprisingly small at first sight, giving the impression of being a scale model of itself, but it is magnificently weird and, like the Odin Stone, its destroyed holed counterpart which once stood on Orkney's Mainland, generously endowed with folklore. It's not even clear what sort of a monument this is. Today the site looks like a row of three stones, with the holed slab set in the centre, but there are other megaliths here: one or two further standing stones and six fallen ones (some of which are buried), and some of the stones have been moved. Archaeologists have speculated that this is all that remains of a circle of 20–22 stones.[133]

One face of the holed stone is flat and smooth, while the other one is more rounded and bevelled, implying that it originally lay flat at the top of a rock stack with the rounded face uppermost, a rock basin catching rainwater that eventually wore the hole right through. There is another holed stone very like it still in situ on Zennor Carn.[134] It's been pointed out that most water basins will erode through their sides rather than through the base, so naturally holed stones like these are very rare, and the Mên-an-Tol will most likely have been perceived as special by the people who brought it here.[135]

We'll never know how the stone was used in prehistory, but there's plenty of more recent folklore about its healing and even

STONE LANDS

oracular powers. When the antiquary William Borlase visited the Mên-an-Tol in 1749, a local farmer told him that people would crawl through the hole as a cure for back or limb pain, and pass through children suffering from rickets. They also used the stone for divination, leaving brass pins crossed on its top edge and returning to observe whether the pins were as before or moved or vanished.[136] In 1870, the folklorist William Bottrell recorded a custom of crawling nine times widdershins through the hole for the cure of lumbago, sciatica and other 'cricks and pains in the back'; for this reason the Mên-an-Tol was known as the Crick Stone.[137]

The weather changes fast on this peninsula jutting out into the churning Atlantic. One minute we have blue skies, the next the horizon is dissolving and rain is coming down in great drenching gusts. There's a short video, just a few seconds long and blurred with raindrops, of Stephen, Alex and Ava, their hair plastered against their scalps, crouching against the ancient wall of stone and earth at the bottom of Mên Scryfa's field. Alex has his T-shirt half-pulled over his head; Ava is squirming away from the rain, burrowing into her dress, a pretty summer one patterned with sunflowers. Stephen is looking directly at the camera – at me – but he's not smiling, he looks a little sad and it's as if he has a sense of what will happen. It's as if he can see me right now, across the years. Make the most of it, he seems to be saying: this is our one life and it's wondrous.

A track leads through the grass up to Mên Scryfa, which stands tall on the horizon, piercing the sky and from this angle matching the height of Carn Galva, the twin-peaked rock outcrop peeping balefully over the horizon. Mên Scryfa means

This is a World of Wonder

'engraved stone', named for the Latin inscription carved on it some time in the 5th to 8th centuries: RIALOBRANI CUNO-VALI FILI – 'Rialobranus [or perhaps 'Royal Raven'], son of Cunovalus'. We trace with our fingers the lettering of this memorial carved onto a stone that could have been standing for 2,000 years before Royal Raven died. The stone is thickly crusted with spiky sea-green lichen and knobbled with glittering quartz.

Then on to the Nine Maidens – and oh the joy of tracking a stone circle through water-logged gorse and purple-belled heather, the larks singing their hearts out, the children darting ahead, hopping over the boggy bits! The tower of Ding Dong on the far horizon is a signpost leading us onwards. We glimpse a standing stone and leave the main path to follow this clue. The stone turns out to be part of a destroyed cairn: a discernible circle of old stones, but not the one we're looking for.

And at last... there they are! The Nine Maidens, as the stones of Boskednan circle are known, although there have never been nine of them. Whether there were 19 or 20 or 22 stones in the circle originally (no one seems to know), 11 of them survive today, standing or lying on the ground. These granite pillars crown the rising land, encircled by soggy ground in which the clouds float and the sun is captured. We are in the heart of the moor, the far-off sea visible as a swathe of deeper blue cradled by hills, no sound of cars or other humans, only the delirious lark song, like a tumbling mountain stream. The sense of peace and spaciousness is wonderfully uplifting. When I turn to look back the way we've come, I see how the tallest upright stones of the ruined circle appear to offer a gateway to Carn Galva, which seen from here dominates the moorland. The portal stones

STONE LANDS

framing Carn Galva glint silver, bright against that sinister black pyramid across the gorse.

Rock Deities on the Skyline

'The life of a region depends ultimately on its geologic substratum,' wrote Ithell Colquhoun in *The Living Stones*, her magical memoir of post-war West Penwith; for the structure of the rocks not only determines the plants, animals and types of humans who live there, but also the land's psychic nature.[138] And it is that stern stuff granite that defines the character of this peninsula, creating the towering cliffs and the carns, fantastically weathered rock stacks that command the skyline like giants' castles.

Archaeologists Christopher Tilley and Wayne Bennett believe that William Borlase, though much derided for his bloodthirsty speculations about Druidic human sacrifice at prehistoric sites, was not so far off the mark when he wrote of Cornish outcrops 'of that grandeur, remarkable shape and surprising position, as can leave us in no doubt but that they must have been the Deities of people addicted so much to the superstition of worshipping Rocks'. The hills and tors, Tilley and Bennett suggest, could have been seen as places of spiritual power, each with its own supernatural character. And perhaps Neolithic dolmens such as Chûn Quoit and Mulfra Quoit were deliberately constructed to replicate the appearance of the carns. Breaking the skyline from a distance, these stone-walled chambers with their huge single capstones do look remarkably similar to the natural rock stacks.[139]

This is a World of Wonder

It is at Tregeseal circle, on Kenidjack Common outside St Just, that the awesome power of West Penwith's granite tors is most apparent. Above the stone circle the moorland rises straight to Carn Kenidjack, a crazy eruption of rock that rules over the naked northern skyline, its boulders heaped up like the towers of a ruined citadel. There is absolutely nothing else up there but a communications mast, a weedy modern upstart, and it's impossible not to be impressed by the weird, grim cluster of massive boulders looming above. Carn Kenidjack is called the 'hooting carn', for the wailing the wind is said to make blowing through its rocks; and the common below it, a sea of gorse and heather in which a stone circle, a row of holed stones and several tumuli are set, was once thought to be haunted, a place of demons and malevolent fairies. Even the miners were scared to cross it at night, it was said, for fear of the Devil who rode wild horses there in pursuit of lost souls.[140]

Of all the stone circles of West Penwith, Tregeseal is the one I have visited most often, and usually alone and at dusk. Since that first summer camping trip, we came back to Cornwall year after year to rent a cottage in St Just for the October half-term; and after a day out, the kids would settle down with their screens, Stephen would get in some guitar practice and I would go for a run. This run always involved an ancient site: to Ballowall Barrow above the cliffs west of St Just, or through the Cot valley to the cairns on the coastal path (where I once encountered a woman who was walking from St Ives to Plymouth and had pitched her tent inside one of the cairns, unbothered by the idea of ghosts), or – most frequently – north-west to the stones of Kenidjack Common.

STONE LANDS

I run past the plen-an-gwary, the medieval amphitheatre where miracle plays were once performed, past St Just's church with its ancient crosses, its 14th-century tower glowing pink in the fading light, down the steep footpath to the jabber of jackdaws and the urgent cawing of crows, and up into the country along a lane fringed by sinister giant rhubarb. I run through Hailglower Farm and onto the moor that rises to Carn Kenidjack, and there's a tinge of fear to add excitement: the fear of dogs running out from the farm, of cows blocking access to the stones, of the desolate common and who I might meet there, of wraiths rising from the barrows, of being caught out on the moor after dark.

There were once two stone circles here, and possibly even three, but just one circle survives today, its stones arranged in a higgledy-piggledy, somewhat inauthentic way, dipping down into a hollow created by 19th-century quarrying. Inauthentic or not, who cares, these stones seem alive and conscious to me, as if they've just come together to form their untidy ring. I walk around the circle touching each one in turn and notice they all have pointed tops, as if they were large, friendly dogs reaching up to snuffle their noses into my palm.

The sun gilds the granite pillars and their shadows reach into the interior of the circle. The luminous russets, garnets and golds of bracken, gorse and grass glow warm and rich, like stained glass. I sit within the circle, listening to the larks and the crows, watching the cloud shadows flit across the moor. Sun follows shadow follows sun, and the stones stay calmly present through it all.

This is a World of Wonder

I run along footpaths through bracken and gorse, past broken-down burial mounds, to find a row of four holed standing stones, and another holed stone a little further north. This is the Kenidjack stone row, the only row of prehistoric holed stones known in Britain. I ponder the delightful mystery of these holes. They're much smaller than the Mên-an-Tol opening, certainly not big enough to pass a baby through, and just a few inches off the ground – too low to sight anything through. I can just about insert my hand into them, but someone else (with a bigger hand) might not be able to. In 1842 all these stones were lying on the ground and now they are upright; were they originally recumbent? Have they been re-erected wrong end up, or on their sides or set too deep? It's not even known for sure if the holes were made in prehistoric or later times. Despite all these questions, Sandy Gerrard's Stone Rows of Great Britain website categorises this row as a plausible though unique ancient site, set as it is in this landscape of stone circles and cairns, with the grassy hump of a barrow swelling on the skyline to the south-west.[141]

From the stone row, Carn Kenidjack is almost entirely hidden by rising ground, its tip just protruding above the horizon. Is this reduction of the rock deity to manageable proportions relevant, the just-about-visible-ness the very point of the row's location?

STONE LANDS

Hunting for Leys and Alignments

In West Penwith, I'm constantly being surprised as I catch sight of landmarks way off in the distance: St Buryan's church tower seen from the Pipers or Boscawen-ûn, echoing the shape of a megalith on the horizon; or St Michael's Mount glimpsed through an opening in the hedge at the top of the grove that shelters Sancreed holy well. Many of the standing stones are inter-visible, if you know where to look: you can see the Boskednan stones from Mên-an-Tol, for example, and (apparently, though I've not managed it myself) the Pipers and the Merry Maidens from Boscawen-ûn. Glimpses of distant carns and standing stones, of church towers and mine stacks, seem to lend an extra dimension to the landscape. It's as if these perspectives offer a glimpse of another realm that exists in tandem with our everyday reality, an otherworld that may be accessed from significant places or by walking on the lines between them.

It was John Michell, author of *The View Over Atlantis* (1969) and many other books on archaeoastronomy and earth mysteries, who popularised the still on-going cult of alignment hunting in West Penwith. In *The View Over Atlantis*, Michell developed amateur archaeologist Alfred Watkins's idea of leys (straight lines linking prehistoric sites and natural landmarks which Watkins believed marked the routes of prehistoric paths) into an ambitious theory of a worldwide network of ancient sacred places, centres of a lost prehistoric science that were linked together by leys. After publication of *The View Over Atlantis*, criticism that it contained no actual proof sent Michell to West Penwith, to survey the archaeology there and find hard evidence of leys by plotting lines of intervisibility between prehistoric sites.

Michell's research was hampered by the disappearance of many of the sites, but as he tried to connect one ancient place with another, he found what he believed to be lost prehistoric standing stones, fallen or hiding unnoticed in hedges. Walking from stone to stone, following lines plotted on his map and seeing how on the ground one site after another came into view, Michell became convinced of the reality and precision of alignments connecting ancient places.[142] He published his findings in *The Old Stones of Land's End*, a beautifully produced survey of the megalithic sites of the peninsula and the alignments that connect them, which elegantly marshals all his evidence: photographs, drawings, plans, fold-out maps and detailed description of the stones.[143]

Archaeologists don't have much truck with ley lines that link prehistoric sites with millennia-younger features such as churches, or with ideas about lines of earth energy, but they do often creatively embrace the concept of alignments, believing it's possible to intuit prehistoric preoccupations by observing how a monument is positioned in relation to other sites and to the surrounding landscape, especially to features on the horizon that mark the position of the sun and moon at key turning points of the year. Carolyn Kennett is one such: an archaeoastronomer who researches the relationship of Cornwall's prehistory with the sky, who combines modern computer analysis with painstaking on-the-ground observation, and who leads sunset and night-time walks to allow people to get some insight into these sites as they may have originally been intended.

When I asked Carolyn if there seemed to be any overall pattern to the alignments she'd observed in West Penwith, she said that she believed the megalithic monument builders there were above all interested in the winter solstice. 'I think that's in part because of the spine of granite outcropping that runs north-east–south-west through the peninsula. The sites are often aligned to this rocky spine, and south-west marks the position of the midwinter sunset. The alignment between Chûn Quoit and Carn Kenidjack is a good example: if you stand at Chûn Quoit at the winter solstice, you see the sun set into Carn Kenidjack.'

Carolyn points out that while Chûn Quoit was built in the Neolithic, the interest in the winter solstice can also be seen in the monuments put up in the Bronze Age on the land below Carn Kenidjack. 'As you drop down the hill, the sea views get more restricted and by the time you reach Tregeseal, the sea view is very limited and what it frames, in the right weather conditions, is Scilly. If you'd been standing at the two stone circles there at winter solstice, what you would have seen in this small frame was the sun going down over the Isles of Scilly.

'From the perspective of the mainland, Scilly is a liminal space. On a clear day with high pressure, the isles just pop. They look close up and it's magical. On other days, Scilly is just not there, or it can be coming in and out of view. The people who built the Tregeseal stone circles could have had a perception of Scilly as an otherworldly, liminal place, perhaps a place of the dead (even if they weren't actually transporting their dead there), and so they tagged it with this alignment.'

I am amazed and moved when I hear this. In all my many visits to Tregeseal, my attention has always been focused uphill, on Carn Kenidjack, and I have never paid much attention to the strip of blue sea over the hedge and beyond the field where the other stone circle used to stand. It had never occurred to me that in certain conditions, it might be possible to see Scilly from here (you have to climb up by the hedge which otherwise obscures the view; in that hedge are some suspicious large stones, possible survivors of the lost western circle). It feels very significant to me that there is this link between West Penwith and Scilly, both places that have been so incredibly special to Stephen and me, both of them magical realms and both now linked, for me, through this alignment to winter solstice, to ideas of the return of the light, of death and rebirth.

In 2023 Carolyn was part of a team excavating the Kenidjack holed stones, and she has an idea about how they could have been used, with the caveat that it is just a theory, especially as the stones are not necessarily all in their original positions (the fifth stone, the smaller one set to the north of the row, is definitely in the wrong place): 'As the sun rises, a shadow will form behind the stones. On certain days of the year, the sun is going to rise and shine through the hole, so you'll suddenly get a sunbeam on the shadow, and that effect will occur on about 20 days. As you go down the line of stones, the holes are oriented in different directions, so this phenomenon will occur behind different stones on different dates, starting in late October and leading up to December. So the monument could have worked as a sort of countdown calendar to the winter solstice.

'I do think what we have here is a winter solstice landscape. A number of monuments tag each other for the winter solstice all the way down West Penwith's granite spine. At Nine Maidens, you can watch the midwinter sun set over Boswens Menhir; at Chûn Quoit, you can watch it set over Carn Kenidjack; and at Tregeseal, you can watch it set over the Isles of Scilly.'

Somewhere in the field to the left of the path you take through Hailglower Farm to reach Tregeseal stone circle is a chambered tomb that's famous in archaeological circles for the urn that William Copeland Borlase (William Borlase's great-great-grandson) found there in 1879. I have long wanted to visit the site but have been too nervous to go into the open fields so close to the farmhouse without asking for permission, and there has never been anyone around to ask. Now I'm all the keener, given what Carolyn told me: 'The passage of the entrance grave is aligned to winter solstice sunrise. At the far end of the passage Borlase found a cist, and in that cist was a large, highly decorated urn. When he flipped the urn, he saw a cross set into the circle of the base. This cross wasn't for stability; it would actually have made the urn *less* stable. A cross within a circle is a solar symbol, like the gold lunulae (sun discs) found in Ireland and in west Cornwall.'

She summarises what this symbolism means: 'So the cremated remains of the dead were left in the upside-down urn, with the solar symbol on top, in the darkness of this entrance grave aligned to the winter solstice. It's as if they were inviting light into the darkness – as if they were showing the dead the way back to life.'

A Legend that Enchants a Landscape

As the story of the witch, the king and his army transforms a Cotswold hill and some weathered oolitic limestone megaliths into the stuff of Rollright legend, so the tale of 19 maidens turned to stone has soaked into the fields, hedges and ancient granite between St Buryan and Penzance, and permeated this entire landscape with magic.

It is a fresh, bright summer morning that promises a hot day, and I have managed to exit the tent in my running gear without rousing Stephen or the children, or anyone in the neighbouring tents or their dogs. Adventure is in the air. I set off down a sun-dappled avenue to the next cove along from the campsite, then up onto the headland and along a grassy field path between two tall hedges, swallows swooping overhead, and then onto the mystic B3315. I say 'mystic' because this morning that is how it strikes me, this road that links up ancient sites like pearls on a necklace: early medieval crosses; the Tregiffian entrance grave; a standing stone with a hole that's used as a gatepost; the awesome stones that stand in fields on either side of the road – Gun Rith, the Merry Maidens, the Pipers. The B3315, empty at this hour, is lit up by a blinding sun dazzle that bounces off damp

STONE LANDS

tarmac and turns my onward path to silver. I am in the land of legend, this road a processional way heading directly for the stones.

I enter the field to find the Merry Maidens dancing on the skyline above me. This is a lovely circle, elegant and symmetrical, the 19 pillars evenly spaced (apart from a wider gap to the east, which may be an entrance) and regular in shape. So this is the Dans Maen, the 'stone dance', here are the girls who one Sabbath evening, instead of going to church, were tempted into sinful behaviour by two evil spirits in the form of pipers:

> The excitement increased with the exercise, and soon the music and the dance became extremely wild; when, lo! a flash of lightning from the clear sky transfixed them all, the tempters and the tempted.[144]

The haze thickens on the horizon and downward-slanting lines indicate that rain is falling over a sweep of upland to the north. The sun keeps shining on the Merry Maidens though, and a few moments later a rainbow curves across the blackest cloud, emerging in the sky like that fatal lightning bolt and plunging down into the stone circle, right above one of the petrified girls.

A little further eastwards along the B3315, I find the Pipers who led the Merry Maidens astray, standing stock-still among the waving grasses. These stones are giants compared with the Maidens, both of them over 4 metres tall. They must have seen the girls turned to stone and run for their lives, and this is as far as they got before divine retribution caught up with them. One moved faster than the other, so now each Piper stands in a field of his own.

The rule was no dancing or any other profane activity on Sunday, the holy day, and standing stones all over the country demonstrate the fate of Sabbath-breakers, this folklore developing alongside the rise of Sabbatarianism from the start of the 17th century.[145] Stanton Drew in Somerset is a petrified wedding party, rings of guests still dancing in the field, while the bride, groom and priest are frozen in the garden of the Druid's Arms pub; the Nine Maidens in north Cornwall is a row of dancing girls, their fiddler fallen 750 metres away; and the stones of Tinkinswood chambered tomb in South Glamorgan are also women who dared to dance on a Sunday. Duddo stone circle in Northumberland, the Shearers near Hownam in the Scottish Borders and the three Moelfre stones in Gwynedd are all labourers turned to stone for working on the Sabbath. On Bodmin Moor, the three Hurlers stone circles are men struck down while playing at hurling.[146]

The legend of dancing girls turned to stone applied to other circles on the peninsula – Boscawen-ûn, Tregeseal and Boskednan have all been called the Nine Maidens (though predictably there were never nine stones at any of them – see page 251) and Tregeseal is also known as the Dancing Stones. At the Merry Maidens, the story of dancing girls doesn't seem to be at all ancient; William Bottrell wrote in 1870 that 'the old folk only know it from having it repeated to them by visitors, who have seen it in books' and he said that the Pipers used to be known as

STONE LANDS

the Hurlers, because they were used as goalposts in the game.[147] Yet the Maidens' tale has put down roots and spread through the landscape, so that today it seems as if it's always been there. It makes sense: here is the ring of dancing girls, and here are the two Pipers, and here, in a hedge bordering a field a little way west of the Merry Maidens, is Gun Rith, who was the party's fiddler.

What's more, on the A30 two miles or so to the north of the Merry Maidens stands another petrified musician: the Blind Fiddler. Could he have fled all that way from the disaster at Boleigh, thinking he'd escaped, only to meet his fate in a field next to what is now Land's End's main thoroughfare? His stone head peeks over the hedge at the cars and caravans speeding past. A mile further east along the A30 and you find the field belonging to the two sisters of Drift, hooded and shawled and possibly stragglers from one or another of the illicit Sabbath gatherings. Scores of stone people are scattered over the nine-mile length of the peninsula.

One late October, Stephen, Alex, Ava and I arrive at the Merry Maidens to find that someone has left a red apple on every stone, and that seems to me magical and wonderful. We lie among the stones and soak up their energy, and then we follow Walk Eight in Ian McNeil Cooke's *Journey to the Stones*.[148] I've found this book in our rented cottage and am obsessed with it: in my opinion it's the best guidebook ever, combining nine walks – nine is a mystical number for McNeil Cooke – around the ancient sites of West Penwith with features on stone circles, folklore, fogous, early crosses, holy wells, ley lines, and much more.

Today, inspired by this book, I am feeling afresh the joy of standing stones and all their mysteries, as if I were learning about all of this for the first time. I feel delight in the turning of the seasons and the ways people mark these, and in the walking, which is itself a sort of magic, binding us together. The children are remarkably uncomplaining. Something goes wrong with the route directions on the way back from the coastal stretch, and we have to climb over a gate that's plastered with warnings to trespassers: I'm nervous but Stephen insists we proceed, taking a principled stance against landowners who fail to maintain rights of way, and delighting Alex and Ava.

We regain the route and search for two stones we've never seen before (designated 'St Buryan 4' by McNeil Cooke): a menhir standing between furrows in a stubbly field,* and another dubious one, which takes us a while to find: a slab leaning in the hedge. Alex collapses against it, burying his face into the rock in exhaustion and exasperation, and perhaps just a hint, though he would not admit it, of stone hugging.

Later I write in my diary: *I must continue to find joy in this wondrous world, in my children, in the connection between me and Stephen.* It is just three months before Stephen is diagnosed with cancer and the last time we'll ever go to West Penwith together.

---

* This stone, less than half a mile from the Merry Maidens, is also known as Boscawen-Ros East and starred in its own biopic, *A Year in a Field* (2023).

STONE LANDS

The Healing Power of Quartz

Imagine coming upon a stone circle a few days before Samhain, when the thinning of the veil between this world and the otherworld is made tangible by a mist that hides the uplands and makes the enclosure of the stones, separated by a hedge from the ocean of bracken outside, feel entirely apart from everyday life. Through the mist comes joyous lark song, and the distant rumble of the A30 that serves only to remind you that you have left the ordinary world behind. Nineteen stones, 18 of granite and one of glittering quartz, stand in a ring around a central pillar that leans at an angle of 45 degrees, as it perhaps has always done. As you slip into the circle, the larks intensify their song, and you feel welcomed there, and cleansed and empowered. The feeling of otherworldliness is so intense that the hairs on the back of your neck actually stand up.

Boscawen-ûn is one of my favourite stone circles, perhaps my very favourite, and we come here without fail every time we visit West Penwith. Whenever I go, I find myself greeting the quartz block like an old friend. I can shut my eyes now and recall the feel of it under my palms and cheek: smooth and cool and soothing. The leaning central stone, marked low down with carvings of axes (or perhaps they are feet with circles or breasts) that are fully illuminated only at summer solstice,[149] makes the whole monument seem like a sun dial; this pillar is surely a stone of the sun, while the luminous, silvery quartz stone belongs to the moon. To me, the circle feels complete, bringing together as it does sun and moon, male and female.

This is a World of Wonder

It is special for others, too. Archaeoastronomer Carolyn Kennett, who was here day and night over the course of a year when she was taking observations of the circle's solar and lunar alignments, loves Boscawen-ûn so much that she had a handfasting ceremony here when she got married. 'My husband Jamie has been visiting that circle since he was five years old, so it's super-special to him too,' she says. This is also folk singer and megalith enthusiast Angeline Morrison's favourite standing stone site and when I asked her why, she said: 'It just feels so perfect to me. I am not sure I can put into words the deep connection I feel when I go there. I feel as though time stops, and that I'm a tiny part of a very vast, very complicated web of life that stretches into eternity in every direction. I love the central stone and its angled stance – for some reason it reminds me of a stylus and I like to imagine the music that might be channelled through it, with the sky as the vinyl.' She has a special love for the quartz stone too, and its associations with healing, the moon and women.

One May Day morning, Angeline made a pilgrimage to Boscawen-ûn to perform a ritual: 'I wanted to dance a solo Morris jig for the stones. I've always loved the Bledington jig "Lumps of Plum Pudding", but I hadn't danced it in a while. So while I was on tour I watched YouTube videos of various dancers doing the jig, and practised as much as I could whenever I got little moments alone. The evening before, I went out to gather sticky buds to make a crown for the dance, and I gathered bunches of campion, which were growing abundantly in the hedgerows, to be my Morris hankies. When I'm dancing out in nature by myself, I like to use whatever is seasonal as the theme for my kit that day.

'When my friend Rosie – the amazing musician Rosie Vanier – and I got to Boscawen-ûn, it was deserted so we communed with the stones for a while, and then I danced for them. It felt very special.'

Aubrey Burl thought the quartz stone might have been used as a marker for observing the May Day sunrise.[150] If that is the case, then I wonder if the ritual that Angeline performed at Boscawen-ûn at Beltane sunrise could have echoed in any way those that were performed here millennia earlier. The idea of pilgrimage and carrying on through time a tradition of visiting a sacred place is one that resonates with her.

'Pilgrimage is very important to me,' Angeline says. 'The idea that many others have walked the steps that I am now taking on my own pilgrimage contributes to a feeling of sacredness. The energy of so many other human souls going to the same place for the same reasons creates layers of significance. You can feel a connection to these other pilgrims, even though you have never met them. There is a power in that imagined community.'

Cheryl Straffon is a local Pagan, writer and megalith researcher, who since 1986 has published *Meyn Mamvro*, the magazine of ancient stones and sacred sites in Cornwall. She believes that it is the interaction between people and stones in West Penwith that makes the sites there seem so special. 'Very often if you visit an ancient site down here, you will be the only person visiting them. Also, because there are a lot of like-minded people who care about these places and look after them, and use them for spiritual purposes, there's an interaction between people and sites, and others can pick up on that energy and that specialness. It's that relationship that we have with the sites that's important. It brings them alive again. They're not frozen in time, but relevant to us today.'

Cheryl is interested in the effect of quartz stones, such as the block at Boscawen-ûn, which she told me is known as the Healing Stone, and those at Duloe in north Cornwall, where an entire stone circle was built out of quartz. 'Quartz has what is known as the piezoelectric effect, in which it gives off a small electric charge, so it could have seemed to ancient people that the quartz in stones was alive. We view creatures as alive and stone as dead, but ancient people might not have made that distinction. Quartz runs through the granite of the standing stones here; people have experienced small electric shocks from some of the Merry Maidens, for example. I do wonder if this is where the tradition of being passed through the Mên-an-Tol came from. People still crawl through nine times in great seriousness, in the hope of healing their back problems. That practice has endured for a very long time and it wouldn't have done if it hadn't been thought to work. Perhaps there really is something about going through the quartz in that stone which is healing.'

Cheryl had a strange and touching experience connected with the Boscawen-ûn quartz stone. 'We had a cat that had gone missing and I was very upset, because I was very attached to this cat. We went down to Boscawen-ûn, to the Healing Stone, and I asked that whatever had happened to the cat, its spirit should pass peacefully. That night I had this very vivid dream of the cat turning up at our back door – although normally it would come in through the cat flap in the front door. I woke up and I thought, *Oh yeah, that was a strong dream, but it was just a dream*. Then about an hour or so later, I heard a little scratch, scratch, scratch at the back door. And I opened it and there was the cat. It had obviously had an accident, been hit by a car or something, so we rushed it to the vet and it lost its tail, but it survived. I've often wondered if my interaction with the stone at Boscawen-ûn provoked the dream and offered me a doorway into a subconscious world, where this information about my cat was passed on. Maybe it had crawled away to die, but somehow it managed to get back to the house. I treated that quartz stone with respect after that.'

Cheryl is in her mid-70s now and has been visiting standing stones all her adult life. 'I still get a real buzz from ancient sites. I'm like a little girl in a sweet shop, you know. I go to these places and I get a buzz every time.'

This is so inspiring to hear. The buzz has not yet faded for me either, and I hope it never will.

The Way to Scilly

Just north of Land's End, the most westerly point in mainland England, is Sennen Cove, where at the south end of the bay a cluster of fishermen's cottages shelter behind the sea wall in the protective lee of Pedn-men-du headland, and a glorious crescent beach – known as Whitesands for obvious reasons – curves northwards for almost a mile to the next headland. When conditions are right, the Atlantic breakers roll in one after another and the water is full of surfboards. Often, when we came in October, conditions were not right, and Stephen would proclaim, 'Flat as a pancake *again*', as our car edged down the cliff road to the car park, but he loved getting in the water anyway, swell or no swell. I think that was when he was at his happiest, floating on his surfboard, sensing the aliveness of the ocean, taking an off-shore perspective on the green flank of land rising to the sky, all troubles irrelevant for the moment and far away. And when he caught a wave, it would be as if he were flying, nothing existing but his body rushing through spray, the swell urging him onwards. He told me once that he used to dream about this, and it was like nothing else on earth.

Sometimes the rip is running strongly and the red flag goes up, and then it is too dangerous to get in. I have seen the sea here wild and angry, frothing and hissing, the foam whipped solid and the pebbles cracking in the undertow, while the lighthouse beyond Land's End moaned eerily. Perhaps that doleful call was the Hooper – Sennen Cove's guardian spirit – who hides in the mist and hoots to warn of approaching storms and peril on the sea.[151] We climbed up on Pedn-men-du to watch the mountains of spray and, edging too close to the cliff in an attempt to film this, I was drenched by a huge rogue wave coming over the headland, to the hilarity of the kids. Stephen was upset and then angry at my idiocy: when the wave came over I vanished completely and for a moment he thought I had been swept away.

STONE LANDS

One time, while Stephen was surfing and the children attempting to ride boogie boards down the dunes, I lay on the sand here, the drumming of the sea in my ears, and watched the sky resolve itself into patterns like a kaleidoscope, feeling on the point of breaking through to some profound revelation, as if my gaze was piercing veil after veil to penetrate ever deeper into reality – or as deep as my feeble powers to focus would allow me to go. An echo of the previous night, when first one star, then two, then a constellation, then a whole swathe of the Milky Way had been revealed to me outside our cottage, and as I stared up one of those stars had detached itself to shoot off and burn up in the ether. It was as if here, in West Penwith, it is possible to look for signs and find them.

I discover a historical link to Scilly, to Lyonesse. Sennen men used to go over to Scilly for the summer fishing, and the port at Sennen Cove was once called Porth Goonhilly – Goonhilly being the old name for the Eastern Isles of Scilly. The shortest possible distance between Scilly and the mainland is a line drawn between the Eastern Isles and Sennen, so it's possible that Sennen was once the main port for Scilly traffic. What's more, Sennen's beach car park now occupies the site of the medieval Chapel Idne, founded, so the legend goes, by the Lord of Goonhilly, the ruler of Lyonesse, after he escaped from the flood that submerged the land.[152]

In the evenings, dolphins play in the surf at Sennen. Perhaps these are the very same creatures that leap alongside the *Scillonian* as it ploughs the waves to and from St Mary's.

We came back to St Just in October the year after Stephen

died. I managed to drive us all the way to West Penwith from London in one day – a proud achievement. In one of my bags was a jar containing Stephen's ashes.

The first thing I noticed, when we got back into that little cottage in St Just and closed the door behind us, was the silence. And in that silence, cleansing and restful to the soul, it was possible to hear the echoes of our four voices coming through from all the years before.

It is a red flag day, the day that we put Stephen's ashes into the sea at Sennen, and so, although there is barely a cloud in the sky, the water is empty of boards and the horizon a clean edge of curling wave eternally crashing into froth. Above the churning water hangs a dazzling web of spray that makes the whole seascape seem unearthly. There is something soothing about the raging of the water, as if the sea is acknowledging our emotions and showing us that they are natural, just another part of life. I track across the sand, with Alex, Ava and Stephen's cousin Will, to the northern end of the beach, across the stream that flows down through the dunes, to the place where the rocks begin and the top arm of the bay curves round. The lifeguard is wandering with a dog among the boulders and we wait for him to move off. There is no one else around.

I am feeling anxious. Should I have checked the tide – which is coming in – or arranged to do this on a less windy day, or on a non-rip day when swimmers are allowed in the water so I could wade further out? Is it odd to do something so solemn so casually? Should I have devised a formal ceremony, invited Stephen's friends and relatives? Stephen's cousin Will is here because he lives with his partner Rebecca close by on the

STONE LANDS

peninsula, though Rebecca herself is away working in London. No one else knows what we are doing.

And yet somehow it all feels right and perfect. We all think of our own message for Stephen, then I take off my shoes and socks and wade a few steps into the surf, take the jar out of its wrapping and let the ashes float free. It's done in a moment, this setting free of the heavy, grey, granular ashes that are now Stephen's physical presence in this world, all that remains, in material form, of a living, breathing, loving, wonderful man. I am reminded of seeing his body in the funeral parlour and knowing that what lay there was not his spirit but a shell; whatever it was that made Stephen a human being had gone elsewhere.

In the end, there is no trouble with the wind or the current. The ashes ripple through the water and then immediately they are off, out to sea. I had imagined them swirling into the shape of a man – or a selkie – and darting away through the water, and somehow it is exactly like that.

I think of Stephen diving among the seals and dolphins, swimming from Sennen to Scilly along the old fishing route. I think of him following the sunken paved roads between those islands he loved so much.

Later, after Will has gone back to work, the children and I pay a visit to Boscawen-ûn. The circle is incredibly beautiful that day, the stones enclosed by yellow-flowering gorse, russet fronds of bracken and hawthorn trees laden with red berries. It feels like a secret place that belongs to us. Alex and Ava lean against the quartz stone and press their faces into it, and then they scuffle on the ground like over-grown puppies, pushing each other over. Alex is very like how Stephen was at his age, Will had told me earlier. Introverted yet self-assured and curious about the world. And funny. It feels good to be there with the two of them. The darkness throws the light into relief.

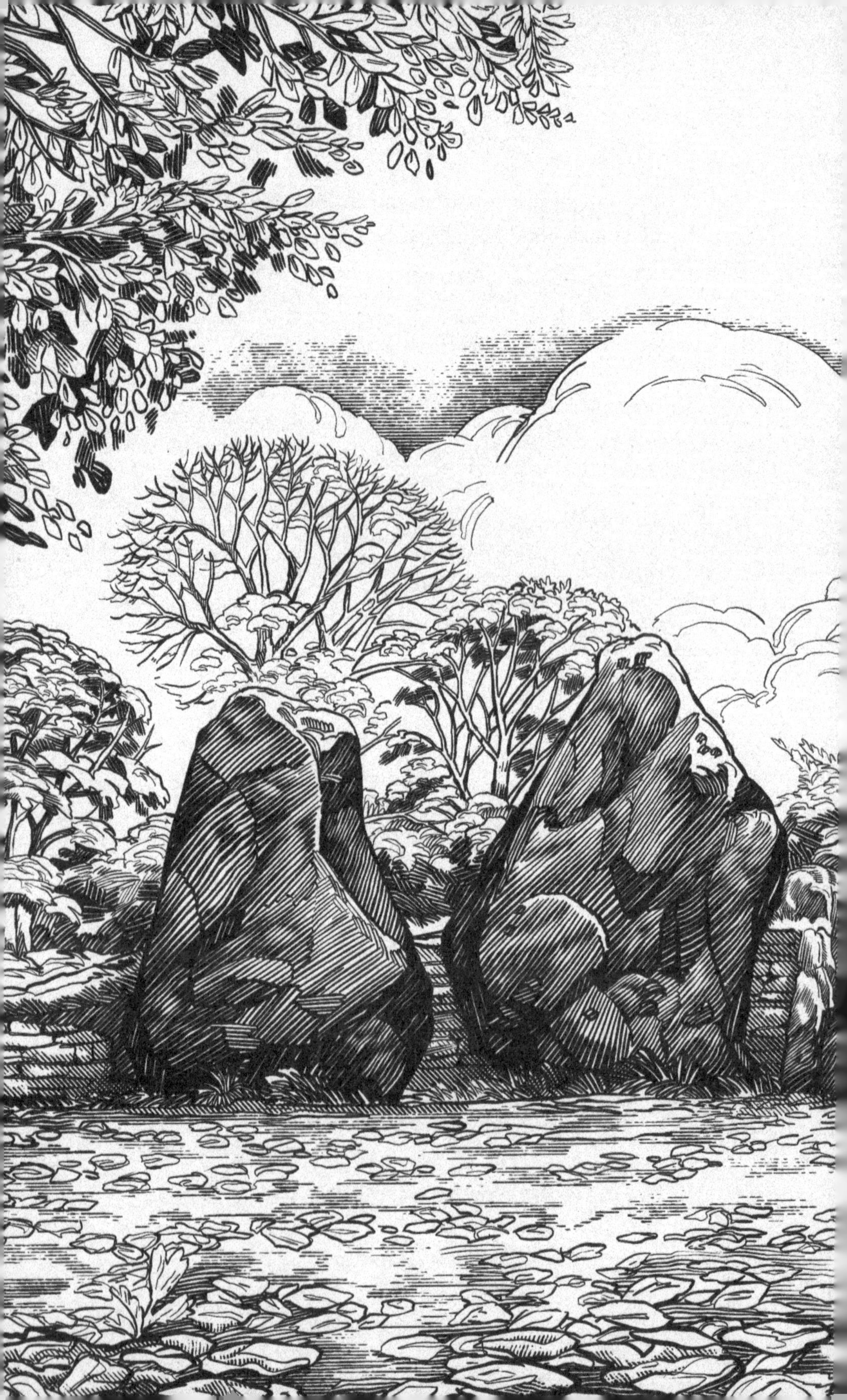

Chapter 12

THE PAST IS ALWAYS WITH US

- c.3700 BCE: Windmill Hill causewayed enclosure + West Kennet long barrow built

- c.3590–3555 BCE: Wayland Smithy I built

- c.3460–3400 BCE: Wayland Smithy II built

- c.3000–2200 BCE: Avebury henge and stone circles/avenues built in phases, with activity intensifying c.2500 BCE

- c.1380–550 BCE: Uffington White Horse first cut

- c.800–700 BCE: Uffington Castle and Barbury Castle built

The White Horse and Wayland's Smithy,
OXFORDSHIRE

THE PAST IS ALWAYS with us. We just have to listen for its echoes.

It is not long after May Day and I am walking the Ridgeway, boots on chalk, following an ancient track towards old stones. (And in my view there is no higher pleasure than that.) Delicate white hawthorn flowers are clustered in the hedgerows, a sprinkling of stars. I have walked this way before, with Stephen one blazing August weekend not long after we'd first met, an orange gerbera threaded through the front of my backpack. It was our first standing stones adventure: a two-day hike along the Ridgeway past the White Horse of Uffington and Wayland's Smithy and on to Avebury. And now, 20 years later, I am doing it all again. Duncan and Lisa have come to London for the weekend to look after Alex and Ava, because for this trip I need to be alone; you notice your surroundings more when there's no one there to talk to and I want to concentrate on catching a glimpse of the two of us marching determinedly through the summer haze all those years ago.

I spent the night in the 16th-century White Horse pub at Woolstone and when I left, the young woman who took my payment at the bar said, 'There's something about walking on the Ridgeway, I can't describe it, it's incredible . . .' She told me she'd walked the whole route in five days, from Avebury to Ivinghoe Beacon. It was the sense of freedom that made Ridgeway walking special, we decided, the feeling of leaving the world and your troubles behind to follow in the footsteps of many others along an ancient path. For some reason I felt extremely moved by this exchange and had to depart hurriedly before I embarrassed myself by starting to cry.

Actually, it is not necessarily the case, when you put one boot in front of the other on the Ridgeway, that you are walking a path that has been trodden since prehistoric times. The National Trail known as the Ridgeway stretches for 86 miles from Overton Hill in Wiltshire to Ivinghoe Beacon in Buckinghamshire, and has been claimed as the oldest continuously used road in Europe, the western part of the route linking up an incredible series of ancient sites: the Uffington White Horse and Wayland's Smithy as well as Bronze Age barrow cemeteries and a string of Iron Age hillforts. Unfortunately for this very appealing theory, aerial photographs have shown that the Ridgeway cuts across prehistoric and Romano-British field systems and farmsteads, meaning that the present route could not have existed before the late Iron Age or perhaps even medieval times. In fact, before the Enclosure Acts of the late 18th century, there

The Past is Always With Us

was probably a network of tracks over the hillside, rather than the one distinct route we have today.[153] What's more, the Ridgeway has never run to Avebury, passing by 2 miles to the east in its journey to the modern end-point at the Sanctuary, the site of the destroyed stone circle on Overton Hill.

With all these slightly dispiriting caveats in mind, it nonetheless remains true that some stretches of the Ridgeway must be very old indeed. The Ridgeway is mentioned by name in the 10th-century bounds of West Woolstone and Blewbury, so there has been a high-level route of this name near White Horse Hill since at least the Anglo-Saxon era, and the chronicles record that it was used by the Saxons and Vikings to transport their troops. Prehistoric tracks must have passed very close to the position of the present path; Uffington Castle hillfort had two opposing entrances that the Ridgeway probably ran through, and the same is true for other late Bronze Age/early Iron Age hillforts such as Rams Hill, Segsbury Camp, Liddington Castle and Barbury Castle.

The norm is to walk the Ridgeway from west to east – something to do with prevailing winds. I can't understand this, personally. I'd always want to be walking *to* Avebury rather than away from it. The last two days of the western end of the route is where you get all the really interesting prehistoric stuff, so why not save the best for last? I can't remember exactly where Stephen and I joined the trail that August weekend two decades ago; I know we took the train from Paddington to Swindon, and then a bus from Swindon to somewhere close to the Ridgeway, north of White Horse Hill.

STONE LANDS

Renewing the Past

Some 2,800 years after it was first built, the rampart of Uffington Castle hillfort is still epic in scale, a massive earthwork enclosing three hectares of empty space on the highest point of Oxfordshire. This spring morning the county spreads sunlit to the blue horizon, a bright quilt of yellow and green squares, and the fort's ramparts are being put to good use by runners and dog-walkers. No one is in the vast interior, as if we have all agreed to leave that space for the spirits of the herders, traders and soldiers who once passed through the fort's gateways. It's impossible to come here and not to wonder what went on here all those centuries ago, not to fill this arena with the smell of smoke and roasting meat, the sound of haggling, arguing, laughing, singing, drumming. Or perhaps with ritual: is it possible that the bank could have allowed spectators to view ceremonies taking place on an immense circular stage, perhaps connected to the White Horse that gallops across the hillside just below the fort? Excavation suggests that the hillfort was rarely and seasonally used, which raises the question of why it was built in the first place.[154] Perhaps it was only ever a ceremonial enclosure, for those who gathered seasonally to care for the White Horse.[155]

I scramble down the bank and into the interior of the fort, with a slight sense of trespassing. Somewhere in here Stephen and I spread out our roll mats and ate our sandwiches. The grasses were long that day and full of wildflowers. I remember it felt like we'd made a nest for ourselves and were quite alone,

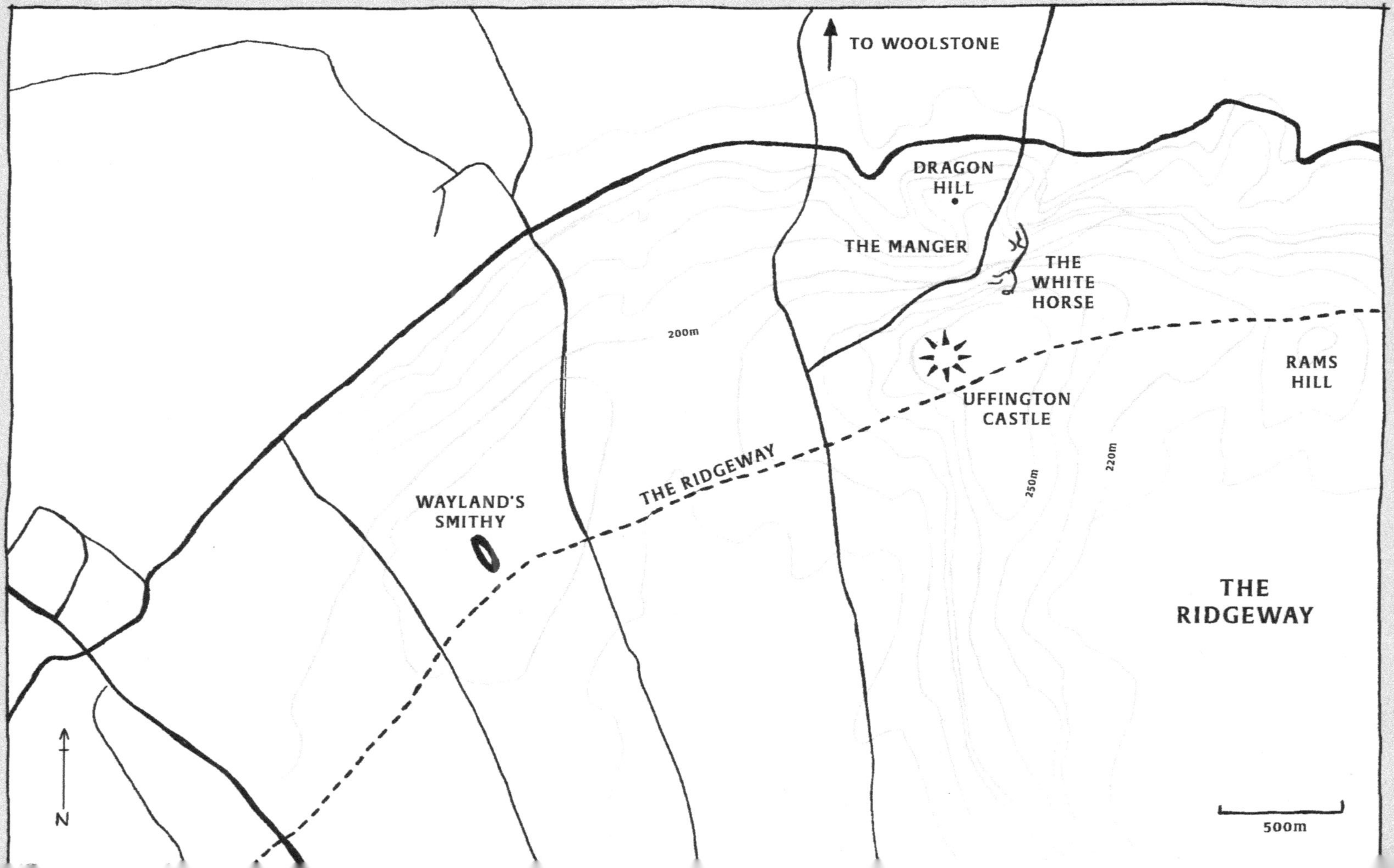
TO WOOLSTONE
DRAGON HILL
THE MANGER
THE WHITE HORSE
200m
UFFINGTON CASTLE
RAMS HILL
THE RIDGEWAY
WAYLAND'S SMITHY
250m
220m
THE RIDGEWAY
N
500m

STONE LANDS

insignificant as mice under the huge Uffington skies. I also remember that my eyes were itching madly and soon swelled up from the rubbing, and I couldn't stop sneezing.

Beyond Uffington Castle, the land falls away and, looking straight down the steep-sided coombe known as the Manger (because this is where the White Horse feeds), you get a vertiginous feeling of thin air under your heels. There's a distinct urge to jump, because if flying is going to be possible anywhere, it's here. Below, a magnificent ocean of chalk downland surges in waves, and from the rippling chaos rises Dragon Hill, a natural mound that looks, with its top that was artificially flattened in prehistoric times, entirely man-made. Perhaps this was another stage for ritual within a ceremonial landscape. This is the place where St George fought the dragon, and the creature's poisonous blood so scarred the earth that today there are still bare patches where no grass will grow.

This landscape takes my breath away. It seems impossible that the people who first carved the figure of a horse into the chalk escarpment and who crowned the hill with a great fort could not have been moved by its drama. Did elaborate rituals, transformative for the watchers and the watched, once play out over the whole hillside? Perhaps Dragon Hill was not a stage for ceremony but rather a stand for an audience, in which case the point would have been not to look down but to look *up*. Up to the White Horse itself.

The White Horse of Uffington is strangely elusive. We all know its iconic image, replicated on T-shirts, beer bottles, book covers, fridge magnets, keyrings, etc.: an elegant stylised horse with a slender body and long tail, caught in the act of galloping

The Past is Always With Us

across the downs with a few bold, disjointed brushstrokes that are reminiscent of modern art as much as Iron Age coinage. But because of the way the figure curves over the brow of the hill, it's impossible in real life to get a good, straight-on, non-foreshortened view of the horse, unless you are taking a drone's-eye view.

This May morning, I have climbed a footpath from Woolstone Wells, the springs where the White Horse is said to come to drink, up to the top of Dragon Hill and then higher still. The horse is always present, yet at no point is fully visible to me. This creature is clearly more concerned with the sky than with us in the valley below.

Now I've made my way up above the horse's head and I'm standing in the exact same spot as when I came here with Stephen. The horse's eye is easy to make out, staring beadily up into the heavens, and I can also see the ear and the mane, but the rest of it, from this perspective, is a muddle of curving white lines. People used to believe it was lucky to make a wish while standing on the White Horse's eye,[156] and National Trust Area Ranger Andrew Foley told me that they still sometimes bury coins there, which have to be removed given that this is an archaeological site. Standing on the eye is definitely not encouraged, and I would feel odd about standing on a horse's eye anyway, even a chalk one.

The White Horse was first recorded as a place name in documents of the late 11th or 12th century, and, like the Rollright Stones, is listed as one of Britain's foremost wonders in the Tractatus de Mirabilibus Britanniae, along with a mysterious 'foal' not mentioned in any other source.[157] But it is much older than that. Of all Britain's hill figures, the Uffington White Horse is the only one proven (via optical stimulated luminescence dating that analyses when the deepest layers of chalk were last exposed to light) to have been first created in prehistoric times – in the late Bronze Age or early Iron Age, between 1380 and 550 BCE, and possibly at the same time the hillfort was built. What's more, geophysical surveys and excavations have proved that it looks much the same today as it has always done, though, due to erosion and repeated scourings (cleanings), somewhat higher up the hill than formerly.[158]

The marvel, according to the Tractatus de Mirabilibus Britanniae, was that the grass would not grow over the shape of a horse – but of course that's not it at all. The marvel is how people have, over many, many centuries, repeatedly done the scouring of the artwork and the pounding of fresh chalk to replenish the lines that was necessary to keep the horse alive. A standing stone may take a lot of effort to raise, but once you've got it up, if you've done the job properly and bedded it in deeply with packing stones, it stays up. A chalk hill figure, on the other hand, needs to be constantly renewed, otherwise it will soon be washed away and grown over. The marvel is the sheer amount of effort that people thought worth putting in over 3,000 years. The marvel is that the tradition was handed from one generation to another and the horse was renewed over and over again. Three thousand years is a long time to keep remembering.

There are records of scourings taking place between 1677, when Thomas Baskerville wrote of the obligation on farmers to 'repair and cleanse this landmark, or else in time it may turn green like the rest of the hill, and be forgotten'[159], until the great

The Past is Always With Us

Pastime of 1857 described by Thomas Hughes in *The Scouring of the White Horse*. That year the scouring was accompanied by a festival that drew 20,000 revellers, with horse racing, pig racing, wrestling, greasy pole climbing, blindman's buff and a breakneck chase down the Manger after a cartwheel for the prize of a cheese. These days, the preservation of the White Horse is in the hands of the National Trust, who encourage the public to take part in the yearly scouring and chalking. They couldn't do it without them – it's a big job. Ranger Andrew Foley explained some of the complexities to me: the chalk, extracted on site, is processed through a stone crusher and fed into ton sacks which are deposited around the horse. Then people are given club hammers and they bash the palm-sized chalk lumps into the surface. Because the horse flows over undulating ground, different parts of the horse are treated in different ways. The head and neck are kept smooth like a billiard table, the fresh chalk pounded into the shape to create a gleaming white effect. Where the ground is very steep, however, such as at the bottom of the neck and the tail, the chalk needs to be kept bulky and looser, to discourage sheep from walking over it and to ensure rain flows through the chalk rather than washing it away.

Andrew Foley is grateful for the help, though he's bemused by what some visitors drawn to this area by its legendary and mystical associations get up to. 'The one word we don't use here,' he says, 'is "why". Why did someone haul six big wardrobe mirrors up White Horse Hill and position them in a circle? Why did someone take all their clothes off and leave them in a neat pile by the side of the road? Why did someone put a hundred rocks in a ring on the top of Dragon Hill?' Without himself believing in the supernatural, he feels a profound sense of wonder about the land he looks after: 'I'm in awe of the landscape, the history, the geology of this place – what's known, what isn't known, the enigma of it all. It's not somewhere I could ever get tired of.'

Artist Ben Edge is also in awe of this place, and of the enduring folklore and customs associated with it. The Scouring of the White Horse is the sort of thing he loves to make art about and he's written a book about his journey through the community customs that take place through the year all around Britain. Its title – *Folklore Rising* – captures his conviction that the growing enthusiastic participation in folk customs represents ordinary people's resistance to political repression, climate peril and disposable capitalist monoculture. He terms this resistance 'folklore activism', and told me: 'There's a new generation of people asking their own questions about big issues and folklore is a vehicle for doing that. In the past, the interest in folk customs tended to be more academic and people looked for the first-ever historical record to define this or that tradition. But history is written by the rich. The working classes keep history alive through folk art, rituals, song, storytelling. People are getting interested in these things because they offer a sincere and inclusive way of connecting to nature, to the stones, to each other.'

He took part in one of the National Trust chalkings: 'The atmosphere up there is incredible. The sound of the hammers breaking the chalk is like a herd of horses running over the hill. It's really moving to be there, chalking the horse and thinking of all the people who've done it over thousands of years.'

As Ben was hammering the chalk to break it up, his hands

became covered with white dust. 'I saw the dust on my hands and thought, *I'll have to do something with that.* There was a magical quality to it.' He brought home a chunk of chalk, wrapped it in his Uffington White Horse tea towel and smashed it with a hammer, then added the dust to a base of white oil paint. It was too lumpy at first, so he hammered it down into a finer dust and it worked much better. He then used the chalk paint to create the image of the White Horse in his painting *The Vale of the White Horse* (2022).

'That chalk has been on a journey that goes back millions of years, to the time when the remains of mollusc shells and plankton accumulated on the sea bed and were gradually compressed into a layer of chalk, which was then sculpted by ice and tectonic movement and forced up onto White Horse Hill, to then be collected by me and become part of my painting. The idea that there's a little piece of the White Horse in my painting makes me feel that there's a kind of magic locked into it.'

Why was the White Horse created in the first place? Over the centuries, it has been associated with the Saxon warriors Hengist and Horsa, who legend tells fought under the flag of a white horse during their invasion of Britain, and also with King Alfred, whose 871 victory over the Danes at Ashdown was once believed to have been commemorated by the White Horse. More recently, the view has been that it was carved out of the hillside as a tribal badge and stamp of land ownership, but for archaeologist Josh Pollard that doesn't make sense. Even factoring in the slight upward migration of the horse since it was first cut, if its creators had wanted a tribal symbol clearly visible from afar, there would have been plenty of better places to have sited it on the escarpment. What was important to the White Horse's creators, Josh Pollard suggests, was to show it running westwards up the ridge, along the east–west path tracked by the sun across the sky. People standing on top of Dragon Hill at dawn at midwinter would have seen – and can still see today – the sun rise behind the horse and appear to roll along its body. Pollard believes the White Horse could have been a sun-horse, like the one that draws the Trundholm sun chariot, the amazing Bronze Age wheeled statue found in a Danish bog, which depicts a horse pulling a disc that is gilded on one side (to represent day) and left dark on the other (to represent night). A sun-horse pulls the sun through the sky, ensuring that day will follow night and that at midwinter the days will begin to lengthen again.[160]

This ancient horse stamped into the Berkshire Downs and born anew each year is, then, an enduring symbol of memory and of hope. It tells us that the past echoes on, through this three-millennia-old custom of scouring and chalking, and it connects us to those who lived before us as well as those who are yet to come. And, like the ray of light that penetrates Maeshowe each year, this sun-horse reminds us of nature's endless renewal: it is a pledge carved out of chalk that light will follow darkness.

Layers of Time

A mile south-west down the Ridgeway and I reach Wayland's Smithy, which is where the Uffington White Horse goes to get its new shoes. This Neolithic chambered long barrow has been associated with Wayland (the Norse god Weland) since at least 955 CE, when a charter listed *Welandes smiddan* as a boundary landmark. If your horse loses a shoe on the Ridgeway, so the legend goes, just leave it alone by the Smithy with a coin for payment. When you return, you'll find the coin gone and your horse newly shod.[161]

Coming up towards Wayland's, the ground rises somewhat and my backpack begins to feel heavier, and I wonder if this is where Stephen and I stopped for a breather, and I moaned about my blisters and about the heaviness of my bag, and Stephen got a bit annoyed because I was wearing sandals and what did I expect. He was also, looking now at the relative size of our bags in the photos, carrying the tent and all the cooking equipment, though I don't remember him complaining about that. We'd only just met and had never gone away together, so this trip was a bit of a risk – what if we hadn't got on? It would have been pretty miserable. Luckily, apart from this minor blister-related clash, we did.

There are lots of people on the trail this morning: runners and hikers, dog-walkers and cyclists. I don't remember meeting anyone at all during that entire first trip with Stephen, but perhaps we were too wrapped up in each other to notice. Today, the beech grove in which Wayland's Smithy is set is alive with yellow-green butterflies, the grassy mound covered with buttercups. One of the beeches has been cut down since my last visit and its bisected trunk is patterned like an old map. It makes a good seat from which to observe the stones, and the people coming and going.

The trees' long, silver-skinned limbs are decked out in fresh green lace and creak gently in the breeze, their shadows crisscrossing the four great standing stones that front the barrow and dramatically flank the entrance to the tomb's passage. One of these façade megaliths is pockmarked with round holes in which coins have been left, offerings for the Smith. When I came here with Stephen, it was high summer and sunlight slanted through a full canopy of leaves onto the old stones as if it were falling into the nave of a country church. When I came back with Ava, in the autumn of the diagnosis year, the leaves had turned to orange and the branches were sparsely covered, and yet the atmosphere of the grove was the same: tranquil, even sacred (despite the constant stream of visitors), a place set apart from everyday life, as if time in here is running on a different loop to that of the world outside the gate.

I have a sensation of layers of time collapsing, as if I am back here with Stephen on a summer's afternoon, entering Wayland's Smithy, heart in mouth, for the first time. As if I am here with Ava, eating our packed lunch among the falling leaves. We took photos of each other inside the passage to send to Stephen and Alex, and then Ava worked out that if she struck a pose on top of the capstone, and I stood a few metres in front of the sarsen façade with my hand held up at exactly the right height, I'd be able to get a shot of her dancing like a fairy in my palm. It took us a few goes to get it right. We WhatsApped the photos, and Stephen sent back a cheery reply. You'd never have thought, looking at his message, that he only had a few weeks left to live.

If ever a place was a palimpsest, Wayland's Smithy is one. Not only do my own experiences of it overlay one another, but its previous incarnations are superimposed one on top of the other too. Excavations in 1962–3 revealed that within the chambered mound is an earlier barrow – 'Wayland Smithy I' – which has been dated to 3590–3555 BCE.[162] The first structure on this site was a wooden mortuary house, a kind of box with a lid through which bodies were deposited, which was then closed by an oval mound of chalk and earth. This initial barrow was then covered by Wayland Smithy II, the long barrow that we see restored today, which was four times as long as the first mound and double its height, with a stone passage leading to two chambers. This grand new barrow was edged with kerbstones and given an imposing façade of huge standing stones.

Why did Wayland Smithy II look so different to Wayland Smithy I? What did the builders mean by it? Archaeologists have suggested that the style of the second long barrow, with its façade of huge stones like those at West Kennet long barrow, and unlike anything else to be found in southern England, was deliberately chosen to associate Wayland Smithy's builders and those buried there with the heroic generation who'd constructed West Kennet some 150 years earlier. Perhaps the impressive façade of four megaliths was put up in memory of the 11 men, two women and one child who had been buried in the first barrow. Some leaf-shaped flint arrowheads were found lying with the bones, and the tip of a flint projectile was embedded in one pelvis, indicating that at least one of these people, and perhaps four of them, met a violent death.[163] Whatever their millennia-old tragedy, they are part of the story of this place.

In his series of paintings 'Children of Albion', Ben Edge seeks to capture how the contemporary and historical co-exist at standing stone sites. He told me: 'I want to show all the layers of history still present in these 5,000-year-old places. I want to paint the stories people tell and the spectres in the landscape.' And his paintings are indeed full of spectres and stories – William Stukeley haunts the Rollright Stones, the shade of a Druid presides over Bryn Celli Ddu on Anglesey and at Wayland's Smithy a shadowy figure is shoeing a spectral horse. Standing alongside the ghostly smith is a visitor in present-day clothes – Ben's wife Rose Spencer. 'Rose grew up in the Vale of the White Horse. She even had the image of the White Horse on her school uniform. I wanted to show that this monument has been in use for thousands of years and it's still being used now.'

For Ben, prehistoric sites are good focal points for those who want to create a more inclusive society. 'The history of these places goes back so far that it's free of the baggage of Empire. Once you understand about the movement of peoples across continents in prehistory, the notion of a single British race is dissolved. If you want a more inclusive society, the idea that these places are open to all is an exciting one. At Wayland's Smithy, the mix of legends from different eras – the White Horse, King Alfred, King Arthur, the Norse tale of Weland the Smith – mimics the true nature of Britain itself, our mongrel nation of people and traditions.'

You can't see the White Horse from Wayland's Smithy but Ben included both sites in his painting *The Vale of the White Horse* because of the on-going mythic relationship between them. As he points out: 'It's no coincidence that there's a legend about a smith when there's this 3,000-year-old horse a mile up the Ridgeway.'

The Past is Always with Us

Opposite Wayland's Smithy, on the other side of the Ridgeway, is a little wood where people have stacked fallen branches against tree trunks to make dens. The sight of them makes me wish Alex and Ava were here with me, although they have outgrown dens really. Stephen used to build dens with them and then he would hoist them right up into the branches of the tree and climb up after them.

The past echoes on. The echoes of all the younger iterations of our current selves, of the people we have loved and lost. The echoes of all those who passed this way before us, stretching way back to the earliest times, with whom we may have no ties of ancestry but whose presence we can still sense. My dad came to London from Scotland, my mum from Croatia, so the people who built the sites along the Ridgeway are not my blood ancestors. And yet I feel their places belong to me, too. The stories of these sites are my stories. Whatever our origin, I believe we can each forge our own connection with the land, with ancient places and with the people of the past. That feeling of awe or sense of the sacred inspired in us by an old stone monument connects us with all the people who through thousands of years of history have come here and shared those feelings too. We can never know the truth of what we intuit, but we can imagine and through imagining our lives are enriched. And we might even come to realise that what we thought we had lost is still with us.

I find the place where Stephen and I camped. I was not

expecting this. Actually, it turns out to be quite obvious, as it is not that easy to find a wild camping spot on this particular stretch of the Ridgeway, surrounded by open fields that offer no shelter from irate landowners. An upturned grassy bowl rises among the crops. It looks a bit like a burial mound, but it is not, it's much bigger and for scale there is an actual burial mound in the field next door. Excitement rising, I follow a path through the wheat, then turn onto a grassy strip to access the hill. There's a footpath worn into the side of the hill, so it's clear that other people have come this way, but it's still a discreet place to camp, with a fringe of shrubs at the bottom of the hill, and at the top a depression, like the sunken top of a pudding, that would hide a tent from anyone passing on the Ridgeway below.

It's the same place, I know it, because of the concrete trig point. I have a 20-year-old photo of our tent standing next to this trig point. I also know it because of the view over Swindon. I remember the feeling of relief that we'd installed ourselves here without being accosted, and the cosiness of getting out Stephen's set of billy cans and the little camping stove to heat up our dinner, and the lights of the town coming on as dusk fell, emerging gradually like the stars in the post-sunset sky. The feeling that we were passing through a mythic terrain on our journey to Avebury, and everything around us – the hillforts, the burial mounds, the stones, the lights of Swindon, too – were part of it. The feeling that I'd never been happier.

I discover that someone has, quite recently, left a bunch of flowers by the trig point, and this makes me cry. Pairs of butterflies – yellow ones, tortoiseshell ones – are dancing their love dance. There's a roaring from a car rally somewhere below, and the constant rumble of the M4. A little further along the Ridgeway is the bridge where Stephen and I crossed over the motorway the morning after our camp. We always used to look out for this bridge – 'our bridge' – when we were driving back from visiting his mum in South Wales.

I get out my lunch – a limp cheese sandwich that has been in my backpack since Friday afternoon – and as I eat it, I'm looking out at the 360-degree view over the chalklands. There's a heart-stopping flash of golden-brown feathers, and a huge bird of prey wheels around the concrete pillar, wing tips vertical. Beside me, Stephen gasps and reaches for his binoculars. I catch a glimpse of white, red, gold; the creature is gloriously bright and alive, and close enough to see the individual feathers. And then it swings up into the ether and circles the hillside while I stare at it, mouth open, and then it is off before I can get a proper look at its silhouette.

'Is it a red kite?' I say aloud, but there's no one there to answer me.

Next to the flowers, I leave a beech nut that I picked up and put in my pocket at Wayland's Smithy. And then it's time to leave this place.

I am trying to recapture what Stephen and I saw, what we talked about. The first day, we must have both been nervous. Would we find somewhere to camp? Would the conversation dry up? Would we get on each other's nerves? I remember the sense of lightness and joy as we crossed the motorway bridge the next morning, bathed in sunshine, joking about something: we'd got away with the wild camp, we'd got along brilliantly. We were on our way to Avebury.

STONE LANDS

After the M4, the ramparts of Liddington Castle hillfort loom on the horizon under dark skies. A flock of crows starts up from the newly ploughed field, thousands of exposed flints its only crop. There must be some ancient arrowheads among that lot. I don't remember these uplands at all; Stephen and I must have hurried by on our way to Avebury, unaware or unbothered that there was a big Iron Age fort a short detour away.

I do remember the long and slightly boring tree-lined section approaching Ogbourne St George, where this time around I have booked a B&B for the night. The branches that screen off the downlands are threaded through with pink and white apple blossom; the verges are full of bluebells. The rapeseed in the fields is a strident bright yellow, the smell exotic and sweet.

It's morning and I'm setting off on Day 2, with that magical feeling of walking along the spine of England, of passing through enchanted terrain, of getting ever closer to the source of the magic – to Avebury. I feel it now and I remember feeling it then and this buoys me up, my boots as light as air as I stride onward. The Ridgeway passes right through the double ramparts of Barbury Castle and out the other side. The banks are pretty impressive now and how much more so would they have been when they were first built back in the Iron Age, much higher, much steeper and faced with sarsen stones. This morning there's a group of people sprawled over the bank with music and bottles, who look to have been there all night. Lucky them, I think, as I have a breather and a snack, and survey the great grassy arena. A good place for a party.

The Ridgeway is a white scar gouged across the land by the feet of all who have passed this way. It is really living up to its

The Past is Always With Us

name today, as I pass into Wiltshire, running right up on top of the ridge and offering extensive views on either side, especially to the north-west where the escarpment drops steeply into a wide valley. Today, storm clouds have heaped up like drifts of dirty snow over the uplands on the far side of the valley and there's an ominous rumble of thunder. I pass by gorse-covered burial mounds and sinister copses of beech trees, their branches heavy with the messy, noisy nests of crows.

I eat my sandwich in drizzle at the Polisher stone on Fyfield Down. Alex, Ava and I had gone looking for this stone just a few months earlier. It was a cold, grey day in February and I dragged the two of them on a long hike from Silbury Hill to West Kennet long barrow, and then up the Ridgway and onto Fyfield Down. After 30 minutes of wandering on the down among identical-looking sarsen stones in search of the one with prehistoric markings, they mutinied and intimated that any more of this would amount to child abuse, so swallowing (somewhat ungracefully) my bitter disappointment, we retreated back to Avebury without finding the Polisher.

Actually it turns out that, despite all the very complex instructions shared online, the Polisher is quite easy to locate. You simply exit the Ridgeway eastwards through the gate at the point on the OS map marked 257, walk along the footpath a little way, look out for the prominent pyramid-shaped stone and then weave through the sarsens to find the Polisher lying very close by the triangular marker. It is a marvellous stone, with parallel grooves and a dish-shaped indentation ground into the sandstone by people shaping and polishing axe-heads 5,000 years ago. The grooves are strong and deep, and the stone

STONE LANDS

is smooth and slippery, turned to marble by the repeated action of stone on stone. I run my fingers down the grooves and try to feel the presence of those who made them and to imagine why they chose this particular stone, in this particular place, to finish their axes and make them special. The whole down is littered with sarsen stones – grey wethers, they are called, for their resemblance to sheep. Why was this one chosen? Faint tracks run through the grass to the Polisher, desire paths created by megalith enthusiasts. Perhaps they also mark routes taken to this stone by the people of the deep past.

This is a mythic landscape, teeming with legends and ghosts. The invisible smith and his sky-horse, St George and his dragon, King Alfred, Hengist and Horsa. The shades of the people who were buried at Wayland's Smithy, of those who polished their axes at certain stones on Fyfield Down, and of those who dragged the stones down into Avebury and set up circles within circles and made avenues of megaliths march across the land. Of those who carved a horse in chalk on a hillside and those who renewed it over 3,000 years. Of those who laboured to shift ton upon ton of chalk and rubble, building the henge at Avebury, and Silbury Hill, and the great forts up on the ridge. Of one who walked with me along the Ridgeway and who no longer can be found anywhere on this earth but who accompanies me wherever I go.

What did the monuments of stone – the standing stones, the stone circles, the burial chambers – mean to the people who built them? In a prehistoric world where life was precarious and could be stamped out at any moment, and where there were no written records, surely these structures built of this most imperishable

The Past is Always With Us

of materials were above all about memory, about literally setting in stone what would otherwise be lost. Were these monuments the prehistoric equivalent of books, the stones encoded with information and stories? We know that standing stones were often used to mark the turning cycles of sun and moon, so what else could they have meant? They could have reminded people that they were part of a community with shared ancestors and myths; they could have helped forge that community when people came together to raise them. Perhaps, as books do today, they allowed entry into the mythic realm and an escape from workaday concerns. At a time when the tendency of all else was to fail and decay, these monuments of lasting stone could have been more important than anything else. Perhaps today a sense of the extraordinarily high value once placed upon standing stones echoes down to us, and that is why they seem so meaningful, although also enigmatic, to us now. We intuit that they were special, without really understanding why.

As I write this book, I've been thinking a lot about what standing stones mean for us today. All the technology and comforts of our modern world do not protect us from the reality that our lives are not stable, that we are still subject to change and decay and death. At any moment, the illusion can shatter and everything can change. And everything *will* change – it's just a question of when. The prehistoric stones are no more eternal than anything else, yet nonetheless they have survived into our era, metaphors for strength, hope and endurance. They seem to represent the best human qualities. Battered by the storms of millennia, they are still standing. To me, this is

STONE LANDS

endlessly inspiring and touching, and all the more so now that I have weathered a terrible storm of my own.

Standing stones remind us that there is much that we don't know. Like lightning rods, they attract magical theories of earth energies and healing powers, and who knows, some of them may be true. These days, many people are striving to create their own spirituality and looking to find the sacred in nature, or in the past, when we were a part of nature. We can never know what the standing stones really represented in prehistoric people's cosmology but today they seem to tell us that there is much wonder in life still, and in the impossible fact of us existing here in this universe, and that we can re-enchant our world, if we choose to do so, through imagination and storytelling and being open to mystery and magic.

Standing stones tell us that the past echoes on and that memory is stronger than death. They remind us that the past is still with us, and that every awesome thing we have experienced, all the love we have given and received, is preserved in our past and cannot be taken away from us. Standing stones are markers of the endless dance of the planets, reminders that the world is always swinging from darkness to light and back again, and that there are seasons in our own lives, too.

The realisation that everything changes has been liberating for me. Alongside the records of stones expeditions in my old holiday diaries are many expressions of anxiety about how quickly the precious days are slipping away. Perhaps I had some inkling of what was to come, and that there was not, in fact, going to be an unending supply of these blissful family camping trips. These days, I think I'm better able to appreciate what

I have right now, instead of the moment being spoiled by worrying that it will come to an end. I already know that it *will* come to an end, so what is there to worry about, right? In some ways I'm a nicer person now, no longer so fierce in reacting to perceived slights, which after all, in the great scheme of things (given that we all will die and maybe sooner than we think), really don't matter. On the other hand, I find myself less tolerant than I used to be of things like moaning. Unless you're being bombed or shot at, or you're staring down the barrel of a terminal diagnosis, what is there to moan about? Come on, we're alive, we're here. It's not over yet. Look at this incredible world! Wake up! Can we try to make the most of this one crazy, wonderful, heartbreaking, beautiful life?

I started writing this book when Stephen was still here and I didn't know how the story was going to end. All the time he was ill, I was hoping for, and expecting, a miracle. Telling this story of our stone hunting has kept him beside me, it has focused me on him instead of on grief, it has given me a purpose. To be honest, I'm scared about what will happen now. I don't want to finish the story because it feels like another goodbye.

I wish I'd known we'd have so much time together and no more. From 4 June 2003 to 8 December 2022, there were 7,127 days. That's a lifetime for some, but it didn't seem so long to us. If I'd known, I'd have done things differently.

Now I come to the place where the Ridgeway meets the track known as the Green Street, where you turn off if you want to go directly down into Avebury. The sky is steel grey shading to black, the clouds sagging heavy with rain, and ahead, in the direction of the Sanctuary on Overton Hill, mist is rising from

STONE LANDS

the valley like vapours from the underworld. The fields are covered in buttercups and dandelions, thousand upon thousand of them, bright sparks that relieve the gloom and speak hopefully of the summer to come. Today I am continuing straight on, following the Ridgeway to its terminus at the Sanctuary, but I pause for a while at the junction, rain pattering on the hood of my anorak, and watch as through the drowsy sunlight of a hot August afternoon a young man and woman, chalk-dusty, sweaty, a little bowed under their packs, walk hand in hand down the hill to Avebury. I keep watching as the two of them get smaller and smaller, and finally disappear.

Acknowledgements

A MASSIVE THANK YOU . . .

To Joanna Swainson, for taking on this weird project and helping me to work out what it actually was, and for all the on-going support. Also to Hana Murrell and Lucy Malone at Hardman Swainson.

To Emma Smith at Little, Brown, for enthusiastically commissioning the book and wise early guidance. To Tamsin English, for the super-helpful editing and advice and for becoming such a fantastic champion of *Stone Lands*. To the whole brilliant Little, Brown team: project manager Rebecca Sheppard, designer, art director and map artist Ben Prior, designer Clare Sivell, copy-editor Alison Tulett, proofreader Elizabeth Dobson, production controller John Fairweather, marketing manager Aimee Kitson, publicity manager Gabriella Drinkald, rights director Jessica Purdue and everyone else involved!

To Philip Harris, for the outstandingly beautiful illustrations, which have made all the difference.

To my archaeology editor, Andy Burnham, for the very detailed checking and inspired suggestions. To Josh Pollard and Sigurd Towrie, for invaluable archaeological information and corrections. To Tom Muir, for the Orkney folklore. To Bernie Bell, for the wonderful site suggestions.

To Adam Gordon, for the insightful initial edit, and to Hazel Medd, Jon Tee, Catherine Grout, John Jefferys, Tracy Bettinson and Vicky Hartley, for all the feedback. To the Book Club, for being so encouraging and supportive.

To everyone who sent me stories about your experiences of standing stone sites. The book has changed a lot since I started researching it, so there is so much I couldn't include, but all your input inspired me hugely.

To all of you who generously gave me your time in interviews and allowed me to share your words and ideas.

To Damian Walford Davies, for permission to quote from the introduction to *Megalith*. To Joseph Fasano, for permission to quote from your poem about the winter solstice.

To Weird Walk, Ben Edge, Josh Pollard, Daisy Buchanan, James Canton, Oliver Smith and Angeline Morrison, for your support.

To my colleagues at Watkins, for being so enthusiastic about the book.

To my parents Nella and Robert, for nurturing a love of

Acknowledgements

history and the hills in me in childhood. And for your support and love ever since.

To Duncan and Lisa, for being just so behind *Stone Lands* and me!

To my friends and family, for helping me through a very dark time. And for your endless encouragement as I wrote this book.

To E. and E., for your patience, tolerance and fantastically good company on so many stones trips. May there be many more (sorry!).

To Stephen, for our stones adventures and all the love.

Endnotes

Chapter 1

1 entandaudiologynews.com/development/potters-soapbox/post/the-barber-surgeon-of-avebury
2 Aubrey, J. Edited and with an introduction by John Fowles. Annotated by Rodney Legg. *Monumenta Britannica. A Miscellany of British Antiques.* Boston and Toronto: Little, Brown and Company, 1980, pp.18–19.
3 Piggott, S. *William Stukeley: An Eighteenth-Century Antiquary.* New York: Thames & Hudson, 1985 (1950), p.45.
4 Stukeley, W. *Abury, A Temple of the British Druids, with Some Others, Described.* 1743. Project Gutenberg.
5 Pollard, J. and Reynolds, A. *Avebury: The Biography of a Landscape.* Stroud: The History Press, 2010 (2002), p.30.
6 Ibid., p.50.
7 Ibid., pp.103–4.

8 Aubrey, J., op. cit., p.38.
9 Ibid., p.50.
10 Stukeley, W., op. cit.
11 Gillings, M. and Pollard, J. 'Authenticity, artifice and the Druidical Temple of Avebury'. In Kolen, J., Renes, J. and Hermans, R. (eds) *Landscape Biographies*, pp.117–42. Amsterdam University Press, 2015.
12 Nash, P. *Fertile Image*, London: 1951, p.11.
13 Nash, P. 'Landscape of the megaliths', *Art and Education*, March 1939, p.8.
14 aveburypapers.org/avebury-people/
15 Dames, M. *The Avebury Cycle*. London: Thames & Hudson, 1977, p.141.
16 Dames, M. *The Silbury Treasure: The Great Goddess Rediscovered*. London: Thames & Hudson, 1976.
17 Smiles, S. 'Thomas Guest and Paul Nash in Wiltshire: Two Episodes in the Artistic Approach to British Antiquity'. In Smiles, S. and Moser, S. (eds), *Envisioning the Past: Archaeology and the Image*, pp.133–57. Malden, MA: Blackwell, 2005.
18 *Weird Walk* Number 1, Beltane 2019.
19 Stukeley, W., op. cit.

Chapter 2

20 Evans, A. J. 'The Rollright Stones and their Folk-Lore'. *Folklore* 6, no. 1 (1895), pp.6–53.
21 Stukeley, W. *Abury, A Temple of the British Druids, With Some Others, Described*. 1743.
22 Evans, A. J., op. cit.
23 Ibid.
24 Ibid.
25 Ibid.
26 Wright, T. 'Legend of the Rollright Stones'. *The Folk-Lore Record* 2 (1879), pp.177–9.
27 Manning, P. 'Stray notes on Oxfordshire folklore'. *Folklore* 13, no. 3 (1902), pp.288–95.

Endnotes

28 'Oxfordshire legend in stone'. *The Illustrated Magazine of Art* 1, no. 5 (1853), p.291.
29 Manning, P., op. cit.
30 Palmer, R. *The Folklore of Warwickshire*. London: B. T. Batsford, 1976, pp.83–4.
31 Hamerow, H. 'A conversion-period burial in an ancient landscape: a high-status female grave near the Rollright Stones, Oxfordshire/Warwickshire.' In Langlands, A. and Lavelle, R. (eds) *The Land of the English Kin: Studies in Wessex and Anglo-Saxon England in Honour of Professor Barbara Yorke*, Brill, 2020, pp.231–44.
32 Walford Davies, D. *Megalith: Eleven Journeys in Search of Stones*. Llandysul: Gomer Press, 2006, p.2.
33 Devereux, P. *Places of Power: Secret Energies at Ancient Sites: A Guide to Observed or Measured Phenomena*. London: Blandford, 1990, p.58, pp.190–92.

Chapter 3

34 Maclean, J. P. *History of the Island of Mull*. 1923.
35 Martlew, R. D. and Ruggles, C. L. N. 'The North Mull Project (4): Excavations at Ardnacross 1989–91'. *Archaeoastronomy* 18 (1993).
36 Ellis, C. 'Monks, priests and farmers: a community research excavation at Baliscate, Isle of Mull'. *Scottish Archaeological Internet Reports* 68 (2017).
37 Darvill, T. 'White on blonde: quartz pebbles and the use of quartz at Neolithic monuments in the Isle of Man and beyond'. In Jones, A. and Macgregor, G. (eds) *Colouring the Past: The Significance of Colour in Archaeological Research*, pp.73–91. Oxford: Berg, 2002, p.85.
38 Pennant, T. *A Tour in Scotland, and Voyage to the Hebrides, 1772*.

Chapter 4

39 The Megalithic Portal, edited by Andy Burnham, *The Old Stones*. London: Watkins, 2018, pp.15–17.
40 Fyfe, R. M. and Greeves, T. 'The date and context of a stone row: Cut Hill, Dartmoor, south-west England'. *Antiquity* 84, no. 323 (March 2010), pp.55–70.
41 stonerows.wordpress.com/gazetteer/region/brecon-beacons/bancbryn/
42 stonerows.wordpress.com/gazetteer/region/dartmoor/hingston-hill/
43 Grinsell, L. V. *Folklore of Prehistoric Sites in Britain*. Newton Abbot and North Pomfret: David & Charles, 1976, p.97.
44 devonlive.com/news/devon-news/dartmoor-landowner-shut-vital-car-8156673
45 theguardian.com/environment/2023/jan/13/dartmoor-estate-landowner-alexander-darwall-court-case-right-to-camp
46 righttoroam.org.uk
47 theguardian.com/world/2023/aug/07/first-edition-right-to-roam
48 righttoroam.org.uk

Chapter 5

49 Darvill, T. *Stonehenge: The Biography of a Landscape*. Stroud: Tempus Publishing, 2006, p.139.
50 Ibid., p.140.
51 Parker Pearson, M., Bevins, R., Ixer, R. et al. 'Craig Rhos-y-felin: A Welsh bluestone megalith quarry for Stonehenge. *Antiquity* 89, no. 348 (2015), pp.1331–52.
52 scientificamerican.com/article/circles-for-space/
53 Geoffrey of Monmouth. *The History of the Kings of Britain*. London and New York: Penguin Books, 1966, pp.195–8.
54 Darvill, T., op. cit., p.35.
55 Pitts, M. 'The Henge Builders'. *Archaeology* 61, no. 1 (2008), pp.48–55.
56 Ibid.

Endnotes

57 Pollard, J. 'Substantial and significant pits in the Mesolithic of Britain and adjacent regions'. *Hunter Gatherer Research*. V.3. 2017.
58 Parker Pearson, M. *Stonehenge: Exploring the Greatest Stone Age Mystery*. London: Simon & Schuster, 2012, pp.244–5.
59 bbc.co.uk/news/uk-england-27405147. 'Summer solstice: how the Stonehenge battles faded'.
60 The Megalithic Portal, edited by Andy Burnham, *The Old Stones*. London, Watkins: 2018, pp.91–3.
61 Nash, D. J., Ciborowski, T. J. R., Stewart Ullyott, J., Parker Pearson, M., Darvill, T., Greaney, S., Maniatis, G. and Whitaker, K. A. 'Origins of the sarsen megaliths at Stonehenge'. *Science Advances* 6, no. 31 (2020).
62 Clarke, A. J. I., Kirkland, C. L., Bevins, R. E. et al. 'A Scottish provenance for the Altar Stone of Stonehenge'. *Nature* 632 (2024), pp.570–75.
63 Parker Pearson, M., Pollard, J., Richards, C., Welham, K., Kinnaird, T., Shaw, D., Simmons, E. et al. 'The original Stonehenge? A dismantled stone circle in the Preseli Hills of west Wales'. *Antiquity* 95, no. 379 (2021), pp.85–103.
64 Parker Pearson, M., Pollard, J., Richards, C. et al. 'How Waun Mawn stone circle was designed and built, and when the bluestones arrived at Stonehenge: A response to Darvill'. *Antiquity* 96, no. 390 (2022), pp.1530–37.

Chapter 6

65 Thomas, C. *Exploration of a Drowned Landscape: Archaeology and History of the Isles of Scilly*. London: B. T. Batsford, 1985, p.9.
66 Ibid., pp.264–94.
67 Charman, D., Johns, C., Camidge, K., Marshall, P., Mills, S., Mulville, J., Roberts, H. and Stevens, T. *The Lyonesse Project: A Study of the Evolution of the Coastal and Marine Environment of the Isles of Scilly*. Truro: Cornwall Archaeological Unit, 2016, p.10.
68 Thomas, C., op. cit., pp.58–9.

STONE LANDS

69 Borlase, W. *Observations on the ancient and present state of the islands of Scilly, and their importance to the trade of Great-Britain. In a letter to the Reverend Charles Lyttelton [. . .]*. 1756.
70 Thomas, C., op. cit., p.55.
71 stonerows.wordpress.com/gazetteer/region/rest-of-england/higher-town-bay
72 Thomas, C., op. cit., pp. 48–9.
73 Charman, D., Johns, C., Camidge, K., Marshall, P., Mills, S., Mulville, J., Roberts, H. and Stevens, T., op. cit., p.10.
74 Borlase, W., op. cit., pp. 30–33.
75 Sawyer, K. *Isles of the Dead? The Setting and Function of the Bronze Age Chambered Cairns and Cists of the Isles of Scilly*. Oxford: Archaeopress Publishing, 2015, p.117.
76 Charman, D., Johns, C., Camidge, K., Marshall, P., Mills, S., Mulville, J., Roberts, H. and Stevens, T., op. cit., p.10.
77 Sawyer, K., op. cit., p.vii.
78 Ibid., p.73.
79 Ibid., pp.66–7.
80 www.redxpharma.com/our-pipeline/rxc004-porcupine. 'Zamaporvint (RXC004, Porcupine Inhibitor). Designed to unlock the potential of Wnt pathway blockade in oncology'.

Chapter 7

81 Toghill, P. *The Geology of Britain: An Introduction*. Marlborough: Airlife, 2000, pp.21–22.
82 Richards, C., Challands, A. and Welham, K. 'Erecting Stone Circles in a Hebridean Landscape'. In Richards, C. (ed.) *Building the Great Stone Circles of the North*. Oxford: Windgather Press, 2013.
83 www.geolsoc.org.uk/GeositesCallanish.
84 Richards, C. 'The Sanctity of Crags: Mythopraxis, Transformation and the Calanais Low Circles'. In Richards, C. (ed.), op. cit.
85 Cope, J. 'Margaret at the Stones: Megalithic Astronomy at Lunar Callanish'. In *The Modern Antiquarian: A Pre-Millennial Odyssey*

through Megalithic Britain including a Gazetteer to Over 300 Prehistoric Sites. London: Thorsons, 1998, pp.57–72.
86 Ashmore, P. *Calanais: The Standing Stones*. Edinburgh: Historic Scotland, 2012 (2002), p.50.
87 Roy, R. *Stone Circles: A Modern Builder's Guide to the Megalithic Revival*. White River Junction and Totnes: Chelsea Green, 1999, pp.165–6.
88 Ponting, G. and Ponting, M. *New Light on the Stones of Callanish*. Callanish: G & M Ponting, 1984, pp.46–52.
89 Sheridan, A. 'Calanais in context: new light on a ceremonial landscape in Lewis'. Glasgow RKO Archaeological Society Lecture. 15/09/2022.
90 archaeocosmology.org/eng/ShortDescription.htm 'Some things explained which happen between heaven and earth'.
91 Ponting, G. and Ponting, M., op. cit., p.45.
92 callanishblackhousetearoom.com
93 callanish.archaeoptics.co.uk
94 Burl, A. *The Stone Circles of Britain, Ireland and Brittany*. New Haven and London: Yale University Press, 2000, pp.205–6.
95 Richards, C. 'The Sanctity of Crags: Mythopraxis, Transformation and the Calanais Low Circles'. In Richards, C. (ed.), op. cit.
96 canmore.org.uk/site/82977/lewis-cnoc-an-tursa
97 Sheridan, A., op. cit.
98 Richards, C. 'The Sanctity of Crags: Mythopraxis, Transformation and the Calanais Low Circles'. In Richards, C. (ed.), op. cit.
99 Richards, C., Challands, A. and Welham, K. 'Erecting Stone Circles in a Hebridean Landscape'. In Richards, C. (ed.), op. cit.

Chapter 8

100 newsweek.com/prehistoric-stone-circle-sanctuary-predate-stonehenge-700-years-1900038.
101 Cummings, V. *The Neolithic of Britain and Ireland*. Abingdon and New York: Routledge, 2017, p.56.
102 Garrow, D. and Wilkin, N. *The World of Stonehenge*. London: The British Museum, 2022, p.72.

103 Lewis-Williams, D. and Pearce, D. *Inside the Neolithic Mind.* London: Thames & Hudson, 2005, p.255.
104 Cummings, V. *The Neolithic of Britain and Ireland.* Abingdon and New York: Routledge, 2017, p.224.
105 Farrah, R. W. E. *A Guide to the Stone Circles of Cumbria.* Kendal: Hayloft Publishing, 2016, pp.68–9.
106 Bradley, R. *The Significance of Monuments. On the Shaping of Human Experience in Neolithic and Bronze Age Europe.* Abingdon: Routledge, 1998, p.121.
107 Ibid., p.128.
108 Lewis-Williams, D. and Pearce, D., op. cit., p.262.
109 Cummings, V., op. cit., p.169.
110 Farrah, R. W. E., op. cit.
111 Grinsell, L. V. *Folklore of Prehistoric Sites in Britain.* Newton Abbot and North Pomfret: David & Charles, 1976, pp.164–5.
112 Archaeological Services Durham University, on behalf of Altogether Archaeology. 'Long Meg and Her Daughters post-excavation full analysis'. Durham University, 2016.
113 Farrah, R. W. E., op. cit., pp.96–8.

Chapter 9

114 Neil, S., Evans, J., Montgomery, J., Schulting, R. and Scarre, C. 'Provenancing antiquarian museum collections using multi-isotope analysis'. 2023. *Royal Society Open Science* 10: 22078.
115 Grinsell, L. V. *Folklore of Prehistoric Sites in Britain.* Newton Abbot and North Pomfret: David & Charles, 1976, p.63.
116 Downes, J. et al. 'Investigating the Great Ring of Brodgar, Orkney'. In Richards, C. (ed.) *Building the Great Stone Circles of the North.* Oxford: Windgather Press, 2013.
117 Parker Pearson, M., Pollard, J., Richards, C., Welham, K., Kinnaird, T., Shaw, D., Simmons, E. et al. 'The original Stonehenge? A dismantled stone circle in the Preseli Hills of west Wales'. *Antiquity* 95, no. 379 (2021), pp. 85–103.

Endnotes

118 bbc.co.uk/news/uk-england-derbyshire-66669485.

119 Blease-Bourne, A. *Guarding Sacred Sites: The Nine Ladies Anti-Quarry Campaign*. Heart Stone Press, 2016.

120 Ibid.

121 Barnatt, J. W. 'Excavation and restoration of the Doll Tor stone circle, Stanton, Derbyshire, 1994'. *The Derbyshire Archaeological Journal* vol. 117 (1997), pp.81–85.

122 Burl, A. *The Stone Circles of Britain, Ireland and Brittany*. New Haven and London: Yale University Press, 2000, p.299.

Chapter 10

123 *Millennium Stone Circle on Hilly Fields*. The Brockley Society. p.4.

124 Muir, T. and Wilson, B. *The Mermaid Bride and Other Orkney Folk Tales*. Kirkwall: The Orcadian Limited, 2018 (1998), p.xiv.

125 Mackay Brown, G. *Under Brinkie's Brae*. London and Edinburgh: Steve Savage, 1979, pp.122–3.

126 Downes, J. et al. 'Investigating the Great Ring of Brodgar, Orkney'. In Richards, C. (ed.) *Building the Great Stone Circles of the North*. Oxford: Windgather Press, 2013.

127 www.nessofbrodgar.co.uk/stones-of-stenness.

128 Richards, C. et al. 'Monumental Risk: megalithic quarrying at Staneyhill and Vestra Fiold, Mainland, Orkney'. In Richards, C. (ed.), op. cit.

129 *The Ness of Brodgar: Digging Deeper*. The Ness of Brodgar Trust.

130 All these tales and many more can be found in Muir, T. and Wilson, B., op. cit., and in Muir, T. *Orkney Folk Tales*. Stroud: The History Press, 2014.

131 www.aaronwatson.co.uk/dwarfie-stane.

132 See theorkneynews.scot/2021/09/30/you-cant-have-too-much-of-brodgar/ and many other stones-themed articles in the *Orkney News* by Bernie Bell, including this one about a winter solstice walk she and Mike took around Stenness and Brodgar: theorkneynews.scot/2021/12/24/21-12-21/

STONE LANDS

Chapter 11

133 Burl, A. *The Stone Circles of Britain, Ireland and Brittany*. New Haven and London: Yale University Press, 2000, p.171.

134 McNeil Cooke, I. *Journey to the Stones: Ancient Sites & Pagan Mysteries of Celtic Cornwall*. Penzance: Men-an Tol Studio, 1996 (1987), p.83. He supplies the Ordnance Survey Explorer grid reference for the holed stone on Zennor Carn: 463382.

135 Tilley, C. and Bennett, W. 'An archaeology of supernatural places: the case of West Penwith'. *The Journal of the Royal Anthropological Institute* vol. 7, no. 2 (2001), pp.335–62.

136 Borlase, W. *Antiquities, Historical and Monumental, of the County of Cornwall*. 1769.

137 Bottrell, W. *Traditions and Hearthside Stories of West Cornwall*. 1870.

138 Colquhoun, I. *The Living Stones*. London: Peter Owen, 2020 (1957), p.57.

139 Tilley, C. and Bennett, W., op. cit.

140 Blight, J. T. *A Week at the Land's End*. 1861.

141 stonerows.wordpress.com/gazetteer/region/rest-of-england/kenidjack-common

142 Michell, J. *The Old Stones of Land's End*. Megalithomania Lecture (Audio). 2006.

143 Michell, J. *The Old Stones of Land's End*. London: The Garnstone Press, 1974.

144 Hunt, R. *Cornish Folklore*. Penryn: Tor Mark Press, 1988 (1871), p.21.

145 Hutton, R. 'Megaliths and memory'. In Parker, J. (ed.) *Written on Stone*. Newcastle upon Tyne: Cambridge Scholars Publishing, 2009, p.13.

146 Grinsell, L. V. *Folklore of Prehistoric Sites in Britain*. Newton Abbot and North Pomfret: David & Charles, 1976.

147 Bottrell, W., op. cit.

148 McNeil Cooke, op. cit.

149 Kennett, C. *An Astronomical Examination of Boscawen-ûn Stone Circle*. 2016/17, p.82.

150 Burl, A., op. cit., p.31.

151 Bottrell, W., op. cit.

152 Thomas, C. *Exploration of a Drowned Landscape: Archaeology and History of the Isles of Scilly.* London: B. T. Batsford, 1985, pp.166–7.

Chapter 12

153 Bradley, M., Ford, A. and Evans, T. L., with contributions by Latour, R., Bashford, D. and Lindsay-Gale, L. *White Horse Hill Oxfordshire: Archaeological Landscape Survey.* Oxford: The National Trust, 2005.
154 Ibid.
155 Miles, D. *The Land of the White Horse: Visions of England.* London: Thames & Hudson, 2019, p.184.
156 Grinsell, L. V. *White Horse Hill and the Surrounding Country.* London: The Saint Catherine Press Ltd, 1939, p.3
157 Woolner, D. 'New light on the White Horse'. *Folklore* 78, no. 2 (1967), pp.90–111.
158 Bradley, M., Ford, A. and Evans, T. L., op. cit., p.9.
159 Woolner, D., op. cit.
160 Pollard, J. 'The Uffington White Horse geoglyph as sun-horse'. *Antiquity* 91, no. 356 (2017), pp.406–20.
161 Ellis Davidson, H. R. 'Weland the Smith'. *Folklore* 69, no. 3 (1958), pp.145–59.
162 Wysocki, M. P., Bayliss, A. and Whittle, A. 'Once in a lifetime: the date of the Wayland's Smithy Long Barrow'. *Cambridge Archaeological Journal* 17 (S1) (2007), pp.103–21.
163 Wysocki, M. P., Bayliss, A. and Whittle, A., op. cit.

Bibliography

Books and articles

archaeocosmology.org/eng/ShortDescription.htm 'Some things explained which happen between heaven and earth'.

Archaeological Services Durham University, on behalf of Altogether Archaeology. 'Long Meg and Her Daughters post-excavation full analysis'. Durham University, 2016.

Ashbee, P., and Thomas, C. 'Scilly's statue-menhir rediscovered'. *Antiquity* 64, no. 244 (1990), pp.571–5.

Ashmore, P. *Calanais: The Standing Stones.* Edinburgh: Historic Scotland, 2012 (2002).

Aubrey, J. Edited and with an introduction by John Fowles. Annotated by Rodney Legg. *Monumenta Brittanica. A Miscellany of British Antiques.* Boston and Toronto: Little, Brown and Company, 1980.

Aubrey, J. *The Natural History of Wiltshire.* 1847 (written 1656–91). gutenberg.org/ebooks/4934.

Barnatt, J. W. 'Excavation and restoration of the Doll Tor stone circle, Stanton, Derbyshire, 1994'. *The Derbyshire Archaeological Journal* vol. 117 (1997), pp.81–5. archaeologydataservice.ac.uk/library/browse/details.xhtml?recordId=3202689&recordType=Journal.

bbc.co.uk/news/uk-england-27405147. 'Summer solstice: how the Stonehenge battles faded'.

Blease-Bourne, A. *Guarding Sacred Sites: The Nine Ladies Anti-Quarry Campaign.* Heart Stone Press, 2016.

Blight, J. T. *A Week at the Land's End.* 1861. archive.org/details/weekatlandsend00blig/.

Bloom, J. H. *Folk Lore, Old Customs and Superstitions in Shakespeare Land.* White Press, 2016 (1929).

Borlase, W. *Antiquities, Historical and Monumental, of the County of Cornwall.* 1769. archive.org/details/bim_eighteenth-century_antiquities-historical-_borlase-william_1769/page/n353/mode/2up.

Borlase, W. *Observations on the ancient and present state of the islands of Scilly, and their importance to the trade of Great-Britain. In a letter to the Reverend Charles Lyttelton [. . .].* 1756. archive.org/details/bub_gb_xZvHAAAAMAAJ/page/n31/mode/2up.

Bottrell, W. *Traditions and Hearthside Stories of West Cornwall.* 1870. gutenberg.org/ebooks/41761.

Bradley, M., Ford, A., and Evans, T. L., with contributions by Latour, R., Bashford, D. and Lindsay-Gale, L. *White Horse Hill Oxfordshire: Archaeological Landscape Survey.* Oxford: The National Trust, 2005. eprints.oxfordarchaeology.com/4114/1/UWHHTS%2004.pdf

Bradley, R. *The Significance of Monuments. On the Shaping of Human Experience in Neolithic and Bronze Age Europe.* Abingdon: Routledge, 1998.

The Brockley Society. *Millennium Stone Circle on Hilly Fields.*

Burl, A. *A Guide to the Stone Circles of Britain, Ireland and Brittany.* New Haven and London: Yale University Press, 2005 (1995).

Bibliography

Burl, A. *The Stone Circles of Britain, Ireland and Brittany.* New Haven and London: Yale University Press, 2000.

buxtonmuseumandartgallery.wordpress.com/2021/12/10/dancing-stones-and-peeing-giants-the-folklore-of-ancient-sites-in-derbyshire.

Camden, W. *Camden's Britannia newly translated into English, with large additions and improvements; publish'd by Edmund Gibson [. . .].* 1695 (first published in Latin 1586). archive.org/details/bim_early-english-books-1641-1700_camdens-britannia-_camden-william_1695.

Charman, D., Johns, C., Camidge, K., Marshall, P., Mills, S., Mulville, J., Roberts, H. and Stevens, T. *The Lyonesse Project: A Study of the Evolution of the Coastal and Marine Environment of the Isles of Scilly.* Truro: Cornwall Archaeological Unit, 2016.

Clarke, A. J. I., Kirkland, C. L., Bevins, R. E. et al. 'A Scottish provenance for the Altar Stone of Stonehenge'. *Nature* 632 (2024), pp.570–75. nature.com/articles/s41586-024-07652-1.

Colquhoun, I. *The Living Stones.* London: Peter Owen, 2020 (1957).

Cope, J. *The Modern Antiquarian: A Pre-Millennial Odyssey through Megalithic Britain including a Gazetteer to Over 300 Prehistoric Sites.* London: Thorsons, 1998.

Cummings, V. *The Neolithic of Britain and Ireland.* Abingdon and New York: Routledge, 2017.

Dames, M. *The Avebury Cycle.* London: Thames & Hudson, 1977.

Dames, M. *The Silbury Treasure: The Great Goddess Rediscovered.* London: Thames & Hudson, 1976.

Darvill, T. *Stonehenge: The Biography of a Landscape.* Stroud: Tempus Publishing, 2006.

Darvill, T. 'White on blonde: quartz pebbles and the use of quartz at Neolithic monuments in the Isle of Man and beyond'. In Jones, A. and Macgregor, G. (eds) *Colouring the Past: The Significance of Colour in Archaeological Research*, pp.73–91. Oxford: Berg, 2002.

Devereux, P. *Places of Power: Secret Energies at Ancient Sites: A Guide to Observed or Measured Phenomena.* London: Blandford, 1990.

devonlive.com/news/devon-news/dartmoor-landowner-shut-vital-car-8156673.

Edge, B. *Folklore Rising: An Artist's Journey through the British Ritual Year*. London: Watkins, 2024.

Edmonds, Mark. *Orcadia: Land, Sea and Stone in Neolithic Orkney*. London: Head of Zeus, 2019.

Ellis, C. 'Monks, priests and farmers: a community research excavation at Baliscate, Isle of Mull'. *Scottish Archaeological Internet Reports* 68 (2017). doi.org/10.9750/issn.2056-7421.2017.68.

Ellis Davidson, H. R. 'Weland the Smith'. *Folklore* 69, no. 3 (1958), pp.145–59.

Evans, A. J. 'The Rollright Stones and their Folk-Lore'. *Folklore* 6, no. 1 (1895), pp.6–53.

Farrah, R. W. E. *A Guide to the Stone Circles of Cumbria*. Kendal: Hayloft Publishing, 2016.

Fyfe, R. M. and Greeves, T. 'The date and context of a stone row: Cut Hill, Dartmoor, south-west England'. *Antiquity* 84, no. 323 (March 2010), pp.55–70.

Garrow, D. and Wilkin, N. *The World of Stonehenge*. London: The British Museum, 2022.

Geoffrey of Monmouth. *The History of the Kings of Britain*. London and New York: Penguin Books, 1966.

geolsoc.org.uk/GeositesCallanish.

Gillings, M. and Pollard, J. 'Authenticity, artifice and the Druidical Temple of Avebury'. In Kolen, J., Renes, J. and Hermans, R. (eds) *Landscape Biographies*, pp.117–42. Amsterdam University Press, 2015.

Gillings, M. and Pollard, J. 'Breaking Megaliths'. In Parker, J. (ed.) *Written on Stone: The Cultural Reception of British Prehistoric Monuments*, pp.36–48. Newcastle upon Tyne: Cambridge Scholars Publishing, 2009.

Gray, W. G. *The Rollright Ritual*. Cheltenham: Helios Book Service, 1975.

Grinsell, L. V. *Folklore of Prehistoric Sites in Britain*. Newton Abbot and North Pomfret: David & Charles, 1976.

Grinsell, L. V. 'The legendary history and folklore of Stonehenge'. *Folklore* 87, no. 1 (1976), pp.5–20.

Grinsell, L. V. *White Horse Hill and the Surrounding Country*. London: The Saint Catherine Press Ltd, 1939.

theguardian.com/environment/2023/jan/13/dartmoor-estate-landowner-alexander-darwall-court-case-right-to-camp

Hamerow, H. 'A conversion-period burial in an ancient landscape: a high-status female grave near the Rollright Stones, Oxfordshire/Warwickshire'. In Langlands, A. and Lavelle, R. (eds) *The Land of the English Kin: Studies in Wessex and Anglo-Saxon England in Honour of Professor Barbara Yorke.* Brill, 2020, pp. 231–44.

Henderson, M. P. *Folktales of the Peak District.* Stroud: Amberley, 2011.

Hunt, R. *Cornish Folklore.* Penryn: Tor Mark Press, 1988 (1871).

Hunt, R. *Popular Romances of the West of England; or, The drolls, traditions, and superstitions of old Cornwall.* London: Chatto & Windus, 1908. archive.org/details/popularromancesoohuntuoft.

Hutton, R. 'Megaliths and memory'. In Parker, J. (ed.) *Written on Stone*, pp.10–22. Newcastle upon Tyne: Cambridge Scholars Publishing, 2009.

Kennett, C. *An Astronomical Examination of Boscawen-ûn Stone Circle.* 2016/7, p.82. www.academia.edu/33532903.

Kipling, Rudyard. *Puck of Pook's Hill.* 1906.

Lambrick, G. *An Illustrated Guide to the Rollright Stones.* Oxford: The Rollright Trust Ltd, 2022 (2017).

Lively, P. *The Whispering Knights.* London: William Heinemann Ltd., 1971.

Mackay Brown, G. *Under Brinkie's Brae.* London and Edinburgh: Steve Savage, 1979.

Maclean, J. P. *History of the Island of Mull.* 1923. archive.org/details/historyofislandoo1macluoft.

Manning, P. 'Stray notes on Oxfordshire folklore'. *Folklore* 13, no. 3 (1902), pp.288–95. doi.org/10.1080/0015587X.1902.9719315.

Martin, M. A description of the Western Islands of Scotland. 1703. archive.org/details/descriptionofwesoomart/page/n3/mode/2up

Martlew, R. D. and Ruggles, C. L. N. 'The North Mull Project (4): Excavations at Ardnacross 1989–91'. *Archaeoastronomy* 18 (1993). articles.adsabs.harvard.edu/cgi-bin/nph-iarticle_query?bibcode=1993JHAS...24...55M.

McNeil Cooke, I. *Journey to the Stones: Ancient Sites & Pagan Mysteries of Celtic Cornwall.* Penzance: Men-an Tol Studio, 1996 (1987).

STONE LANDS

Megalithic Portal, The, edited by Andy Burnham. *The Old Stones*. London: Watkins, 2018.

Michell, J. *The Old Stones of Land's End*. Megalithomania Lecture (Audio). 2006. youtube.com/watch?v=GTYz7Jds5zU.

Michell, J. *The Old Stones of Land's End*. London: The Garnstone Press, 1974.

Miles, D. *The Land of the White Horse: Visions of England*. London: Thames & Hudson, 2019.

Morgan Ibbotson, D. *Cumbria's Prehistoric Monuments*. Stroud: The History Press, 2021.

Muir, T. *Orkney Folk Tales*. Stroud: The History Press, 2014.

Muir, T. and Wilson, B. *The Mermaid Bride and Other Orkney Folk Tales*. Kirkwall: The Orcadian Limited, 2018 (1998).

Nash, D. J., Ciborowski, T. J. R., Stewart Ullyott, J., Parker Pearson, M., Darvill, T., Greaney, S., Maniatis, G. and Whitaker, K. A. 'Origins of the sarsen megaliths at Stonehenge'. *Science Advances* 6, no. 31 (2020). doi.org/10.1126/sciadv.abc0133.

Nash, P. *Fertile Image*. London: 1951.

Nash, P. 'Landscape of the megaliths'. *Art and Education*, March 1939.

Neil, S., Evans, J., Montgomery, J., Schulting, R. and Scarre, C. 'Provenancing antiquarian museum collections using multi-isotope analysis'. 2023. Royal Society Open Science 10: 22078. doi.org/10.1098/rsos.220798.

newsweek.com/prehistoric-stone-circle-sanctuary-predate-stonehenge-700-years-1900038.

ourwarwickshire.org.uk/content/article/the-murder-of-my-great-great-grandmother-ann-tennant-of-long-compton-part-one.

ourwarwickshire.org.uk/content/article/the-murder-of-ann-tennant-of-long-compton-part-two.

Palmer, R. *The Folklore of Warwickshire*. London: B. T. Batsford, 1976.

Parker Pearson, M. *Stonehenge: Exploring the Greatest Stone Age Mystery*. London: Simon & Schuster, 2012.

Parker Pearson, M., Bevins, R., Ixer, R. et al. 'Craig Rhos-y-felin: A Welsh bluestone megalith quarry for Stonehenge'. *Antiquity* 89, no. 348 (2015), pp.1331–52. doi.org/10.15184/aqy.2015.177.

Bibliography

Parker Pearson, M., Pollard, J., Richards, C. et al. 'How Waun Mawn stone circle was designed and built, and when the bluestones arrived at Stonehenge: A response to Darvill', *Antiquity* 96, no. 390 (2022), pp.1530–37.
Parker Pearson, M., Pollard, J., Richards, C., Welham, K., Kinnaird, T., Shaw, D., Simmons, E. et al. 'The original Stonehenge? A dismantled stone circle in the Preseli Hills of west Wales'. *Antiquity* 95, no. 379 (2021), pp.85–103. discovery.ucl.ac.uk/id/eprint/10127155.
Pennant, T. *A tour in Scotland, and Voyage to the Hebrides, 1772*. archive.org/details/tourinscotlandv001penn.
Piggott, S. *William Stukeley: An Eighteenth-Century Antiquary*. New York: Thames & Hudson, 1985 (1950).
Pitts, M. 'The henge builders'. *Archaeology* 61, no. 1 (2008), pp.48–55.
Plot, Dr. R. *The Natural History of Oxfordshire*. 1677. archive.org/details/naturalhistoryofo0plot.
Pollard, J. 'Substantial and significant pits in the Mesolithic of Britain and adjacent regions'. *Hunter Gatherer Research*. V.3. 2017. eprints.soton.ac.uk/412730/1/2017_009_POLLARD_final.pdf.
Pollard, J. 'The Uffington White Horse geoglyph as sun-horse'. *Antiquity* 91, no. 356 (2017), pp.406–20. doi.org/10.15184/aqy.2016.269.
Pollard, J. and Reynolds, A. *Avebury: The Biography of a Landscape*. Stroud: The History Press, 2010 (2002).
Ponting, G. and Ponting, M. *New Light on the Stones of Callanish*. Callanish: G & M Ponting, 1984.
Potter, C. 'The barber-surgeon of Avebury'. entandaudiologynews.com/development/potters-soapbox/post/the-barber-surgeon-of-avebury. 2019.
redxpharma.com/our-pipeline/rxc004-porcupine. 'Zamaporvint (RXC004, Porcupine Inhibitor). Designed to unlock the potential of Wnt pathway blockade in oncology'.
Richards, C. (ed.) *Building the Great Stone Circles of the North*. Oxford: Windgather Press, 2013.
Richards, C. and Cummings, V. *Stone Circles: A Field Guide*. New Haven and London: Yale University Press, 2024.
Roy, R. *Stone Circles: A Modern Builder's Guide to the Megalithic Revival*. White River Junction and Totnes: Chelsea Green, 1999.

Sawyer, K. *Isles of the Dead? The Setting and Function of the Bronze Age Chambered Cairns and Cists of the Isles of Scilly*. Oxford: Archaeopress Publishing, 2015.

scientificamerican.com/article/circles-for-space-german-'stonehenge'-marks-oldest-observatory.

Scurr, R. *John Aubrey: My Own Life*. London: Penguin Random House, 2015.

Sheridan, A. 'Calanais in context: new light on a ceremonial landscape in Lewis'. Glasgow RKO Archaeological Society Lecture. 15/09/2022. youtube.com/watch?v=7v3NUpG8mXQ.

Smiles, S. 'Thomas Guest and Paul Nash in Wiltshire: two episodes in the artistic approach to British antiquity'. In Smiles, S. and Moser, S. (eds), *Envisioning the Past: Archaeology and the Image*, pp. 133–57. Malden, MA: Blackwell, 2005. tate.org.uk/research/tate-papers/03/thomas-guest-and-paul-nash-in-wiltshire-two-episodes-in-the-artistic-approach-to-british-antiquity.

Stukeley, W. *Abury, A Temple of the British Druids, with Some Others, Described*. 1743. www.gutenberg.org/ebooks/64626.

The Ness of Brodgar: Digging Deeper. The Ness of Brodgar Trust.

Thomas, C. *Exploration of a Drowned Landscape: Archaeology and History of the Isles of Scilly*. London: B. T. Batsford, 1985.

Thurnam, J. 'On Wayland's Smithy and on the traditions connected with it'. *Wiltshire Archaeology and Natural History Magazine* 7 (1862), pp.321–33. biodiversitylibrary.org/page/33969055.

Tilley, C. and Bennett, W. 'An archaeology of supernatural places: the case of West Penwith'. *The Journal of the Royal Anthropological Institute* vol. 7, no. 2 (2001).

Toghill, P. *The Geology of Britain: An Introduction*. Marlborough: Airlife, 2000.

Walford Davies, D. *Megalith: Eleven Journeys in Search of Stones*. Llandysul: Gomer Press, 2006.

Weird Walk Number 1, Beltane 2019.

Weird Walk. *Weird Walk: Wanderings and Wonderings through the British Ritual Year*. London: Watkins, 2023.

westerngeomancy.org/swinside-and-sighthill-in-stellarium.

Bibliography

Woolner, D. 'New light on the White Horse'. *Folklore* 78, no. 2 (1967), pp.90–111.

Wright, T. 'Legend of the Rollright Stones'. *The Folk-Lore Record* 2 (1879), pp.177–9.

Wysocki, M. P., Bayliss, A. and Whittle, A. 'Once in a lifetime: the date of the Wayland's Smithy Long Barrow'. *Cambridge Archaeological Journal* 17 (S1) (2007), pp.103–21. clok.uclan.ac.uk/323/1/323_wysocki.pdf.

Websites

This is not an exhaustive list of stones resources but simply a list of websites I personally found helpful in planning trips and researching this book.

aveburypapers.org. Digitising, exploring and sharing the archive of the Alexander Keiller Museum at Avebury.

cadw.gov.wales. The Welsh historic environment service.

callanish.archaeoptics.co.uk. Explore the Calanais stones in 3D from the comfort of your own home.

canmore.org.uk. The Scottish historic environment service.

dartmoorwalks.org.uk. Self-guided walks to prehistoric sites on Dartmoor.

english-heritage.org.uk. Pages on all the many sites managed by English Heritage.

heritagegateway.org.uk/gateway. The English historic environment service (formerly Pastscape).

megalithic.co.uk. The Megalithic Portal online database of standing stone sites around the world, with input from thousands of stones enthusiasts (the associated iPhone app is Pocket Guide – Megaliths).

meynmamvro.co.uk. The magazine of standing stones and sacred sites in Cornwall.

themodernantiquarian.com. Recently refurbished online database linked to Julian Cope's iconic book of the same name.

nessofbrodgar.co.uk. The latest research into the complex at the Ness and Orkney's other ancient sites.

STONE LANDS

thenorthernantiquarian.org. Online database with a focus on the folklore, traditions and customs associated with sites across Britain.
northernearth.co.uk. Magazine exploring archaeology, folklore, antiquarianism and psychogeography.
theorkneynews.scot. Lots of articles on the prehistory of Orkney by Bernie Bell.
righttoroam.org.uk. Campaigning to bring a Right to Roam Act to England so that millions more people can have easy access to nature, and the physical, mental and spiritual health benefits this brings.
rollrightstones.co.uk. The Rollright Trust website.
stonerows.wordpress.com. The Stone Rows of Great Britain, providing information on all the known stone rows in the country.
theurbanprehistorian.wordpress.com. Dr Kenneth Brophy's blog about his experience of prehistoric sites in urban contexts.

Index

A
Achaban House, Isle of Mull 74
Alderley Edge, Cheshire 47
Alfred, King 335, 340, 346
alignments 97, 99–100, 133, 186, 190–1, 193–4, 210–12, 302–7
Allfrey, Dr Fran 22, 23
Alps, Italian 208
Altair 194
Altar Stone, Stonehenge *136*, 138
Ambrosius, Aurelius 126
Amesbury Archer 127
Andle Stone, Peak District *242*, 248
angels 79
Anglesey, Wales 64, 340
Anglo-Saxons 327

Annet, Scilly Isles 152
Apollo 127
Arbor Low, Peak District 254–5
Archaeoptics 191
Ardlair, Aberdeenshire 64
Ardnacross, Isle of Mull 75, 76
Arosio, Paola 240
art, Neolithic 212, 220–1, 277
Arthur, King 47, 118–19, 126, 135, 147, 151, 340
Ashdown, Battle of (871) 335
Aspers Field stone, Lake District 224
Assycombe, Dartmoor 110
Atlantis 150
Aubrey, John 8–9, 135

Monumenta Britannica 8, 20
Aubrey Holes, Stonehenge 116, 135, *137*, 139
autumn equinox 50, 194, 211, 280–1
Avalon, isle of 152
Avebury, Wiltshire 2, 3–33, *16*, 97, 324, 346
   Beckhampton Avenue *16*, 19, 21, 25
   the Cove 19, 20
   Fox Covert 21
   Longstone Cove *16*, 19, 21
   the Obelisk 19
   Overton Hill 19, 29–30, 326, 327, 349
   pilgrimages to 128–9
   Ridgeway and 325–7, 349–50
   Sanctuary *16*, 19, 20, 21, 29–30, 327, 349–50
   sarsen stones 3–4, 18
   Silbury Hill 2, 6, 20, 25, 26, 30, 32, 273, 279, 345, 346
   Swindon Stone 22
   Waden Hill 6, 17
   West Kennet Avenue *16*, 19, 21, 22–3, 25–6, 29
   Windmill Hill 2, 17–18, 29–30, 324
Avebury Papers project 22
The Avenue, Stonehenge 133–4, *137*, 277
The Avenue, West Kennet, Avebury *16*, 19, 21, 22–3, 25–6, 29
axes, stone 208–9

Aylesford, Battle of (455) 234
Aylward, Martin, *Awake Where You Are* 68

B
Balfarg, Fife 212
Baliscate stone row, Isle of Mull 76–7
Ballowall Barrow, West Penwith 299
Balnuaran of Clava 265
Bamford Moor, Peak District 253
Bancbryn, Carmarthenshire 98
Bant's Carn, St Mary's 156
Barbury Castle, Wiltshire 324, 327, 344
Barnhouse Stone, Orkney 258, 268, 270
Barpa Langass, North Uist 196, 198–9
Baskerville, Thomas 332–3
Battle of the Beanfield (1958) 130, 132, 134
Beaghmore, Cookstown 128
Becket, Thomas 232
Beckhampton Avenue, Avebury *16*, 19, 21, 25
Bedd Arthur (Arthur's Grave), Preseli Hills 117–18
Bell, Bernie 285–6
Beltane 50, 314
Ben Buie, Isle of Mull 59, 62–3, 88
Bennett, Wayne 298
Berkshire Downs 336
Bernadette, St 122–3

Index

Birmingham 245
Blake, William 160
Blease-Bourne, Aimee 246–8
Blencathra, Lake District 206, 211
Blewbury, Oxfordshire 327
Blind Fiddler, West Penwith 310
Blue Bell Hill, Kent 230, 232, 233
bluestones, Stonehenge 116, 117–18, 120, 135, *136*, 138–41, 208, 238
Bodmin Moor, Cornwall 309
Bonfire Carn, Bryher 158
Borlase, William 153, 155, 296, 298, 306
Borlase, William Copeland 306
Boscawen-Ros East, West Penwith 311n.
Boscawen-ûn, West Penwith 302, 309, 312–16, 320–1
Boskednan, West Penwith 297, 302, 309
Boswens Menhir, West Penwith 306
Bottrell, William 296, 309–10
Bournemouth 208
Boyne Valley, Ireland 77, 265
Bradford, Emma 42–3, 53
Bradley, Richard 211
Brendan, St 78
Brigid, St 81
Brisworthy circle, Dartmoor 112–13
Brittany 14
Brockley, London 260–2
Brophy, Dr Kenneth 100
Brown, George Mackay 267–8

Bryher, Scilly Isles 147–9, 151–9
Bryn Celli Ddu, Anglesey 340
Buckfastleigh, Devon 205
Buddhism 15, 68
Burl, Aubrey 185, 240, 314
Burnham, Andy 239–41
 The Old Stones 64, 239–40
Burr, Beckie 110–11

C
Cailleach na Mòinteach, Isle of Lewis *see* Sleeping Beauty
Calanais, Isle of Lewis 179–99, *182*, 210, 273
Calgary Bay, Mull 88
Callanish3D modelling project 187, 190
Camden, William 151–2, 221
 Britannia 48
Canmore 74
Canterbury, Kent 232
Capella 194
Carew, Richard 152
Carn Galva, West Penwith 296, 297–8
Carn Kenidjack, West Penwith 299–301, 304–5, 306
Carn Menyn, Preseli Hills 117–20
Carreg Samson, Pembrokeshire 121
Carthy, Eliza 69
Carty, Alistair 191
carvings, Neolithic 212, 220–1
Castlerigg, Lake District 205–13, 215, 274
chalk 330–6

379

STONE LANDS

Chapel Idne, Sennen Cove 318
Chilham, Kent 230
Christianity 72, 77, 281
Chûn Quoit, West Penwith 298, 304, 306
Clach an Truishall, Isle of Lewis 197
Clach Mhic Leoid, Isle of Lewis 197–8
Clava Cairns, Scotland 128, 265
Cnoc an Tursa, Calanais *182*, 186–7, 189, 195–6, 198
Cnoc Ceann a'Ghàrraidh, Calanais 181
Cnoc Fhillibhir Bheag, Calanais 181, 189
Cnoc nan Aingeal, Isle of Mull 79
Coffin Stone, Kent 234–5
Coldrum long barrow, Kent 230–1
Colquhoun, Ithell, *The Living Stones* 298
Columba, St 72, 77, 78, 79
Comet Stone, Ring of Brodgar 280
Cope, Julian 184
   The Modern Antiquarian 184–5, 240
Copt Howe, Lake District 212, 221
Cork Stone, Peak District *242*, 247, 249
Cornwall 14, 151–2, 190, 263, 293–321
Cornwood Maidens, Dartmoor 105–6, 107
Cot valley, West Penwith 299
Cotswolds 38, 53–4, 307

Council of British Druid Orders 135
Countless Stones, Kent 235
Countryside and Rights of Way Act (2000) 108
Cove, Avebury 19, 20
Covid-19 pandemic 123, 177, 239, 254, 285
Cranborne Chase 28–9
Crick Stone, West Penwith 296
Croatia 341
Cumbria 203–25, 263, 264
Cunningham, Maud 23
Curtis, Margaret 184–7, 189–90, 193, 195, 210
Curtis, Ron 185, 186–7
Cut Hill, Dartmoor 97–8
Cuween Hill cairn, Orkney 285, 286
Cynegils of Wessex 253

D
Dames, Michael 25, 97
   The Avebury Cycle 25
   The Silbury Treasure 25
Danes 335
Dans Maen, West Penwith 308
Dartmoor, Devon 89–93, 97–113, 205
Darvill, Timothy 77, 118, 127
Darwall, Alexander 105–7, 108
dating stone circles vi
Denmark 336
Derbyshire 235–7, 241–55, *242*
Devereux, Paul 54

380

Index

Devil 214, 251, 299
Devon 87–113
Dickinson, Steve 208n.
Ding Dong mine, West Penwith 294, 297
Doll Tor, Peak District *242*, 243, 249–51
Down Tor, Dartmoor 89–93, 97, 99–101, 111–12, 113
Downes, Jane 273
dowsing 215–16
Dragon Hill, Oxfordshire *329*, 330, 331, 333, 336
Drift, West Penwith 310
Drizzlecombe, Dartmoor 110
Druids 8, 9, 10, 21, 132, 134, 135, 298, 340
Druid's egg 142–3, 178
Druim Dubh, Isle of Lewis 185
Duddo stone circle, Northumberland 309
Duloe, Cornwall 315
Dwarfie Stane, Orkney 283–4

E
East Kennet, Wiltshire 30
Eaval, North Uist 199
Eden, River 220
Edge, Ben 334–5
  'Children of Albion' 339–40
  Folklore Rising 334
  The Vale of the White Horse 335, 340
Edwin of Northumbria 253
Elizabeth II, Queen 160

Ellis, Dr Clare 76–7
Elmlea, Isle of Sheppey 88
Enclosure Acts (18th century) 326–7
Endcliffe quarry, Peak District 245–6
English Heritage 98, 130, 135
equinoxes 50, 194, 211, 280–1
Evans, Arthur J. 38, 45–7, 48

F
Facebook 237
fairies 47, 79
Fairy Stone, Hordron Edge, Peak District 253
Fasano, Joseph 262–3
Fiennes, Celia 221
Finisterre 294
Fionn mac Cumhaill 198
Foley, Andrew 331, 333–4
foot-and-mouth disease 241
Forster, E. M. 7
Fox Covert, Avebury 21
France 14, 15, 148
Fraser, Jackie 63–4
Froggymead, Dartmoor 109–10
Fyfield Down, Wiltshire 345–6

G
Gardner, Grahame 189–90
Garn Turne, Pembrokeshire 97
Geoffrey of Monmouth 139
  The History of the Kings of Britain 126
George, St 330, 346

STONE LANDS

Gerrard, Dr Sandy 98–9, 301
Giant's Ring, Mount Killaraus 126
Gib Hill, Peak District 255
Glengorm stone row, Isle of Mull 75–6
gneiss 181–3
Goddess worship 25
Goggleby stone, Lake District 224
Goodweather, Kaz 130–1
Goseck, Germany 124n.
Great Goddess 25
Great Langdale, Lake District 212
Great Trilithon, Stonehenge 133
Greece 150
Green Bay, Bryher 153, 157
Green Man 38
Green Street 349
Greta, River 210
Grimes Graves, Norfolk 209
Grinsell, Lesley 235
Grooved Ware pottery 277
Gruline, Isle of Mull 65–6
Gugh, St Agnes 157
Gun Rith, West Penwith 307, 310
Gweal Hill, Bryher 158–9
Gwern-y-Cleppa, Newport 65

H
Hailglower Farm, West Penwith 300, 306–7
Hall, Monty 90 and n.
hallucinogens 212–13
Hardy, Thomas, *Tess of the d'Urbervilles* 125
Harris, Isle of 197–8
Hathersage, Peak District 235–7, 253
Haywood, James 48–9
Healing Stone, Boscawen-ûn, West Penwith 315–16
Hebrides 59–83
Hecataeus of Abdera 127
Heckels, Fiona 130–1
Heel Stone, Stonehenge 126, 133, *137*, 138
Hell Bay, Bryher 148, 159
Helvellyn, Lake District 206, 211, 220, 221
Henderson, Dolly 48
Hengist 234, 335, 346
Herne the Hunter 233
High Seat, Lake District 206
Hillsons' House, Dartmoor 107
Hilly Fields, Brockley, London 260–2
Hogboy 266
Holley, Rebecca 108–10
the Hooper 317
Hordron Edge, Peak District 252–4
Horsa 234, 335, 346
Hownam, Scotland 309
Hoy, Orkney 268, 272, 283–4, 287–8
Hugh Town, St Mary's 155
Hughes, Thomas, *The Scouring of the White Horse* 333
Hughes, Will 47
Hulver, Ann 48
the Hurlers, Cornwall 235, 309, 310
Hyperboreans 127

Index

I
Innisidgen Upper burial chamber, St Mary's 160
Instagram 28, 232, 238
Iona 69, 71, 72–83, 89, 181, 204, 266
Ireland 126, 139, 264, 265, 306
Iron Age 29, 148, 326, 327, 332, 344
Isbister, Orkney 285–6
Ivinghoe Beacon, Buckinghamshire 326

J
jadeite 208–9
James, St 76
James, Rev Helen 50–1
 Sacred Journeys videos 50
Jullieberrie's Grave, Kent 230

K
Kant, Immanuel 176
Keiller, Alexander 4, 21–3, 24
Kemp Howe, Lake District 223, 224
Kenidjack Common, West Penwith 299–301
Kenidjack stone row, West Penwith 301, 305–6
Kennet, River 32
Kennett, Carolyn 303–7, 313
Kent 229–35
Keswick, Lake District 204–5
Kinder Scout, Peak District 253
King Stone, Nine Ladies, Peak District 244, 245

King Stone, Rollright Stones 36, 43–9, *44*, 52–4
King's Men, Oxfordshire 36, 38, 43–8, *44*, 53, 129
Kit's Coty House, Kent 230, 232–3
Kittern Hill, St Agnes 157
Kittler, Friedrich 87
Knowth, Boyne Valley 77n.

L
Lake District, Cumbria 203–25, 263, 264
Lambert, Rebecca 100–1
Lammas 25
Land's End, Cornwall 152, 293–321
Langass, Loch 199
Langdale hills, Lake District 212
Langdale Pikes, Lake District 208, 209, 212
Lees Cross quarry, Peak District 245–6
Lewis, C.S., *A Grief Observed* 203
Lewis, Isle of 179–99
ley lines 189, 302–3
Liddington Castle 327, 344
Little Kit's Coty, Kent 230, 235
Lively, Penelope, *The Whispering Knights* 42
Lochbuie, Isle of Mull 60–4, 69, 71–2, 88
London 260–2
Long Compton, Warwickshire 45–9
Long Meg and Her Daughters, Lake District 208, 219, 220–2, 225
Longstone Cove, Avebury *16*, 19, 21

STONE LANDS

Lord of Goonhilly 318
Lose Hill, Peak District 253–4
Lourdes, France 123, 127
Lower White Horse Stone, Kent 234
Lowther, Lady 223
lunar standstill 186–90, 193, 210
Lyonesse 151–3, 294, 318
Lyonesse Project 155, 156

M
Mabinogion 118–19
MacBeth, Lally 238–9
McHardy, Ian 195
Machen, Arthur 7
Mackay, Captain W. 274
McNeil Cooke, Ian, *Journey to the Stones* 310–11
Maeshowe, Orkney 258, 265–8, *270*, 336
Maid Marian 246
Man in the Woods 28–9, 30–1
Manchester 245
Martlew, Roger 74–5, 76
May Day 314
Mayburgh, Penrith 211–12
Medway, Kent 10, 14, 229–35
Meg of Meldon 221
The Megalithic Portal 64, 65, 91–2, 119, 141–2, 154, 223, 239–41, 243, 250–1
Mên-an-Tol, West Penwith 293–4, 295–6, 301, 302, 315
Mên Scryfa, West Penwith 296–7
Meozzi, Diego 240
Merlin 126

Merrivale, Dartmoor 101–5, *103*, 110
Merry, Alison 51–3
Merry Maidens, West Penwith 244, 302, 307–10, 315
Mesolithic 133
Meyn Mamvro 314
Michell, John: *The Old Stones of Land's End* 303
    The View Over Atlantis 302–3
Midhowe, Orkney 258, 284–5
midsummer *see* solstices
Midsummer's Eve 48
midwinter *see* solstices
Milky Way 148–9, 318
Millennium 260
The Modern Antiquarian website 240–1
Moelfre stones, Gwynedd 309
moon 186–90, 193, 210
Morris dancing 51–2, 313–14
Morrison, Angeline 313–14
Mortlake axe 208–9
Moscar Moor, Peak District 253
Mother of the Sea 280–1
Mount Killaraus, Ireland 126
Mount's Bay, Cornwall 151
Muir, Tom 278–81
Mulfra Quoit, West Penwith 298
Mull, Isle of 59–83, 88, 89

N
Nash, Paul 23, 24
    Landscape of the Megaliths 25–6
National Trust 333, 334

384

Index

neo-Pagans 10, 30, 233–4
Ness of Brodgar, Orkney 258, 269–73, *270*, 276–8
New Age Travellers 130, 132, 134, 247
Newgrange, Boyne Valley 77 and n., 265, 268
Newport, South Wales 65
Nine Ladies, Peak District 241–8, *242*
Nine Ladies Anti-Quarry Campaign 245–8
Nine Maidens, West Penwith 244, 251n., 297–8, 306, 309
Nine Stones Close, Peak District 243, 251–2 and n.
North Downs 232
North Mull Project 74–5
North Uist 196, 198–9
Nottingham 245
Nuckelavee 281

O
Obelisk, Avebury 19
Odin 233
Odin Stone, Orkney 295
Ogbourne St George 344
Olcote, Isle of Lewis 185
Old Crockern 107
Old Man of Gugh, St Agnes 157
Old Man of Hoy, Orkney 287–8
Old Woman of the Moors, Isle of Lewis *see* Sleeping Beauty
Old Woman Stone, Bamford Moor, Peak District 253

Orford Ness, Suffolk 282
Orkney 14, 138, 238, 258, 263–89, *270*
Orkney News 285
Outer Hebrides 179–99
Overton Hill, Avebury 19, 29–30, 326, 327, 349
Oxfordshire 37–55, 325–6, 328–46

P
Pairc hills, Isle of Lewis 186
Par Beach, St Martin's 154
Parker Pearson, Mike 101, 134, 139–41
Peacey, Kelly 50–1
Peak District 235–7, 241–55, *242*
Peckham Rye, London 160, 167
Pedn-men-du, West Penwith 317–18
Pembrokeshire 116–22, 139–41, 294
Pendragon, Arthur Uther 135
Pennant, Thomas 79
Penrith, Cumbria 203–4, 210, 211–12, 219, 222, 224, 231
Penzance, West Penwith 307
Pérez Cuervo, Maria J. 129
Philip, Neil 42–3, 53
The Pickwick Papers 245
Piggott, Stuart 22
Pike o'Stickle, Lake District 209
pilgrimages 73–7, 314
Pilgrims' Way 232, 234–5
The Pipers, West Penwith 302, 307, 308–10

385

STONE LANDS

Pitt Rivers, Lt General Augustus 233, 245
Pleiades 194
Plot, Dr Robert, *Natural History of Oxfordshire* 48
Pobull Fhinn, North Uist 198–9
Poit Na H-i stone, Iona 81
Polisher stone, Fyfield Down 345–6
Pollard, Josh 77n., 335–6
Ponting, Gerald 185, 186
Porth Goonhilly, West Penwith 318
Preseli Hills, Pembrokeshire 97, 116–20, 138–43, 208, 209, 238

Q
quartz 51, 76–8, 312–16

R
Rackwick Glen, Orkney 283
Rainham Marshes, Kent 88
Rams Hill, Oxfordshire 327, *329*
Rees, Ceri 107, 108
Reijs, Victor 187, 191
Rennie, Emma 187, 190–3
Richards, Colin 195–6, 273, 275, 279
Ridgeway 4, 28, 70–1, 325–7, *329*, 336–7, 341–5, 349–50
Right to Roam 106–8, 111
Ring of Brodgar, Orkney 128, 258, 269–73, *270*, 275–6, 279, 280, 286
roads 29, 153, 210
Robin Hood 246
Robin Hood's Stride, Peak District 251

Rollright Stones, Oxfordshire 37–8, 42–55, *44*, 128, 129, 235, 307, 331, 340
Roman roads 29
Rothwell, John Timothy 135
Rousay, Orkney 284–5
Rowtor Rocks, Peak District *242*, 247, 251
Royal Raven 297
Ruggles, Clive 74–5, 76
Rylance, Mark 69

S
Sabbatarianism 309–10
St Agnes, Scilly Isles 151–4, 157
St Buryan, West Penwith 302, 307
St Just, West Penwith 299–300, 319
St Martin's, Scilly Isles 151, 153–6
St Mary's, Scilly Isles 147, 149–55, 160, 318
St Michael's Mount, Cornwall 302
St Norbert's Gate, Hilly Fields, Brockley 261
St Peter and St Paul, Trottiscliffe, Kent 229–30
Salisbury, Wiltshire 28
Salisbury Plain 28–9, 97, 118, 125, 132–5, 140, 238
Salt Knowe, Orkney *270*, 273, 279
Samhain 50, 211, 259, 312
Samson, Scilly Isles 152, 153, 156, 157–8
Samson Hill, Bryher 158
Sancreed holy well, Cornwall 302

Index

Sanctuary, Avebury *16*, 19, 20, 21, 29–30, 327, 349–50
Sanctuary, Castlerigg, Lake District 206–7, 208n.
Santiago de Compostela 76
sarsen stones: Avebury 3–4, 18
  Barbury Castle 344
  the Polisher stone, Fyfield Down 345–6
  Stonehenge *136*, 138
Sawyer, Katharine, *Isles of the Dead?* 155–7, 158
Saxons 45, 234, 327, 335
Scafell Pike, Lake District 209
Scillonian III 149–50 and n., 154, 318
Scilly Isles 147–60, 237, 263, 304–5, 306, 318
Scotland 138, 181, 197, 309
Scrabster, Caithness 265
Scridain, Loch 73–4
Seed Sistas 130–1
Segsbury Camp, Oxfordshire 327
selkies 282
Sennen Cove, West Penwith 316–20
Seven Stones of Hordron Edge, Peak District 252–4
Sewell, Zakia 26–7
  Finding Albion 27
Shap, Lake District 222–4, 225
Shaw, Matthew 238–9
the Shearers, Hownam, Scotland 309
Sheffield 245
Sheldon, Aberdeenshire 64

Sheppey, Isle of 88
Shetland 264
Ship of Death, Orkney 285
Shipman Head Down, Scilly Isles 147–8, 157, 159
Shovel Down, Dartmoor 109–10
sightlines *see* alignments
Silbury Hill, Wiltshire 2, 6, 20, 25, 26, 30, 32, 273, 279, 345, 346
Simpson, Dr 223
Sithean Mòr, Iona 266
Skara Brae, Orkney 258
Skellaw Hill, Lake District 223
Skiddaw, Lake District 206, 211
Skye, Isle of 181, 199
Sleeping Beauty, Isle of Lewis 180–1, 186, 188–9
solstices: summer solstice 30–1, 50, 97, 133–5, 187, 211, 233
  winter solstice 10, 30–1, 50, 77, 97, 130–1, 133–4, 187, 211, 260–2, 264–5, 267–8, 277–8, 304–7
Sornach Coir Fhinn, North Uist 198
South Ronaldsay, Orkney 285–6
Spencer, Rose 340
spring equinox 50, 194, 281
Stall Moor, Dartmoor 107
Stalldown Hill, Dartmoor 105–6, 107, 108, 110–11
Stanage Edge, Peak District 236, 253
Stancliffe Stone 245–6
Stanton Drew, Somerset 309

STONE LANDS

Stanton in the Peak, Peak District 247
Stanton Lees, Peak District 247
Stanton Lees Action Group (SLAG) 247
Stanton Moor, Peak District 241, *242*, 245–6, 248–9
Stellarium 191
Stenness, Orkney 258, 269, *270*, 272, 273–5
Stone Club, London 238–9
Stone of Odin, Orkney 274
Stone o' Quoybune, Orkney 279
Stone Pages website 240
Stone Rows of Great Britain website 99, 301
Stonehenge, Wiltshire 101, 116–20, 124–41, *136–7*
   Altar Stone *136*, 138
   Aubrey Holes 116, 135, *137*, 139
   Avenue 133–4, *137*, 277
   bluestones 116, 117–18, 120, 135, *136*, 138–41, 208, 238
   Great Trilithon 133
   Heel Stone 126, 133, *137*, 138
   legends 126–7, 235
   sarsen stones *136*, 138
   and solstices 97, 130–1, 132–5, 264–5
Stones Mailing List 240
Stones of Stenness, Orkney 258, 269, *270*, 272, 273–5
Stour, River 230
Straffon, Cheryl 314–16

Stukeley, William 8–9, 20–1, 25, 32, 221, 340
   Abury 21
Sunkenkirk, Lake District 214
Sunna 233
Sutherland, Graham 229
Swallowhead Springs, Wiltshire 32–3
Swindon 342
Swindon Stone, Avebury 22
Swinside, Lake District 208, 213–15, 235

T

Taoslin stone, Isle of Mull 73
Taransay, Isle of 198
Taversöe Tuick, Orkney 284
Taylor, Ken, *Celestial Geometry* 188
Tennant, Ann 48–9
Tennyson, Alfred, Lord, *Idylls of the King* 152
Teran 280–1
Thames, River 208
Thom, Alexander 210, 211, 215
Thomas, Charles, *Exploration of a Drowned Landscape* 149
Tilley, Christopher 298
Tinkinswood, South Glamorgan 309
Tirghoil stone, Isle of Mull 73–4
Tomb of the Dogs, Orkney 285
Tomb of the Eagles, Orkney 285–6
Towrie, Sigurd 277–8
Tractatus de Mirabilibus Britanniae 331, 332

Index

Tregarthen Hill, Scilly Isles 157
Tregeseal, West Penwith 299, 304–5, 306, 309
Tregiffian entrance grave, West Penwith 307
Tresco, Scilly Isles 151, 152, 153–4, 156, 157
Trosley Country Park, Kent 229
Trottiscliffe, Kent 229–30, 231
Troutbeck, John 153
Trundholm sun chariot 336
tuff 209
Tweed, Chris 240
Twitter/X 249, 262
Tysoe, Warwickshire 49

U
Uffington, Oxfordshire 324–6, 328–36, *329*
Uffington Castle, Oxfordshire 324, 327, 330
Ulie Stane, Ring of Brodgar 280
Unstan, Orkney 258, *270*, 282–3
Usk valley 263

V
Vikings 267, 281, 327
Virgin Mary 123

W
Waden Hill, Avebury 6, 17
Wainwright, Alfred 209
Wales 138–42
Walford Davies, Damian, *Megalith* 52–3

Ward Hill, Orkney 283
Watchstone, Orkney 269, *270*, 279
Watkins, Alfred 302–3
Watson, Aaron 284
Waun Mawn, Preseli Hills 116, 139–42, 178
Wayland's Smithy, Oxfordshire 324–6, *329*, 336–41, 346
Weird Walk 27–8
Weland the Smith 337, 340
Well of Eternal Youth, Iona 81
West Kennet, Wiltshire 2, 18, 25, 30, 32, 324, 339, 345
West Kennet Avenue, Avebury 16, 19, 21, 22–3, 25–6, 29
West Penwith, Cornwall 14, 293–321
West Woods, Wiltshire 138
West Woolstone, Oxfordshire 327
Western Rocks, Scilly Isles 152
Westminster Cathedral, London 122–3
Wheel of the Year 10, 30, 50
Whispering Knights, Oxfordshire 36, 43–7, *44*, 65
White Horse of Uffington, Oxfordshire 324–6, 328–36, *329*, 340, 346
White Horse Hill, Oxfordshire 327, 333, 335
White Horse Stone, Kent 233–4
Whitesands, West Penwith 317
Wiccan 10, 50
Wideford Hill, Orkney 284, 285
Wilson, Gareth 244–5

389

STONE LANDS

Wiltshire 3–33, 124–43
Win Hill, Peak District 253–4
Winchester, Hampshire 232
Windmill Hill, Avebury 2, 17–18, 29–30, 324
witches 45–50
Woolstone Wells, Oxfordshire 331
Works Carn, Bryher 158

Y
A Year in a Field 311n.
Yetnasteen, Orkney 280
Yule 50

Z
Zennor Carn, Cornwall 295
Zotti, George 191